David Thomas Ansted

The great stone Book of Nature

David Thomas Ansted

**The great stone Book of Nature**

ISBN/EAN: 9783743344006

Manufactured in Europe, USA, Canada, Australia, Japa

Cover: Foto ©ninafisch / pixelio.de

Manufactured and distributed by brebook publishing software (www.brebook.com)

David Thomas Ansted

**The great stone Book of Nature**

# THE GREAT STONE BOOK

## OF

## NATURE.

BY

DAVID THOMAS ANSTED, M.A.

F.R.S., F.G.S., ETC.

LATE FELLOW OF JESUS COLLEGE, CAMBRIDGE; HONORARY FELLOW OF KING'S
COLLEGE, LONDON.

PHILADELPHIA:
GEORGE W. CHILDS,
628 & 630 CHESTNUT STREET.
1863.

# CONTENTS.

## Introductory Chapter.

### THE BOOK OF NATURE.

Nature a Library rather than a Book—Unity of Method in Creation—Infinite Resources of Nature—Extent to which the Plan of Nature is made out—The Study of the "Stone Book"—What it means—Necessity of studying the Language of Nature to understand the Book—Meaning of Geology—The Language of Geology a Picture-Language—Facilities for observing in Geology—Method of Nature illustrated from Astronomy—Familiar Causes of Geological Phenomena—The First Lessons to be learnt—Quarries and Cuttings not indispensable............................................................................................. Page 21

## PART THE FIRST.

## THE LANGUAGE OF THE GREAT STONE BOOK.

### Chapter the First.

### THE RIVER-BED AND THE SEA-BEACH.

The River—Its first Traces and subsequent Course—Passage through the Plains—Approach to the Sea—Cause of the unfailing Supply of Water—The Water muddy after Rain—Reason of this—The Bed of the River—How occupied—Passage of a River through a Lake, and the Result—General Result at the Mouths of large Rivers—Illustration in the Case of the Mississippi—The Sea-Beach—How it differs from the River-bed—Formation of a Pebble-beach—Effect of Stones rubbing over each other—Incessant Motion of the Water owing to Tidal Action—The General Circulation of Water through the Earth the Cause of the Incessant Wearing of the Surface ............................ 35

### Chapter the Second.

**THE SUN, THE WIND, THE RAIN, AND THE FROST.**

Result of Drought in cracking the Earth—Subsequent Rain splitting and removing large Fragments—Effect of Winter, Rain, and Frost—The Effect chiefly seen where there is little Cultivation—Effect on an exposed Coast—Effect of Ice—Formation of Glaciers—Removal of Stone by Glaciers—Limit of Glacier Action—Effect of Wind on loose Sand—Effect of Lightning—The Destruction of the Surface perpetual—Incessant Alternation of Heat and Cold—Direct Action of Rain and Frost—Total Amount of Change thus Caused—Rocks—The different Varieties............................................. Page 47

# PART THE SECOND.

## THE STONES OF THE GREAT STONE BOOK.

### Chapter the Third.

**CLAY AND ITS VARIETIES.**

What is meant by Clay—Its Origin—ALUMINIUM—*Alumina*—Forms in which Alumina is known—Its Combination with Silica to form CLAY—Clay always mixed with Water and foreign Impurities—Properties of Clay—Production of *Brick*—Various Kinds of Brick-clay—*Fire-clay*—Its Composition and Use—*Terra-cotta*—How formed—Its Advantages and Disadvantages—*Potter's-clay*—Where obtained, and how used—*China-clay*—Its composition—Whence obtained—How and where used—Floating-bricks and Bath-brick—*Fuller's-earth*—Its Nature and Use—*Lias*—Its peculiar Properties—*Alum-clay*—Its Use—Rarity of Fossils in some Clays—Drainage of Clay-lands—Artesian Springs beneath Clays—Curious Remains of Cuttle-fish and other Animals in Clays—Remains of Reptiles—Fragments of Vegetation—Fruits at Sheppy—Chief Deposits of Clay in England—Characteristics of each—SLATE—Its Nature and Uses—Origin of Slate—Contents of Clay Rocks—Felspar a Variety of Clay—Lava and Pumice of the same Nature—Precious Stones derived from Clay 61

### Chapter the Fourth.

**CHALK.**

The Surface and Landscape in a Chalk District—Features of the Chalk in the British Islands—The characteristic Peculiarities of Chalk as a Rock—Its Contents—Its Identity with deep-sea Mud, or *Ooze*—Its Dissimilarity to other Limestones—Its probable Origin—Flints in the Chalk—Their Position and

Form—Frequent Association with Fossils—How produced **originally**—Bedding of Chalk—Beds often disturbed—Chalk-cliffs of the South **Coast**—Chalk in France—Accumulations of Material covering parts of the Chalk—Portions of the Chalk often **removed**—**Texture of** Chalk—Its Water-content—Uses of Chalk, for **Building, for Lime, and for** dressing Land—The History of Chalk and Flint—Occasional but rare Occurrence of foreign Substances in Chalk—**Chalk a** good Starting-point for the Young English Geologist.......... Page 78

## Chapter the Fifth.

### LIMESTONES AND MARBLE.

**Limestones differ from** Chalk in being more Crystalline—Passage of Limestone into Marble—Limestone only occasionally present on the Earth—Its **Value as a Rock**—Varieties of Limestone—*Carbonates of Lime* (**Limestones Proper**)—*Carbonates of Lime and Magnesia* (Magnesian Limestones) and *Sulphates of Lime* (Gypsum)—Marbles—Oolites—Bedding of Limestones—Limestones in the Quarry—Quarries Picturesque Objects—Underground Quarries—Caverns in Limestone—Stalactites and Stalagmites in Caverns—Bone-contents of Caverns—Human Remains in Caverns—Cliff-scenery of Limestone-rock in Derbyshire and elsewhere—Beds of Limestone—Valuable Minerals found **in** Limestone—Composition of ordinary Limestone compared with that of Chalk—Work of **the** Coral Animal—Position and Locality of Limestone-rock and Marble—*Sulphate of Lime*, Gypsum and Alabaster—Position as Rocks—Localities—Uses—*Phosphate of Lime*—Coprolites—General Conclusion concerning Limestones .................................................................................. 91

## Chapter the Sixth.

### SAND AND SANDSTONE.

Universality of Sand—Gold Sands—Their Wide Range—Silica Sands—Nature of Silica—Varieties of Silica commonly found—Flints—Their Nature and Composition—Appearance under the Microscope—Uses **of** Flint—Flint **common in** Chalk, and other Forms of Silica in other Limestones—Sandstone—**Varieties** of Sandstone—Their Uses—Flagstones—**Footprints** and other Markings **on** Sandstone—Their Origin—Abundance in certain Districts—The Animals **that have made these** Markings—Sandstones of this kind rarely good for Building—Salt in Sandstone Deposits—Gypsum found with Salt in Sand—Bitumen and Asphalte in Sand-rocks—Use of Sandstone in allowing Water to percolate—Fossils found with Sand-rocks—Minerals in Sandstone and Quartz—Gold Sands—Quartz Rocks and their Appearance—General Barrenness of Quartz Sands and Rocks.................................................. 106

### Chapter the Seventh.

#### GRANITE, GRANITIC ROCKS, AND LAVA.

Varieties of Stone not yet treated of—Where Granite is best seen and studied—Reefs and Detached Rocks and Islands—Cliffs—Color as well as Form of Granite peculiar—Rounded Mountains and Pyramidal Peaks of Granite—Granite in Egypt—Buildings of Granite sometimes almost indestructible—Natural Cliffs of Granite sometimes rapidly worn—Composition of Granite—Principal Varieties—Granite Veins—Their Contents—Granite in principal Mountain-Chains—Porphyry—In what it differs from Granite—Extreme Hardness of Porphyry—*Lava*—Its Nature—*Basalt*—Where chiefly found—Properties—*Gneiss* and *Schists*—Rotten Granite—Picturesque Examples of decomposed Granite in Bavaria .................................................. Page 121

## PART THE THIRD.
## THE PLACEMENT AND DISPLACEMENT OF THE STONES IN THE GREAT STONE BOOK.

### Chapter the Eighth.

#### IN THE BRICK-FIELD AND THE GRAVEL-PIT.

Links connecting the Present with the Past—The ordinary Means at Hand to determine such Links sufficient—Brick Clay—How associated—Mixed with Sand—Supposed to be the Result of a Deluge—Section of a Brick-pit—Condition of a Gravel-pit—Marine Shells and similar Fossils found with Gravel—Effects of Water—Large Districts recently under Water—Effect of Torrents of Water or Deluges—Long Duration of Causes producing Diluvial Appearances—Earthquake Action insufficient to account for a Deluge—Time required—History of a Pebble................................................. 135

### Chapter the Ninth.

#### IN THE QUARRY AND THE MINE.

Quarries almost universally accessible—All Kinds of Stone are quarried—Magnitude of Quarries—Points of Interest in Quarries—What Lessons will be inculcated in this Chapter—Nature of Material quarried—Granite Quarries—Only some Portions of the Stone workable—Reason why there is so much Difference in Quality—Joints and Systems of Cracks—Veins penetrating the Mass of Stones—Frequent Improvement of Quality of Stone in descending—

CONTENTS.    9

Slate Quarries—Their Points of Interest—Facility of Splitting, or *Cleavage*, that characterizes Slate—The Sets of Joints—*Limestone Quarries*—Varieties of Limestone—Joints in Marble and Limestone—Different Kinds of Limestone quarried—Limestone generally much broken near the Surface—Fossils common in certain Beds—*Sandstone*—How bedded—Marks of Bedding—Joints—*Basalt*—Picturesqueness of Quarries in this Rock—Columnar Character of the Rock—Proof of Igneous Origin of Basalt—General Result of the Examination of Quarries—Under-ground Quarries at Caen—Mining is a kind of under-ground Quarrying—Mines generally—Mining for Coal—Mining in Mineral Veins for Metals and Ores—Systems of Mineral Veins—Example in Cornwall—Right-running Veins and Cross-Courses—General Summary of the Lessons learned in Quarries and Mines .................................. Page 151

## Chapter the Tenth.

### VOLCANOES AND EARTHQUAKES.

Volcanic Mountains—Their Conical Form—Nature of the Eruptions from them—Examples of Ancient and Recent Eruptions—Elevations at which Eruptions may take place in no way limited—Distribution of Volcanoes in Groups in different Parts of the World—Volcanoes now extinct—Universal Proof of the Reaction of the Interior of the Earth on the Surface—Interior of Africa and Australia less Volcanic than other Countries—Hot Springs and other Proof of High Temperature at a Small Depth—History of a Volcanic Eruption—Noises—Outbursts of Gas and Steam with Sulphur—Slight Shocks and Tremblings of the Ground—Eruption of fine Ashes and Dust—Lava—Nature and Amount of this Substance poured out—Little Difference in the Nature of Volcanic Products—What Volcanoes indicate—Earthquakes—Meaning of the Phenomenon—Duration of an Earthquake—Range of a Single Disturbance—Extent of the Earth's Surface sometimes disturbed—Periods when Earthquakes chiefly occur—More Earthquakes in Cold than in Warm Weather—Changes of Level accompanying Earthquakes—Examples in America and India—Upheavals in the Absence of Earthquakes—Scandinavian Coast known to undergo Changes of Level—Raised Beaches in various Places—Importance of recent Changes—Laws and Theories of Earthquakes ....................... 163

## Chapter the Eleventh.

### THE DISTURBANCE OF ROCKS.

Order observable in Stratified Rocks—Appearance of Stratified Rocks illustrated by the Piling of Books—General Irregularity of the Placing—Most of the Rocks are Slanted—The Railroad from London to Brighton—The Sequence of the Rocks observed, and their Meaning—Disruption of the Chalk—More complicated Examples of Tilted Rocks—Further Disturbances indicated—General Result of Travelling across England—Order of the Rocks sometimes disturbed—The Reason of this—Detached Portions of Rocks—Extent and Range of similar Deposits in various Countries—Australia and Africa contrasted with England—Complications of Rocks in Mountain-Districts—Conversion of one Rock into another under such Circumstances—Great Disturbance involved—Upheaval of the Great Mountain-Chains—The Himalayan Chain and the Alps—The Andes—Older but Lower Mountain-Axes—Results of **Upheaval on** the Rocks—Special Language employed by Geologists in describing such Phenomena—Explanation of Terms—*Dip* and *Strike* of Rocks—*Faults*—*Anticlinal Axis*—*Conformable* and *Unconformable Stratification*—Granite the Central Rock of Mountain-Axes—Granite formed at Great Depth—Derivation of Metamorphic Rocks—Catastrophes not necessarily involved in these Changes—Objection **to assuming that the** Changes that have **taken** place have involved a System of Interferences............................ **Page 181**

# PART THE FOURTH.
## THE PICTURES IN THE GREAT STONE BOOK.

### Chapter the Twelfth.

#### WHAT THE PICTURES ARE, AND WHAT THEY MEAN.

Necessity of Time in explaining Elevation of Rocks—Contents of Rocks—Petrifactions, or Fossils—Mode in which Organic Substances may be **preserved**—Organic Remains—The Pictures in the Stone Book—Abundance of Remains of Life—What Parts are likely to be buried safely—Small Proportion of the Whole that can thus be presented for Examination—Great Variety really found in spite of the Causes of Destruction—Further Illustration of the Use of Fossils by a Number of Books—Real Value of the Geologic Record—Simplest Forms of Organization indicated in a Fossil State—Sponges found fossil in various Deposits—Vegetable Remains found in Coal and the adjacent Rocks—Corals frequently indicated by their **actual** stony Skeletons—Peculiarities of Form of the earlier Corals—Stony Parts of Star-fishes and Sea-urchins—Curious Habits of some of these **Animals** assist in the Dispersion of their Remains—Indications of Worms **and Insects** and of Crabs and Lobsters not rare—Bivalve and Univalve Shells—Remains **of** Fishes and peculiar Structure of such Animals favorable for Preservation—Reptiles, Birds, and Quadrupeds—Circumstances under which **Remains of Quadrupeds** might be retained ................................................ 199

## Chapter the Thirteenth.

### ANCIENT FORESTS AND MODERN FUEL.

The Chain of Mineral Fuel through England—Coal Scenery—Visit to a Coal-mine—Impression made on the Visitor—The Floor of the Mine—The Root-lets of Trees in the Floor—Absence of Under-clay in some Coal-fields—Coal very regular in some Countries—Coal the Remains of Ancient Vegetation—Microscopic Evidence of the Origin of Coal—Coal Strata and its Fossils—Abundance of Ferns indicated—Trunks of Trees—Appearance of an ancient Forest of the Coal Period—Principal Varieties of Trees—The *Sigillaria*, or Scarred-trunk Tree-fern—Its Appearance and Chief Characteristics—The Roots (*Stigmariæ*) and their Peculiarities—The *Lepidodendron* an ancient Arborescent Club-moss—The *Calamite*; its Nature and Peculiarities—Tree-ferns very common—Insects found in the Coal-beds—Origin of Coal—Differences between Wood and all kinds of Coal—Multiplication of Beds of Coal on the same Spot—Upheaval of Coal Deposits—How Coal Forests can have grown in Northern Climates—Climate required—Possible Alteration of Northern Climates by Changes in the Land—Former Archipelago probable—Enormous Quantity of Vegetation needed to produce a Bed of Coal—Origin of Coal—Prospect of continued Supplies .................................... Page 218

## Chapter the Fourteenth.

### THE PRE-ADAMITE WORLD.

Remains of Former Inhabitants of the Earth—Ancient Stone Weapons of Pre-historic Races—Relation of Structure to Habits, the Key to this Part of Natural History—Peculiarities of Structure illustrating this—Extinct Species of Animals found among the Fossils—The Study and Use of Fossils determine the Order of Stratified Rocks, and enable Geologists to identify them—Mechanical Illustration of this Mode of identifying Rocks—Frequent Omissions in the Series of Fossils—Imperfection of the Geologic Record—Number and Variety of Objects found Fossil—Remains of Man and of the larger Quadrupeds—Elephants and gigantic Quadrupeds once common in England—The *Mammoth*—Curious and anomalous Forms found in India—The *Sivathere* and others—Remarkable gigantic Sloth-like Quadrupeds in South America—Gigantic Marsupials in Australia—Curious Quadrupeds of the older Rocks—Birds in a Fossil State—Gigantic Birds of New Zealand—Foot-prints of Birds and Reptiles—Reptiles—Frog-like Reptiles (*Labyrinthodon*)—Flying Reptiles (*Pterodactyl*)—Marine Reptiles—*Ichthyosaur* and *Plesiosaur*—Fossil Fishes, with bony Plates coated with Enamel—Fossil Sharks and Rays—Fossil Cuttle-fishes—*Ammonites* and *Belemnites*—Bivalve Shells—Statement of the Law that Fossils are characteristic of Formations—Kinds of Fossils most useful for this Purpose—Vast Profusion of Nature in the Accumulation and Distribution of Fossils.................................................... 240

## PART THE FIFTH.
## THE TREASURES OF THE GREAT STONE BOOK.

### Chapter the Fifteenth.
#### GLITTERING TREASURES OF THE EARTH.

The Earth contains many beautiful and valuable Objects belonging to the Mineral Kingdom—Object of the present Chapter to describe only One Group—The Gems and their Literature—Various Ways of viewing the Subject—The DIAMOND—Anciently valued for special Purposes—Classical Account of its Discovery—Diamonds associated with Gold—Obtained by Washing—Marco Polo's Account of Diamond-finding—Brazilian Diamonds—Composition of the Diamond—Cutting of the Diamond—Colored Diamonds—Large Diamonds—The Pitt Diamond and the Koh-i-noor—Uses of Diamonds—RUBY and SAPPHIRE—Varieties of these Gems—*Corundum*—Greek Name for the Ruby—The Ruby phosphoric—Remarkable Stones—Sapphire; its supposed Value about the Person—Used to engrave upon—EMERALD—Its Properties—Large Specimens without Flaw very rare—Whence obtained—Superstitions concerning this Stone—Large flat Stones admired in the East—Supposed Medical and other Properties—BERYL, or *Aqua-marine*—Its Appearance and Properties—TOPAZ—The Oriental Topaz a Sapphire—Varieties of Color and Uses of the Topaz—GARNET—The *Carbuncle* a Garnet—Color and Properties—*Hyacinth, Zircon,* and other Stones—MOONSTONE and other varieties of *Felspar*—QUARTZ, and the Gems obtained from it—*Crystal*, a Name for Quartz—*Cairngorm, Jasper,* and *Bloodstone*—*Agate, Onyx*, &c. and *Carnelian*—Use of the Onyx in Cameos—*Cat's-eye*, and other Combinations of Quartz with Water—Cavities in Quartz—OPAL—Its great Beauty and Value—TURQUOISE—Its History—PEARLS—Where and how found—Seed-Pearls—AMBER—How found—Its Value—Medicinal Properties—CORAL—Found in the Mediterranean—Curious Superstitions concerning it—Polish Superstitions concerning Gems—Apostle Gems—*Jet, Malachite,* and *Lapis-lazuli*—*Jade*—The Lessons to be learnt from Gems—Their great Beauty and small apparent Use—The Use of Beauty.................................................................... Page 267

### Chapter the Sixteenth.
#### SOURCES OF METALLIC WEALTH.

How the Metals are met with—Native Metals—Ores—Noble Metals generally found Native—They are comparatively rare—GOLD—How Discovered—Chief Localities—Properties of Gold—Gold-dust, Pepitas, and Nuggets—Sudd

Influx of Gold from Time to Time—Very wide Range of Gold—Gold Leaf and Wire—Gold occasionally combined with other Metals—Transmutation of Base Metals into Gold—Real Quantity of Gold obtained very small, compared with the Quantities of other Metals found—Value of Gold not factitious—SILVER—Its Appearance—Less capable than Gold of resisting Acids—Native Silver—Common Ores of Silver—Combinations with Lead and Copper—Properties and Uses of Silver—Silver a Metal very widely distributed—De-silverization of Lead—MERCURY—A Fluid Metal—Amalgam found with Sulphur—Uses of Mercury in the Arts—Divisions of the Base Metals—Malleable Group—COPPER—Its Properties and Peculiarities—Its History—Occasionally found Pure in large Quantities—Ores—Pyrites and Malachite—LEAD—Common Ores—Galena—Properties and Uses of Lead—IRON—Its History—Sources of Supply—Properties and Uses—TIN—Its Uses, History, and Properties—ZINC—When discovered—Very volatile—Uses—NICKEL—Its Value in making German Silver—Its Properties—COBALT—Its Uses—Ores usually found—ARSENIC—ANTIMONY—BISMUTH—MANGANESE—CHROMIUM—Rarer Metals—Meteoric Stones—Metals in the Sun and Stars.................. Page 293

# Chapter the Seventeenth.

## THE CIRCULATION OF WATER.

The Circulation of Water not necessary to Planetary Existence—Universal Distribution of Water near the Earth's Surface—Water exists in two ways in Rocks—Part of it helps to form all Solids—Part fills up the Crevices and Open Spaces in all Rocks—This State of Things only kept up by the constant Circulation—Phenomena of Springs and Wells illustrate this—Course of Water in its Circulation—Water always in the Air—How supplied—How lifted into the Air by Evaporation from the Sea—Drifted along in Clouds—Falling on the Earth in Rain—Conveyance along the Surface in Rivers—Absorbent Power of Sand and Sandstones, Limestones and Chalk—Total Quantity of Water in a given Volume of Rock—Electrical Action in the Conversion of Water into Steam—The Water that falls as Rain—Its Course when it enters the Earth—No Repose in Nature—Changes that take place in the Earth's Interior—Deposit generally as Mud—Partial Drying under Pressure—Subsequent Depression, and final Re-lifting—Results of these Movements—Destruction and Denudation when Rocks come again to the Surface—Result if the Earth were deprived of Water............................ 313

# THE SHUTTING-UP OF THE GREAT STONE BOOK.

## Chapter the Eighteenth.

### CONCLUSION.

General View of the History of the World—Geology a cumulative Science—No Finality in the Discoveries—Observation of Nature the only Path to Geological Discovery—Observation possible to all—Extreme Importance of accurate Observation—No Mystery in Geology—Discovery of Systems and Laws the Result of accurate Observation—The real Method of Nature may be ultimately made out—Geology the most important Department of Natural History—Certainty of Benefit from the Study of Nature in a right Manner—The one great Lesson of Geology is to enforce the Necessity of a careful Study of existing Methods of Nature .......................................... Page 327

# EXPLANATORY LIST

OF

# ILLUSTRATIONS.

## I. Vignettes.

### The Frontispiece.

This Plate represents a group of figures of vertebrate animals such as have existed on the earth at various geological periods. Species are selected that are among the most singular in form and proportions, and also among those whose remains are sufficiently perfect to justify a restoration of the complete animal. The following are the names by which they are known to naturalists, and the deposits in which they are found. They are drawn as nearly as possible to the same scale. Most of the animals are alluded to in Chapter the Fourteenth.

1. MEGATHERIUM, a Newer Tertiary gigantic Sloth.
2. PALEOTHERIUM, an Older Tertiary animal like the Tapir.
3. DINORNIS, a very modern but extinct gigantic Bird.
4. MEGALOSAURUS, a Middle Secondary gigantic Land Reptile.
5. PLESIOSAURUS, a Middle Secondary gigantic Marine Reptile.
6. PTERODACTYL, a Middle and Newer Secondary Flying Reptile.
7. LABYRINTHODON, an Older Secondary and Paleozoic Frog-like Reptile.
8. DAPEDIUM, } two Secondary Fishes of the Lias Period.
9. PTYCHOLEPIS, }

### The Language of the Book.

A sketch illustrating the atmospheric and aqueous forces tending to modify the surface of the earth at present. In this view distant snow-clad mountains, with glaciers in the valleys, are represented in their relation to a river conveying the worn material to the ocean. The rocks and cliffs enclosing the river are much more widely separated than seems due to the magnitude of the river. Near the sea the destruction caused by the tidal wave is indicated, and thus in many ways the language of the Great Stone Book is taught.

### The Stones of the Book.

The Stones of the Book are indicated by a group of very singular boulders, probably worn by exposure to atmospheric influences generally, rather than by water alone. These large egg-shaped stones have been figured from an American sketch. Similar but more angular boulders are found in various parts of Northern Europe. All rocks are Stones of the Book of the World, and picturesque scenery in every country may be regarded as exemplifying some one or other of them.

### The Placement and Displacement of the Stones.

In this diagrammatic sketch are illustrated some of the more striking phenomena of the disturbance of rocks. In the background is a volcano, the immediate indication of the reaction of the interior of the earth on its external surface. On the right are representations of *anticlinal* and *synclinal axes*, *faults*, and other fractures of strata; and on the left are examples of *conformable* and *unconformable stratification*, tilted rocks, and also of the accumulation of *débris* at the foot of cliffs.

### The Pictures in the Book.

A sketch illustrating some of the more remarkable and better-known varieties of tree-vegetation supposed to afford the nearest resemblance to the vegetation of the Coal Period. The tree-ferns, and the curious varieties of palms and pines, characteristic of islands in the South Pacific Ocean, are those that have been chiefly referred to for form and general appearance. The actual shapes, proportions, and markings of the remains of trees, found fossil in our coal-measures, are taken as authorities for the wide divergence from these modern types. Many of the principal forms are described in Chapter the Thirteenth, on "Ancient Forests and Modern Fuel."

### The Treasures of the Book.

A group of some of the most interesting and picturesque minerals and native metals, drawn from specimens in the possession of Professor Tennant. The following are the references to the Plate:—
  1. A mass of small Crystals of Quartz or Rock-crystal of the most usual form (see p. 109).
  2. A specimen of doubly-refracting Iceland-spar or Crystalline Carbonate of Lime.
  3. A fine Crystal of Emerald in its matrix (see p. 275).

# EXPLANATORY LIST OF ILLUSTRATIONS.

4. One of the finest Nuggets of Australian Gold (see p. 295).
5. A very beautiful specimen of Capillary or hair-like Native **Silver** (see p. 299).
6. A specimen of **Malachite or Carbonate of Copper**, showing the concentric structure (see p. 304).
7. **Crystals of** Specular Iron Ore, from the Island of Elba (see p. 307).
8. **A Crystal of** Galena (Sulphuret of Lead) (see p. 305).

## II. DIAGRAMS.

| | PAGE |
|---|---|
| Section through an **Alluvial Valley** | 39 |
| Effects of Ice on the Banks of the Dwina | 56 |
| **The Head of** Earth, the Sand, and the Clays **in** a Brick-pit | 137 |
| **Section from** London to Brighton | 183 |
| Illustration of "Faults" | 192 |
| Anticlinal and Synclinal Axes | 195 |

# Introductory Chapter.

## THE BOOK OF NATURE.

> "To recount almighty works
> What words or tongue of seraph can suffice,
> Or heart of man suffice to comprehend?
> Yet what thou canst attain, which best may serve
> To glorify thy Maker, and infer
> Thee also happier, shall not be withheld
> Thy hearing."
>
> PARADISE LOST, Bk. vii. lines 112–118.

# The Book of Nature.

ALL know what is meant by the Book of Nature. But Nature is rather a Library than a Book; for it is the general and well-stored receptacle of all that has ever been created,—of all that we know and all we have not yet learned,—of all that is animate and all that is inanimate,—of all that is happening and all that has happened, not only on the earth, but above the earth and within it and around it. Nothing once existing has entirely disappeared. Every thing has been photographed, and is preserved for use and reference somewhere and somehow. Every year something is discovered that was not before known; but there remains so vast an amount of material yet unknown and unrecorded, that we may be quite sure it will never be exhausted, however long the human race may remain on the earth, or however highly the faculties of man may be developed.

Nature offers many of her books for our study;

for every department of knowledge, large or small, may be looked on as a separate volume. Astronomy supplies not a few, Chemistry many more, Zoology and Botany each its quota. Of these a number have been read and studied with more or less success. In a few cases we seem to have learnt something of the general plan of Nature; in others, mere glimpses are made out of local and partial phenomena. Many departments have only lately attracted attention; many, probably, there are which are not yet known to exist. Some, on the other hand, have been in course of development ever since man was an intelligent and observing animal, recording his own experiences for the benefit of future races.

Of all this vast wealth of knowledge, there is one book that long escaped notice and study, although, since it was first opened in modern times, it has attracted so much attention, and been so extensively read, that its name and some of its contents are familiar to all. It is the book which teaches us concerning the structure and composition of the earth we live on,—the history of its gradual progress, and of the inhabitants it has had from time to time. It is, in a word, "The Stone Book." The leaves are the various and successive layers of earth and rock that make up the whole solid mass laid bare occasionally in the cliff and the quarry, but generally concealed beneath the soil, and trodden negligently under foot; its pictures are the picturesque remains of its former inhabitants, now long passed away. The Stone Book is the science of Geology.

When first studied, the facts of Geology—the records of this Stone Book, which can be learned only by careful personal observation and an acquaintance with the language of Nature—were comparatively disregarded, and great stress was laid on inferences and theoretical views of little value, and based on preconceived notions. It is so in all matters. Ignorance is bold, and takes high but useless flights; true knowledge is modest, and limits her flight to what she knows she can accomplish safely. Ignorance, having few facts, loses sight of all in her endeavors to generalize; knowledge, with many facts, finds it difficult so to arrange them as to obtain the conclusions they properly warrant. Even at present, those who study Geology are often more apt to generalize than to study detail; but as the facts multiply the deductions become more sound, though at the same time more difficult. The earth, however, really contains its own history within itself. The leaves of the Stone Book may be carefully conned: what is found in one may be compared with what is indicated in another; the illustrations, ancient and modern, may be studied; and if, in this as in many other books, the early pages should seem dry and barren of incident, still, as we advance, the plot thickens, and the *dénouement*, when reached, interests us all directly and personally, as well as tends to clear up early obscurities in the history of Creation.

By the opening of the Stone Book, I mean the earliest studies of the earth with a view to make out its history, and these studies teach how Nature speaks rather than what she means. First of all, we must learn the language, and even study the dialect, if we may so far carry into detail our literary illustration. And this is so because here, as in various sciences, the class of objects to be studied, and the mode of studying them, must be governed by circumstances. In Geology it is very necessary, in almost all cases, not only to observe, but to infer. In order to infer, careful observations must first be made, and thus there is a double work to be carried on. As each point is made out, and each fact discovered, its meaning and bearing on the whole must be carefully learnt; and all these bearings being brought together, we obtain at last a sound basis on which to rest our conclusions.

There is but one way in which Geology can be understood, and that is by a thorough familiarity with all that is going on now, both in the animate and inanimate kingdoms of Nature. These represent the language in which the Stone Book is written. We may open the book at random, and be astonished, but we cannot be interested or instructed without this: for what is any one the wiser, when he or she has merely stared with astonishment at the strange skeletons in the British Museum, or the still more strange stony monsters perpetually threatening the following night's repose of the visitor to the gardens of the Crystal Palace at Sydenham? He is none the wiser for these visions, if he does not know how and where the bones were found, according to what principles the skeleton was converted into the semblance of an animal, to what period of the earth's history they belong, and what relation they bear to existing and familiar races. What, again, can be learned at the seaside by the examination of a lofty sea-worn cliff, showing varieties of rock utterly unlike similar rock elsewhere, and placed in all kinds of impossible positions, if we have not been taught what is now being done in other parts of the world that may result in a similar cliff? Who can understand the wonderful columns of Fingal's Cave in Staffa, or the Giants' Causeway on the coast of Ireland, who has not familiarized his eye to similar appearances, where their origin is more manifest, and their history clearly made out? Experience and knowledge can alone guide us in these matters.

When, therefore, we speak of the opening of the Stone Book, we allude to all those inquiries and considerations that are preliminary to the study of Geology properly so called. How few persons, comparatively, think of the grand operations that are always going on around us! These operations are silent, but they are incessant; and most of us behave as if the things that go on every day without disturbance were not really going on at all. The regularity of a change, no matter what its amount may be, is quite sufficient to make us fancy that there is no change at all. The sun shines, the rain falls, the wind blows, the summer and winter succeed each other, and we grow old, fancying all the time that there is no difference, and little aware that all Nature is getting older as well as ourselves, and that nothing of us, and little that is around us, is the same, in a material sense, to-day as it was a few years ago. The times change, and we change with the times; and because all change together, we act and talk as if there were no change at all.

Geology is a history of the earth,—a history of what it was, and of how it became what it is,—a history of the successive events in its progress, of the succession of plants and animals that have occupied it. To learn the history, we must know the causes that have operated; and thus we are thrown directly upon the study of existing causes of change. For a long time, no one seemed to imagine that a study of what goes on now could help us to an understanding of the earth's early history. But, if not that, what could? What can we know of forces concerning which we have no experience? How can we judge of the effect of a rush of water, without measuring the effect of the nearest approach to a deluge that comes within our experience?

To understand any thing of rocks, we must learn how they have been formed; and to learn this, we must look out for the nearest approach to such formations at present. So, also, to understand fossils, which are the remains of former animals and vegetables, we must study animals and vegetables now living. The present is the key of the past.

Strictly speaking, the language in which Geology is written is a picture-language, and the pictures are the events going on around us, according to the ordinary course of Nature. The river and the sea, the heat and the frost, the heavy rain and the continual drought, all afford illustrations. In the same way, illustrations are derived from the plants and animals characteristic of our own and other countries.

As in all cases where Nature is to be studied, it is of singularly small consequence where or how the study begins. Every one in his own neighborhood may find enough to amuse, enough to suggest thought, enough to instruct, and enough to puzzle. Who is there who cannot, within a day's excursion, find some cliff, some railway cutting or tunnel, the bed of some stream, some quarry, or some pit, to study? Even the sinkings made for the foundation of a house or church, or any public work, are often sufficient. Wherever and whenever we can see below the vegetable soil—whether reaching gravel, or sand, or stone of any kind—there will be some instructive lesson afforded.

Let us proceed, then, first, to consider what these common appearances mean, and thus become familiar with the hieroglyphic language in which so much of the Stone Book is written. We may then with advantage study the various materials—the rocks, as they are called—which make up the part of the earth presented for our investigation.

There are certain appearances and facts so familiar to all that they are seldom thought of, as being themselves only agents in the great work of Nature. It is, perhaps, the perfection of Nature that, in all stages of her progress, she exhibits at the same time, in different places, the birth or first beginning of her great operations, her work fully developed and in perfect condition, and the same work in a state of commencing decay. The purpose for which it was adapted having been accomplished, the completion of each one operation generally serves as the commencement of a still larger progress in another. An illustration from Astronomy will render this more clear. Our earth of itself gives us, in all points, a perfect habitation,—perfect in its history of the past, perfect in its adaptation to the present. All is in order and harmony, and for long ages men believed, naturally enough, that their habitation was the central and only object of God's care. They thought the sun was made to light them alone by day, and the moon to shine at night only for their benefit,—that the twinkling light of the countless stars served only to give a faint addition to their night's glory, and that the occasional comet rushed through space merely to warn them of coming danger, or astonish and disturb them. They were right in one sense; for all these are, no doubt, real purposes, except, perhaps, the last. But they thought not of the earth being one only of a group of similar bodies, performing a part in Nature comparatively very small,—that myriads of suns existed which they saw not, and perhaps many more myriads of bodies which they never will see or know of, so long as they remain mortal,—that the sun served other earths besides this, and that the earth may be as useful to the moon and stars, and even to the sun and comet, as these are to the earth. The whole of the earth's history may be but as a day in the history of the universe, though each fraction of a moment of that day is fraught with important results to every one of us. It is not, indeed, on that account less real and significant, or less perfect. On the contrary, it is more perfect, and perfect in a higher sense, and is far more significant. Every part illustrates the great whole; every fact in Nature helps to explain every other fact; and by continually learning more and more about the particular planet which was at their disposal, astronomers have at length succeeded in gaining important and definite knowledge about the distant bodies which they can only approach at second-hand.

And just so it is with Geology. Every day's history is the key and the clue to the history of ages long since past. By searching out the meaning and object of the small and apparently unimportant changes that are produced by the ordinary action of familiar causes and known modes of operation, the nature of a deposit of mud, the conversion of mud into stone, the change of stone into some other substance or some other kind of stone, have been successively made out. The history has been obtained by comparing and studying familiar things.

And of all familiar causes, those that are produced by moving water and changes of temperature are incalculably the greatest. Others are occasional, but these never cease; others may be larger and more active at certain times or in certain places, these go on at all times and in all places. Thus the river-bed and the sea-beach, as illustrations of the influence of sun and rain, wind and frost, afford admirable first lessons in Geology. They teach the alphabet and grammar of the language of our Stone Book. They cannot be too often looked to, or too much thought of.

It may seem that the only means of obtaining access to the earth's interior must require some operations of digging or quarrying. No doubt the laying bare the framework of Nature, by breaking through the outer shell or crust, is calculated to teach us much useful information; but we shall see, as we go on, that there are other and sometimes readier methods of opening the book than by the use of the hammer and wedge, the pick and the gad. Many and good lessons may be learnt, and the early pages of Nature's Book may be studied to advantage, even where mines and quarries are not easily accessible.

# PART I.
## THE LANGUAGE of the GREAT STONE BOOK.

# THE GREAT STONE BOOK.

## Part I.

# Chapter the First.

## THE RIVER-BED AND THE SEA-BEACH.

FAR away among the distant hills are the first trace of the great river that rolls along so grandly as it nears the sea, carrying on its broad bosom the ships that come and go and help to communicate with all parts of the world. Very clear and bright is the water that first bubbles out of the earth and runs along the narrow rocky bed. You might step across it easily there, and walk up through the stream without wetting your ankles. A little further on, indeed, there begin to be holes, in which speckled trout love to take shelter; and further on still is the first mill, near where the country opens out at the foot of the hills, and now villages are seen, and corn-fields and orchards. Afterwards other streams join the growing river: each individually is small, but each helps to increase the supply of water; and as the river flows onwards it becomes gradually wider and deeper, and moves with a more even and regular pace, utilized all the way, either to drive wheels or to irrigate the soil, or else made to branch off into some canal, on which the barges are constantly travelling, laden with the produce of the interior or carrying into the country various articles brought from the sea-coast.

The history of a river is often a simple statement of this kind, commencing as a spring of living water, gushing from a hill-side, and finding its way in some natural channel over the surface. By small degrees and successive additions it becomes a considerable body of water, flowing along a well-defined channel and draining a large tract of country. Occasionally, it meets with obstacles, and is swollen into a lake, or it leaps over a cataract before it leaves the hills; and sometimes, after having long occupied a sufficient channel, it enters a rocky or mountain gorge, where it hurries along over rapids, or dashes with resistless force down a precipice into the valley below.

At a certain point in its course, our river, as it approaches the sea, meets a body of salt water forced up by the tide, and there the salt water, alternately forced forward and carried backwards beneath the fresh, produces a corresponding tide of fresh water, interfering with the otherwise uniform course of the river's current. When the fresh water enters the sea, it floats for some time before it becomes so far mixed with the salt as to form a common part of the great ocean.

Throughout its course, whether amounting only to a few miles or continuing for hundreds of miles, the water is constantly running. Whence comes this large supply, and how is it that the river never ceases its flow to the sea, and in many countries never seems to alter much in the depth or width of its channel? The small spring that forms the source would not, if multiplied a thousand times, fill this wide and deep channel. It is in fact, by an almost infinite multitude of small streamlets entering, after every shower of rain, from all the gutters and puddles and drains, not only into the river itself, but into all the smaller rivulets that feed it, that the great body of water is obtained that finds its way to the sea. Every shower thus helps to feed the river, and the rain that falls is sure to find some ready means of getting back to the great reservoir from which it originally came.

If we look at the river after wet weather, we find it muddy: the water is loaded with particles of the soil, and these are carried along as far as we can see. We know that the mountain-rill and the trout-stream are clear and bright, for we can see every pebble at the bottom; and we might be at a loss to know how the mud came into the water, if it were not for the explanation just given. The soil is washed into the river, and part of it is carried by the river a long way.

Now let us look at the bottom or bed of the river. Near its source it consists of large, broken, rough stones—often huge masses of granite, or limestone, or sandstone; and if we watch for a few seasons, we shall see that these do not remain in the same place. They are carried down, perhaps, only a few yards in a year, but still they move. We do not suppose that the force of the stream is strong enough to carry them along, for we can easily keep back the water by the hand, but could not with any effort move the larger stones. The stream, however, works insidiously and undermines as it goes along; for the water is always moving a multitude of small stones on which the larger blocks rest, and from time to time, their floor being taken away, they tumble over—the direction they take in falling being always governed by that in which the water is going. Being constantly rolled over and over, and knocked against by other stones, they are often broken, and as they get down the stream they become smaller and smaller, being more easily and frequently rolled over and broken, till at last they are reduced to pebbles, whose edges are rounded and almost polished by being rubbed constantly one against another. While these pebbles are being made, the smaller particles are converted into still smaller stones and sand. This is the way in which the bed of the brook and mountain stream is produced. It is a mixture of sand and stones of all sizes and shapes, and the whole of it has been obtained by slow degrees from rocks, which were at first hard, solid masses, just like those we now find it so troublesome to climb over to get at the top of the hill.

The bed of the river lower down is made up nearly in the same way, only instead of stones the mud is brought in from the clay lands on the banks. More clay than sand is carried along by the water, because the particles of clay are smaller, and do not sink so fast as the large pieces of stone. It is not that the clay is really lighter than the stone, because if you take a hard lump of clay and throw it into a basin it will sink to the bottom as fast as any stone, but if you mix it well up the water will look dirty. After a time all the little particles of mud will, however, sink, and the water will clear again.

The water carries along the mud and stones with it, and the faster it flows the further of course they travel. At last, if the river enters a lake and ceases to run so fast, they sink down, and the river runs clear from the other end; but if the river flows on to the sea the mud goes with the water, dropping as it goes, but always supplied again at every mile from the banks on each side, till at last the fresh water approaches the great body of salt water in the sea. As the sea only rises and falls with the tide, except where the tide runs up the river, there are no longer the means of carrying on the mud, and it sinks to the bottom.

Do you see now what all this comes to? The river receives muddy water, sand, and stones, and carries all these along a little way; but as it is always receiving some, and always letting some sink, and always carrying some along to the sea, where it all stops, the bed of the river must be constantly getting higher and higher, and at the mouth of the river there must be a great heap of mud, which the river has been bringing down ever since it was a river.

SECTION THROUGH AN ALLUVIAL VALLEY.

a. The hard rock eaten through to form the valley.
b. The alluvial mud deposited by the stream.
c. The present bed of the river.

If you look at the banks of a river you will generally find, as marked in the cut annexed, that they are made of nearly the same kind of mud as the bottom or bed: at least, this is the case near the mouth of the river, and where it runs through open country. In these cases, what are now the banks have been at one time the bottom; and though there seems no change, the channel of the river, or the hollow space along which the water runs, is constantly shifting—perhaps only a few inches in a year, but still enough to keep the course clear. The current of the water is always strong enough to eat away part of the banks or the bed to make room for itself.

The surface of a country is everywhere connected with some one or other of the rivers running through the country, and the whole is constantly being pared away. It is true that the process is slow, but it is incessant; and the mud thus moved is heaped up at the mouths of the rivers, tending to extend the land horizontally, giving a larger surface and reducing the elevations.

This is a great lesson in Geology. Over the whole world the hills and mountains are being gradually moved away bodily, and lowered by degrees, because of the rain which falls on them and runs off to form the rivers; and the stones and mud carried away help to fill up the sea. This is the inevitable effect of rain, and it is not a small effect, for the whole of Holland is entirely formed by the mud thus brought down by the river Rhine; the greater part of Lower Egypt, the most ancient agricultural country in the world, was deposited in the same way by the Nile; an enormous country in India is the result of deposits left behind by the Ganges; and, in America, the city of New Orleans is built on mud which the Mississippi has brought down from the interior of the continent it drains. Every day throughout the year does this great river throw into the Gulf of Mexico sufficient mud to make a conical hill half a mile round at the bottom and sixty feet high.

Let the reader endeavor to imagine what this would have been if the mud had really been collected and piled in heaps half a mile apart. In the course of a thousand years these hills would have occupied a space as large as the whole of the British Islands, France, Belgium, and Holland. And yet the Mississippi is but one of the great rivers of the earth; and all the others, whether great or small, are always doing similar work,—some of them, perhaps, at a more rapid rate.

The river-bed, then, is not to be despised. It represents the result of running streams in removing solid matter all over the earth, and a little consideration shows that a great deal of such work is done.

But it must not be supposed that, having looked at the beds and banks of rivers, we have seen all the effect of moving water. Almost everywhere there is a wide space of comparatively flat land near the river, particularly during the latter part of its course, and all this, too, has been produced by the same cause, though completed long ago. Even far up steep mountains, and away from all rivers, there are often flat patches of cultivated land, and occasionally bogs and marshes; while many rocks, exposed to the action of running water, and formerly bare, are now thickly covered with vegetable soil. Almost everywhere we may see, by a little careful examination, some of the changes that have been produced on the land by this powerful agent, many of them commenced and completed within even that short time during which we have any good maps, or an account we can depend upon.

The sea-beach is covered with pebbles and coarse sand, and sometimes with very fine sand and mud, wherever the bare, naked rocks do not present a strong wall against the inroads of the waves. But the sea-beach is not quite like the river-bed: the pebbles are rounder, more uniform, and more abundant, the broken rocks more jagged, the sands more shifting, the mud is not of the same kind; and altogether there is a sufficient difference to enable any geologist to say at once, if taken to a natural heap of gravel or bed of mud, to which cause the heaping together was due. Sea-beaches are found sometimes inland, so that the difference requires to be learned by the young geologist.

Most persons have listened, at Brighton or elsewhere, to the peculiar and incessant roar of the sea as it breaks upon a pebble shore. Along many miles of beach the restless waves are always either advancing or receding, according as the tide is rising or falling, and every wave carries backwards and forwards a certain breadth of pebbles, which are then made to roll over each other with some force. Now, if stones are rubbed together the corners are knocked off, and they become at last smooth and round, and it is in this way that all pebbles are produced. The particles broken from them form sand; and as there is thus a constant tendency to grind the sea-pebbles into sand, there can be no doubt that in a short time they would all be worn away, if there were not an ample supply constantly provided. It is a curious question where the new pebbles come from, and one not always easily answered. Generally, however, we can trace them readily enough to the rocks not far off. Just as the blocks in the river-bed get broken up and carried away, so those that fall from the cliffs into the sea are turned, after a time, into smaller stones and sand. Where the whole rock is hard the quantity of sand is small, but where the rock is soft, even if it contains hard lumps, there will be a great deal of sand or mud, or both, to mix with the pebbles. But the mud is easily removed, and is generally carried into sheltered nooks, where the tide has little force, and where the water is still. Wherever water is left undisturbed the mud will sink and be found at the bottom, leaving the water itself clear and transparent.

Very large and deep accumulations of gravel and sand exist near the sea, and wells are often dug in such gravel, in places where one would suppose the sea had never been. But a heap of well-rounded beach-pebbles must have been brought to their shape and rolled about in water, so that we are obliged to suppose either that the sea has left that part of the shore, or else that the whole body of the land thereabouts has been upheaved from below; unless, indeed (which is perhaps sometimes the case), the pebbles and sand have been gradually thrown up until they formed a kind of natural wall which the waves do not break through except on very extraordinary occasions. The water in the ocean is just like that in a trough or cistern, the surface of which cannot for any time be kept aslant. It is one of the properties of all liquids to come to a level wherever they are placed, and so the sea must ever retain its level, one part not remaining permanently lower on any coast, unless, indeed, the whole body of water in the ocean were to diminish or become lowered by the deepening of its bed; and of this we should have independent proof.

Almost everywhere, then, in the neighborhood of all the rivers and little streams, by the sea-side, and even in the open country of some parts of the world, there is a constant movement and shifting of the earth's surface. There is a proverb which says, "continual dropping will wear away stone," and it is perfectly true in every sense; for where water is constantly dropping or running or beating, by the action of the waves, stone, however hard, is gradually but surely worn away, while sands and mud are eaten into very fast. But water is wonderfully helped in all these cases by the rubbing together of the stones themselves, which at first it may only be just able to move, but which are soon rolled over and over; and since the water never gets tired of doing its work, but takes advantage of every little chance that comes in its way, we find that, however slow the process at first, an impression is soon made, and in time the hardest granite is turned into the finest mud, and nothing can resist so indefatigable an instrument. It must be remembered, too, that the rain of to-day, falling on the ground clear and running off by a dirty puddle, becomes the cloud of to-morrow by the process of evaporation, but leaves the mud behind. Passing through the air, it may fall again in rain at some other place; so that if it has not a long course, and does not on each occasion perform a large task, it at any rate is soon ready to recommence its work. If it runs long over the earth it is always helping to move solid matter, and when it retires into the bosom of the ocean it is still never at rest. There is, indeed, no such a thing as rest for water, even for a moment, for water is always in circulation here and there and everywhere,—in the sea, in the river, in the air, on the earth, and even within the earth. Not only is it never quiet, but it is always helping to move and disturb and destroy all other created matter.

This account of what water does in the river and on the sea-beach clears up wonderfully some of the great mysteries of Geology. In Geology we have to examine large results, and we cannot judge of them at all without knowing something of the operations now going on upon the earth, since these afford the only means of comparison open to us. In all these water is an important agent. It acts very widely and very powerfully,—without ceasing, and often without much noise. Its effects are easily overlooked, and not very easily done justice to, so that there is little fear of its real importance being estimated too highly.

If we would learn the ordinary language of Nature, we must study the familiar expression of her ways as events pass on from hour to hour, from day to day, and from year to year, with a true regularity, and even monotony, in the midst of the greatest apparent irregularity. To do this, it is absolutely necessary to consider the effect of water as it circulates through the earth, as it passes from the sea to the sky, and as it returns in refreshing showers from the sky to the earth, and so back again to the ocean. It is this circulation more than any thing that serves as the means of communication— the connecting link—between the power and the conveyer of power. It is to the ordinary force of running water that we must refer many changes apparently far too great to be thus brought about. It is to this that we must ultimately refer, even when many other causes act, each of which apparently is much more powerful.

The river-bed and the sea-beach, inasmuch as they illustrate the ordinary action of running water, are beyond a doubt the most instructive and the most interesting of all the studies preliminary to Geology; but, after all, they represent only one of several ways in which water acts upon the earth. They do not include the results of changes of temperature on substances containing water, nor do they refer to the action of ice. Let us pursue the subject, then, a little further in another chapter.

## Chapter the Second.

### THE SUN, THE WIND, THE RAIN, AND THE FROST.

The brook and the wave break up the large stones that fall into the bed of the one from the mountain-side, or come under the action of the other on or near the shore. But how do the large stones first become loosened from the rock, and what are the causes of so much material being supplied to make pebbles, sand, and mud? If we watch the mountain-side or the sea-cliff, we may obtain an answer to these questions.

After a long dry season the earth is parched and cracked at the surface, clays gaping with wide fissures, and some other rocks, such as sandstones, showing open splits of considerable depth. In warm countries these are several feet wide and some yards deep; but even in England, though rarely so wide, being measured by inches instead of feet, they penetrate some distance. This is evidently the effect of the sun's heat in drying and so contracting the surface of rocks. Some things swell with heat and become softened, but earth and rocks losing their moisture shrink and get harder, as any one may satisfy himself by a little observation.

But after long drought comes a shower of rain: the rain pours down at once into the cracks, and penetrates far down into the interior of the rock. The part first moistened cools and swells, and acts as a kind of wedge, splitting the whole into pieces if the rock is at all brittle. Down come large fragments tumbling into the bed of the stream; other detached blocks rest for a time on the hill-side, while others come within the influence of the sea, falling at the foot of the cliff, and these before long are all broken up into smaller stones and converted into pebbles or mud.

But it is not only in summer that the rocks fall to pieces and feed the rivers and the sea. Long-continued rain at any time penetrates through the crevices of rocks and softens the muddy and clayey parts, so that the harder upper beds slip down over the lower ones and fall into the valley below, where they are allowed to disintegrate slowly in the air, or are rapidly broken up by the water. The same result follows: the work begun by the sun or the rain is finished by the river or the sea, and the earth is pared of yet more of its surface.

When the winter comes the effect is similar, but still greater. Water swells a little when it is about to freeze, as most people know who have left a narrow-necked jug full of water exposed in winter weather. Almost every night, therefore, for some months of the year in temperate climates, there is a continual swelling out and shrinking in of the water in rocks, as far as the weather can penetrate. At last, towards spring, the heavy rains come once more and wash down into the lower depths the whole top of the rock, which is then in a state to fall to pieces on the slightest disturbance.

It might be supposed that, with all this movement

constantly going on, the whole face of a country would be changed every year, so that it would be difficult to know where the landmarks had been placed. It must be remembered, however, that in cultivated countries— where the land is drained, where roads and hedges intersect the fields, and where men do all they can to prevent injury to the surface—the effect is comparatively small. Even in places where men do not grow crops, a natural covering of wood or grass is a very great protection to the surface,—the roots binding the soil together, and checking that wearing away that would otherwise be produced by the rain. It is only where the ground is uncultivated that the full effect is seen; and even then the first change, which turns the hard rock into a rotten earthy soil, will in many cases check further destruction, if the soil is not at once carried off by the rain.

At the same time it will be evident that near the sea, or in hills and mountains where rivers take their rise, and where there are steep cliffs, there will generally be a large quantity of broken rock ready to be ground up into pebbles every year; while in other places, exposed to the same weather, there is hardly any amount of alteration or destruction to be noticed.

Many countries are so placed as to have exceedingly cold weather during a large part of the year. This is the case near the poles of the earth, where there are but two seasons,—a short summer, and the long tedious winter; and it is the case also near the tops of several of the great mountain-chains in different parts of the world. Owing to the absence of any quantity of solid earth to get warmed by the sun's rays, these high peaks and ridges are always excessively cold; and when it would rain below, snow there falls at almost all seasons.

Ice, or water in the solid state,—which, in England, is only occasionally formed during cold winters—is always present in these places, and takes the place of water. Let us see what difference this makes in the action of the water.

Those great mountains the Alps, and particularly the parts of the chain situated in Switzerland, are remarkable for being always covered with snow. People who have not actually travelled can hardly form an idea of the exceeding beauty of a distant chain of lofty snow-capped elevations, shooting up into the sky with every variety of jagged and rounded summit. As you get nearer you see large dark patches, where either naked rock juts out, or where are green slopes covered in summer with cattle; and then, as you come close to the mountains and go amongst them, you find besides the top, which is always white with snow, there are numerous patches of snow, covering thick heaps of ice, reaching down quite into the valleys. In winter these cover the whole flank of the mountain, and even occupy parts of the lower valley; but in summer the surface-snow melts, and we can easily examine and walk over vast fields of ice.

I advise any of my readers who have the opportunity, to look carefully at one of these patches, for they show, more clearly than any description, what ice and frost on mountain-sides are able to perform; but those who have not such opportunity may still feel interested by an account of what others have seen. The path of the ice in the larger ice-fields is marked very distinctly on the mountain-side, and there are often many instances, of exactly the same kind, easily seen and examined within a narrow breadth of country. The mountain-side is, in such cases, smoothed towards the valley, and covered with a continued string of stones of all sizes,—the breadth gradually increasing, and terminating at the bottom in a wide and large heap. Just at this point there is, generally, running water, and the heap gradually diminishes during summer. Where the mountain is high and the sides steep, but not too steep to allow the ice to rest on it without falling, there is sometimes no interval at all between these broad strips of broken stone. Where the mountain is steeper, the ice and stones are seen at intervals only, and between them are waterfalls,— numerous white threads of water leaping down hundreds of feet; while very often the bottom of the fall, and the valley beyond and below, are so completely blocked up by the broken rocks that it is difficult to walk along. Millions of tons of stone and rock are seen, all of which have been recently moved, and the ice and water which helped to move this vast quantity are still visible.

The same thing goes on,—the constant breaking away of the mountain continuing during winter by help of the frost in the upper part, where the ice never altogether disappears. The stones and mud are thoroughly mixed with the ice and form a part of it; they gradually come to the top, because the surface of the ice is always being evaporated by the air, and fresh material is supplied by the frozen snows above.

Such masses of ice, and some of them are many miles in length and of great breadth, are called *glaciers*. They look as if they were quite still, and the ice of which they consist is often concealed by newly-fallen snow all through the summer; but they are always in motion,—the ice creeping slowly down the valleys with a peculiar motion, and melting at the lower end. From the foot or lower extremity of glaciers proceed the first germs of the principal rivers in Europe, and the ice is advancing incessantly, bearing down along with it, in its progress, the stones and mud torn away from the mountain top and sides. These, of course, ultimately enter the valley and are broken up by the running water.

A glacier may be formed in any part of the world, provided the mountains are sufficiently lofty and the prevailing winds carry moisture enough to insure frequent falls of snow. But in those high northern and southern lands where cold sufficient to freeze water is hardly ever absent, as on the shores of the Arctic and Antarctic seas, similar but much larger masses of ice, formed in the same way,—taking their origin from the steep cliffs, and coming from the interior and higher land,—push forward, occupying creeks and inlets, until at last they break off and float away.

In some parts of the world the wind combines with the rain and cold, or even acts independently of it, in removing solid matter from one place to another. On the coast of Flanders, between Dunkirk and Ostend, is a tract of country where almost every wind that blows drifts sand to such an extent as to require careful management lest property should be seriously injured. By making nature oppose herself,—by bringing vital energy to bear against mere mechanical force, and fixing the loose sands by causing roots of particular kinds of grass to penetrate them in every direction, the sand-drift is either stopped or seriously checked.

But in Egypt, and over the whole of that wide and large and little-watered tract in North Africa, known as the Great Desert, the moving columns of sand are not checked, and they have already concealed and buried enormous tracts of fertile land, at one time richly cultivated. There no plants seem likely to grow which could fix the sand, nor are efforts made by human intelligence to combat the natural powers at work. A continual advance of the sand towards the east, due to the prevalence of westerly winds, is a fact no less influential, and produces results no less marked, in Northeastern Africa, than the alternate frost and thaw of the northern countries of Europe, or the rain that washes down its millions of tons into the great rivers of Central Asia and America.

Even the lightning-flash, restoring by a sudden and energetic communication the electric equilibrium between the air and the earth, is capable of producing effects which tend to change and disturb the soil and break up solid rock. Instances are on record of considerable disruption of hard sandstones effected in this way; and as rocks once broken or split, however hard they may be, are soon worn down and lost sight of, even this source of change and destruction must not be disregarded.

Sun, wind, and storm,—rain, snow, and hail,—frost and thaw,—summer and winter,—are thus found to be all of them favorable to the process, eternally going on, of smoothing and paring away the rough surface inequalities, and scooping out new channels and furrows on the earth's wide surface.

There is no day and no hour when such forces are not at work; and we have every reason to conclude that this has always been so, and that at all former periods, as much as at the present time, disturbance and change and mechanical displacement are among the inevitable events of Nature. So far as we can tell, they are inevitable results of the course of Nature as it has been settled for the earth; for nothing else could arise from the admixture of the three conditions of matter,—solid, liquid, and gaseous. So long as this has continued, so long must there have been the same equilibrium produced by the same means,—a means admirably adapted, no doubt, to carry out the intention of the Great Creator, but very difficult for us fully to comprehend in the present limited state of our knowledge. Without these conditions, however, all would be still with the stillness of death. Life consists in this incessant play. Life, perhaps, means some struggle of this kind, in which the elements are constantly entering into new combinations, constantly releasing themselves from those in which they have for a time been imprisoned. Certainly life, in the sense in which we inhabitants of the earth understand it, has very distinct reference to the conditions of matter on the earth. Were the latter to be changed,—were the mean temperature of the air to admit the water generally to be fixed in ice or converted into steam,—how enormous would the difference be!—how completely would almost the whole group of animals and plants pass away!

Thus, then, destruction and renovation, effected by

means of air and water, is one of the laws of Nature: it is the law which leads us to all others; it is the thing to be understood if any thing of Nature's ways is to be learnt. We shall see hereafter how clearly this action of water is marked in all, or nearly all, the rocks that have been formed, and how, if it has not really produced them, it has affected their production.

We shall also see, if it is not already plain, that heat and cold must be constantly alternating; that there must be a means of producing incessant change of temperature if these vast changes and reconstructions of the earth are to proceed. We do not really know, and probably never can know, what conditions of temperature are most favorable to the rapid destruction and reconstruction of rocks. Geologists assume, without knowing much about it, that a higher temperature than we have now, even in the tropics, has formerly existed all over the earth, and would do more in a given time to effect and alter deposits than is now done in that time. On the other hand, we know that many of our greatest recent changes have been brought about in a very cold climate. At any rate, climates have altered, and perhaps the alteration itself has been more important than the nature of it.

Not one of the elements and causes of change to which we have alluded in this chapter and the last is without very great influence and meaning. The sun, as the source of heat and the direct cause of other changes independent of heat and of a chemical nature, is one of the chief. The wind or periodic and occasional motion of the air acts in many ways, directly and indirectly, but always with much effect. It distributes heat, moisture, and cloud. It induces changes in the electrical state of the air, and thus affects the supply of rain. When interrupted, it produces great mechanical pressure.

The rain is too manifest a source of movement to require more than mention. The frost splits up the ground and prepares it for further change. The following diagram offers a curious illustration of this, in a part of the world where the changes of weather are very great:—

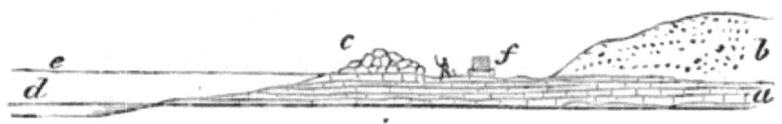

EFFECTS OF ICE ON THE BANKS OF THE DWINA.

*a.* Limestone rock.         *b.* Sand hillocks.
*c.* The limestone broken up by the winter's frost.
*d.* The summer level of the stream.     *e.* The winter level.
*f.* The road on the banks of the river.

Besides all this, every stream of water running over the surface collects the small results and distributes them in order,—carrying some far, leaving others near; while the great ocean, when reached, finally arranges and distributes what is brought down by the river, as well as what it removes by its own waves.

If we could add together the whole annual amount carried along by rivers and left behind before reaching the sea, including the solid rock broken away and converted into boulders, pebbles, sand, and mud,—of cliffs ground into sand and mud by the sea,—of sands drifted by the wind,—of mountain-peaks, jagged rocks, and cliffs thrown down and conveyed away by ice; and if we could multiply this large total by the number of years during which such work has been going on before our eyes, we should understand, better than we can now, the vast importance of considerations of this kind in explaining the great changes that, in the course of that time, have been produced on the earth. Without a careful study of Nature in these matters, in different countries, at various seasons, and under different influences, no one is justified in forming an opinion as to the value of geological evidence,—and, indeed, no one can fully understand the nature of Geology, or the possible extent of changes on the earth's surface in ancient times.

Having now considered these fundamental matters, and learnt something of the mode in which Nature acts at present to produce new things out of old, it will be convenient to pass on at once to consider the materials with which geologists have to deal,—the so-called "*rocks*,"— not always rocky and hard, but, in a word, the materials, whatever they are, of which the earth's external shell is composed. These, of course, vary in different places. They are all, however, reducible to a small number of principal varieties; for they have either been left behind by water, or built up by animals, or accumulated by plants, or they have undergone some chemical change within the earth, or finally they are, or have been for a long while, within the earth in a melted state. The former are of three kinds: they are clays, limestones, and sandstones. The latter are either lavas or granites, or what are called schists.

Let us begin with one of the most common and familiar of all,—the clays that, in one shape or other, are universally spread over the earth. Of all rocks, clays are the most manifestly derived from water, and they are among the least altered from their original condition as mud.

They have, however, undergone many and great changes, and are adapted to illustrate our history of the Stones of the Great Book.

# PART II.
## THE STONES of the GREAT STONE BOOK.

# THE GREAT STONE BOOK.

Part II.

## Chapter the Third.

### CLAY AND ITS VARIETIES.

By clay we understand, not merely the substance commonly so called,—whether in the fields helping to make vegetable soil, or in the pits worked for brick-making, or exported to make porcelain, or for other special purposes,—but also various minerals and rocks derived from it. In this general sense it is a complicated rock of great importance and of great interest.

And, first of all, let us go back to its origin, and connect it, as far as possible, with the element from which it is derived. It is not desirable to do this in all cases in Geology; for many elementary substances, interesting enough to the chemist, are so rare and have so few properties of general interest as not to be worth considering by the geologist. Not so with clay; for the element from which it is derived is already manufactured in sufficient quantity to show that it may hereafter possess importance in the arts, while it is quite remarkable enough to have attracted much attention, and to have been the object of important experiments.

There is a beautiful metal recently brought into use for making bracelets, brooches, and some other personal ornaments; and this metal, while almost of the color of silver, is only about one-fourth its weight,—being in fact no heavier than so much glass. It is called ALUMINIUM; and, although new in one sense, its existence as a chemical curiosity has long been known. This singular substance, called a metal, but in many respects very little like other metals, mixes readily with oxygen gas, and when in the mixed state occurs naturally in several different forms. It is then known as ALUMINA. Crystallized, it becomes a precious ruby or sapphire; half crystallized, but equally pure, it is known as *emery*,—a substance sufficiently rare, but not costly, and found sometimes as a stone, sometimes as a coarse powder. In either form alumina exists ready made in rocks; whereas the metal aluminium is only to be obtained by an extremely expensive and troublesome chemical treatment of some natural ore.

When, however, the comparatively rare mineral, alumina, has combined in nature with another very common substance, *silica* or flint, a third product results, and this is infinitely common and abundant everywhere. This product, mixed with a little water, is, in fact, CLAY.

Clay, then, is derived from alumina, as that is derived from aluminium. It is called by chemists a *silicate of alumina*, to denote its composition, and the form in which one of the metals exists, under ordinary conditions, at the earth's surface.

Silicate of alumina, however, in a perfectly pure state, without water, is hardly found in nature. It occurs in a complicated and ever-changing series of combinations, and when mixed up with a vast variety of other substances as well as water, it is of universal occurrence. It forms a few rare minerals; but we will not here trouble ourselves with the rarities, since the commonest clays are exceedingly useful, and will supply us with ample material for illustration.

The foundation of all natural clays is, we have seen, silicate of alumina combined with water; and the proportion of water varies, according to circumstances, from ten to twenty-five per cent. All clays contain, also, a mixture of sand and some impurities,—these latter, indeed, often giving a distinctive character to the varieties. The common materials met with in clays as impurities are the oxides of iron and manganese, carbon, soda, and potash, and more or less lime and magnesia. Other substances may be present accidentally, but these are all very common; and the quantity of them, and sometimes also the way in which the foreign ingredients are mixed up with the pure mineral, affect the value of the result for those purposes for which the clay is to be used.

One of the properties of clay, which renders it so much more useful than many substances apparently more valuable, and so indispensable to man in almost every state of civilized existence, is its plastic nature,—or, in other words, the property it has of working up into a paste with water, and when once moulded in this state, and exposed to high heat, parting with the water without losing the form given to it. It is in this way that clay becomes *brick*. When it has thus been exposed to great heat, and the water got rid of by burning, clay cannot again be made soft and plastic by merely mixing it with water.

Many stones, if ground very fine and mixed with water, can also be moulded and brought into shape; but in these cases a complete and permanent hardening would not be secured by any heat that the mixture could endure without melting. Some of the clays (though reckoned as among the most refractory and troublesome of all rocks) will themselves melt in the fire which is intended only to harden them; but this is owing to an excess of soda, potash, limestone, or other flux, any one of which ingredients may help to convert the clay, when burnt, into a sort of opaque glass. It must not be supposed that, merely because they may all be moulded, all clays are essentially of the same kind and equally unlike other minerals. There are, for example, various degrees of plasticity,—some very complete, others very imperfect. It has been found, generally, that pure clays, free from all foreign ingredients except pure silica sand, are the most manageable and the best that can be used, since they are not only more easily worked, but the hardest and most beautiful after burning.

Common brick clay fairly illustrates the general properties of the whole group. Some of the best brick clays contain a great deal of sand, and enough oxide of iron to color them deeply. The dark color of such clays is due also, in part, to minute particles of carbon derived from vegetable matter with which they are mixed; but the material that produces the deep bright red so common with burnt bricks is iron, and before burning is generally of a dirty yellow or brown tint.

Besides carbon and iron, and a good deal of sand, brick clay contains lime, potash, and soda. Of all these the less there is the better is the clay,—the less risk is there of the bricks running together in the kiln, and the harder and firmer will they be ultimately. It might be thought that too much sand would be injurious; but this is not the case,—some of the best clays for burning containing the largest proportion of sand. The iron, or rather oxide of iron, may also be abundant without injury.

Very fine clays occur in small quantities in some parts of the country, especially near coal-beds, from which can be made bricks which resist any amount of heat in a wind-furnace. These are the *fire-clays*, and their properties are owing to the almost entire absence of the alkalies and the presence of but little iron. They are often loaded with bitumen, which of course disappears in the kiln where they are burnt. Stourbridge clay from near Oxford, other clays near Newcastle, and others again near Glasgow, are all celebrated for making those bricks which best resist intense heat. They are called fire-bricks, and are made with much greater care than common bricks. Besides the careful working that such clays require before using, they must be exposed for a long time to the air after being taken from the earth, for unless thus seasoned they cannot be depended on. A good deal of the *terra-cotta* work, used commonly enough in buildings and garden-terraces where ornament is required at small cost, is made of these superior varieties of brick clay; but they are all subject to the great disadvantage of shrinking. This they do very much and very unequally, while undergoing the intense heat of the kiln necessary to bake them.

Potter's clay, of a blue color and excellent quality, is obtained from the little peninsula called the Isle of Purbeck, on the Dorsetshire coast. It is also found elsewhere, and its peculiar value depends on the composition.

Some kinds, without much sand, and of very uniform texture, are adapted for the artist's use as modelling-clay; and these, if burnt, are remarkably smooth and beautiful. Other kinds, without iron, make tobacco-pipes, while the iron varieties are used for the common red pottery-ware seen everywhere. There are two kinds of pottery, one being dark red and comparatively soft; the other, called stone-ware, of pale color, and very hard.

China clay is a still finer kind. Formerly the finest China clays were only known to occur in China and Japan, and they are still known by their Chinese names, *kaolin* and *pe-tun-tse*. Large quantities are now obtained from England, France, and Germany, and are much used in the manufacture of the finer kinds of pottery and porcelain. It is a striking thing to see and examine some of the largest and most regular works where the clay is dug, cleaned, and prepared for the market. This clay is principally derived from Cornwall and Devonshire. The process of cleaning and separating the clay from sand and dirt is carried on in pits, where the raw material is conducted by water and allowed to settle. When afterwards dried, it is cut into bricks and sent to the Staffordshire potteries. The operation is tedious, many months elapsing, even in favorable weather, before the clay is ready; for it is extremely necessary that the material sent should be as pure as possible.

There is a kind of clay found in Tuscany, not far from Sienna, and also in France, which has a large admixture of magnesia in its composition, and from which bricks may be made. When either dried or burned, these bricks are much lighter than water, and they are also very efficacious in resisting heat. The common Bath scouring-brick, used for various purposes, is made in the same way, and from somewhat similar materials.

Fuller's earth is another clay possessed of some curious properties. It consists of nearly twenty-five per cent. of water, dissolving almost entirely when mixed with water, and melting when exposed to heat. This clay absorbs grease very readily, in spite of its water, and is much used in cleaning or *fulling* cloth. For this reason it is called fuller's earth.

Some of our clays in England are valuable for purposes that at first they would seem hardly fit for. Thus the *lias*, or "*blue lias*," a common rock in the middle of England, is particularly useful in the manufacture of cement. It is a clay which contains much limestone, and burns into a kind of lime, which when made into a mortar sets rapidly in damp air, and even under water. It is thus extremely convenient for building purposes; and the mortar thus formed is called *hydraulic cement*. It is made from impure clays and limestones, the peculiar properties for which it is valued depending on the presence of foreign substances, so that the impure clays are more valuable than those kinds which are more free from foreign admixture.

Among the blue clays of the Lias, and below them, are certain slaty beds, from which the alum of commerce is obtained. The coast of Yorkshire near Whitby is one of the places where this manufacture is largely carried on. It might have been thought that alum has little to do with clay: this is not so, for the one is derived from the other; and, as we have already had occasion to remark, the apparent impurities and foreign matters in clay are materials of value in certain important manufactures.

It will be evident, then, that the ordinary clays under our feet, forming the soil or subsoil of the earth, contain materials of great interest, which are often largely employed for manufacturing purposes. From some such clays we make bricks,—an admirable substitute for stone as a building material in our climate; from others, apparently little different, we make pottery and porcelain; from others, again, cements are manufactured; while some yield alum by elaborate chemical preparation.

These clay-beds do not (like the limestone) show any marks of having been formed by animal or vegetable help, for clay is not a substance that enters directly into the composition of living beings; and the expressions often made use of in reference to clay as an emblem of mortality are not really very applicable. A vast amount of decomposition and recomposition must, in fact, go on before any kind of substance resembling clay enters into the human frame, or the frame of any animal, as a component part; and even then the essential elements are very small in amount. Carbon in abundance, and lime, and iron, and even some silica, are traceable in the structure of living tissue, but of clay properly so called (pure hydrous silicate of alumina) there is none.

But although this is certainly the case, it is not the less true that clay plays a part in nature hardly exceeded in real importance by any substance. As the soil and subsoil in large districts of cultivated land, its conditions and peculiarities affect all vegetation to an enormous extent. If a clay soil be not well drained, so that the water, when it gets down within the clay, remains for a long time without a chance of absorbing fresh air,—a thing very likely to happen in undrained land,—the result is exceedingly injurious.

The moisture, then, instead of encouraging vegetation, completely poisons it, becoming highly mischievous instead of beneficial. In drained land, when the stiff clay is treated with lime, or mixed with sand, or in any other way rendered accessible to the water and prevented from caking into bricks, a clay soil is good and useful.

Stiff clay retains water on the surface in pools, not allowing it to pass down. Whenever, therefore, a bed of such clay, covered by more open and porous rock, is laid bare by a cliff or railway-cutting, or by the natural slope of a hill, it is very likely that the water should come out on the side of the cutting in natural springs. There are very simple conditions also under which, when beds of clay are bored through, or when borings through other rock reach clay, there should be natural jets of water, such as are called Artesian springs.

Although clay is not formed or separated by animals or vegetables, still many beds of it contain fragments of wood, shells, bone, and other substances, which serve to show very clearly the circumstances under which the deposit was brought together. It is curious enough to find among these many indications, and sometimes whole skeletons, of animals of which all traces have long passed away from the world of life.

Among the shells found in the Lias clay, and in another bed, called Oxford clay, lying over it in some places, there are various kinds that seem to have had a general resemblance to the squids and cuttle-fish now living; but they were provided with a long pen or solid framework different in shape from that of any yet found. The squid now is a soft animal, having a plate of horny or solid matter (generally limestone) for the sake of attaching its muscular system. It has also a very curious apparatus of claws for holding its prey, and a small receptacle of ink, with a tube by which it can shoot out the ink and darken the water. It is not a little curious to find buried in the clay remains of ancient animals of the same kind, such as the thickened and dried ink, the bag in which it was preserved, the delicate little hook by which the creature could touch any thing that came in its way, and the tube conducting to the ink-bag, unemptied at the death of the animal.

Yet more singular remains are found in the same bed. Among them are entire skeletons of large lizards, shaped like fishes, and evidently adapted to live almost entirely in the water, if we may judge by the presence of fins and the absence of legs. Of such animals we find occasionally not only the hard bones and teeth, but the marks of a soft skin and large fins, showing that the animal was not covered with scales, and there are even the contents of the stomach, with fragments of indigested, half-digested, and digested food, and the bones of the latest prey that had been devoured.

The parts of clay-beds that are mixed up with limestone often contain other remains of animals, such as might be expected in that mineral and not in pure clay. Thus, fragments of coral, and little shells like those at the bottom of the deeper parts of the Atlantic, are here found, with scales and teeth of fishes and shells of unfamiliar animals.

The fragments of vegetation found in these beds are generally water-worn or altered. They do not form good coal; but some of them can be, and are, used for fuel when no better can be had. Some of them are changed into jet, and are valued for ornamental purposes. Much of the clay thus loaded with organic matter, and black or brown with bitumen, is now extensively used in the manufacture of mineral oil.

The number of different beds of clay found in England is very large, and they are characterized by very different remains. Thus, at the mouth of the Thames, in the Isle of Sheppy, are numerous fruits of tropical trees, with bones of alligators, large serpents and vultures, and even remains of monkeys, all buried together and lying over the chalk. Inside the chalk range in Surrey and Sussex there are other varieties of clay loaded with very minute valves of a small fresh-water animal. Near Weymouth there are clays, with bad coal, used in making pottery. These clays are below the chalk; and others again, below them, and on which they rest, are worked near Oxford. These extend eastwards to Cambridgeshire and Lincolnshire, and form the well-known Fen country,— out of which rises Ely, on a small island in the middle of a vast level space of such clays. Peterborough is not far off, proving that there must have been some attraction in monkish days to induce a settlement in these rich but uncomfortable and aguish tracts of country.

The Lias, seen well on the coast at Lyme Regis in Dorsetshire, and Whitby in Yorkshire, and extending through the midland counties, is another great and thick clay deposit; and others again are known in places further to the west.

Each of these clay localities is remarkable for some peculiarity by which its clay may be recognized. In many cases the difference in the appearance of the clays is well marked; but, if not, the remains of animals found in them would decide the question. Thus, no fragments of any of the curious and gigantic fish and lizards are met with, except in the group of rocks between the chalk and the coal deposits, while the shells, and even the corals and star-fishes, found in the clay-beds of Herefordshire and Wales, are quite unlike those of the deposits near the middle of England.

We have already said that, by piercing through many of the clays, springs of water are arrived at which reach or approach the surface. This occurs when the water flows beneath sloping beds of which the uppermost is clay, there being tolerably free communication with the surface on the upper part of the slope, but no means of escape for the water from the other end. In such cases the water is under pressure, and when an opening is made it will immediately rush up in the endeavor to find its level.

We have hitherto been regarding clay in its most usual form, as a tough, elastic mineral, and a substance which cannot remain hard after long exposure to wet. Let us now look at it in another light. If we use clay to make bricks, of which we build our houses, we also frequently use slate to cover them; and at the present time large slates, under the name of slabs, are very extensively used for making tanks, billiard-tables, &c., and for a variety of other useful purposes. The only limit to the use of slates and slabs is the power to supply them in sufficient quantity at a reasonable price. They combine so much hardness and toughness, with a perfectly flat natural surface obtained with little trouble; they are so admirably adapted to withstand exposure of all kinds; they are so little absorbent, and affected so little by heat and cold, that for many purposes they could hardly be replaced with advantage by any known contrivance.

England is rich in these, as in so many other sources of mineral wealth; and some of the great slate-quarries of North Wales, Cornwall and Scotland are among the most valuable mineral properties in the world.

Slate of all kinds is, however, nothing more than clay that has undergone an enormous squeezing. The slate is hardly more pure or free from mixture with foreign substances than the clay; but in some way or other it has become so completely altered as to assume a curious kind of half-crystalline appearance and condition which no other known substance presents. To satisfy ourselves that slate is nothing more than clay, we have only to observe the surface of the ground in slate districts. In those parts of the country where slates abound, the roads, and even paths, are generally thick clay; for the constant treading of feet and grinding of wheels on the slate reduce it first to a fine powder, and this mixed with rain produces common clay. But, on the other hand, it is equally certain that slate is a very peculiar condition of clay; for, without being actually ground up with water, no amount of mere exposure to weather on the flat surface seems to have much effect upon it. In its most remarkable characteristic, also, it is singularly unlike clay, for it splits with extreme readiness into thin films when struck in one direction, although it always breaks with jagged edges in every other direction. It is not necessary to direct attention here to the nature of this peculiarity, as it is so universally known; but, although probably only the result of enormous squeezing, the change certainly involves a considerable alteration in the arrangement of the particles. By very simple and familiar means we can reduce slate to clay; we cannot, on the other hand, make slate out of clay by any forces that have yet been brought to bear upon it.

The capacity of splitting, carried to so great an extent in slate, is called its cleavage, and is a property possessed in an imperfect degree by many minerals when they pass into the crystalline condition. In the case before us, however, the clay can hardly be said to be altered otherwise than in texture, whereas most minerals, when they become crystalline, enter into new chemical combinations. Slate is thus an exceptional mineral.

Few simple minerals exist in beds of clay, although some are occasionally met with. Thus, in many places, a peculiar substance called *heavy spar*, used in the arts to adulterate white-lead, occurs in crystalline form in the interstices of clay-beds, while transparent crystals of *selenite* (sulphate of lime) are tolerably plentiful in some of the beds. Hard lumps of the size and shape of a man's skull, occurring irregularly in many clays, consist of impure mixtures of carbonate of lime and clay. These are called *septaria*, because they look as if they had been split into divisions, or *septa*, the cracks being afterwards filled up. Such lumps are often collected, and serve as the foundation of hydraulic cement, which sets, or hardens, under water. But, although there are these exceptions, clay generally is a rock unfavorable for mineral wealth. Slate, on the other hand, especially when near granite, contains some of the richest and most valuable mineral deposits, especially the ores of copper.

In addition to the minerals already alluded to, there are numerous very striking and beautiful substances in nature which are so very largely indebted to the clay element as to deserve special remark. Thus the mineral called *felspar* is also a silicate of alumina; but either soda or potash to the extent of fifteen per cent. is added to the combination.

Now, as in one shape or other felspar and closely allied minerals form the basis of all the granites, and also of all the basalts and lavas, all over the world, it will be seen that clay assumes a still greater importance than we have yet attributed to it. From the natural destruction of granite under certain circumstances are produced the finest clays for the manufacture of porcelain; and from the decomposition either of basalts or lava (the name basalt being understood to mean the same as lava, but employed when the volcano from which it was poured out is absent, and all traces of its origin have disappeared) the finest and richest soils are often obtained. Pumice, as well as lava, is a modification of clay.

Even some precious stones, in addition to the ruby and sapphire, belong to our vulgar clays; for the garnet and carbuncle are silicates of alumina and lime; emeralds are silicates of alumina, combined with a rare earth called *glucina*, and beryl is a mere modification of emerald. A vast variety of comparatively rare minerals have also a similar composition, including all those common in volcanic districts, all volcanic ashes and minerals thrown out during eruptions, and those also which are afterwards found in the clefts and cavities of the hardened masses.

Wonderfully varied, then, are the forms and uses of clay, and the natural combinations of mineral substances of which clay is an essential part. The solid foundations of the earth, or at least all those most solid masses seen near the surface, are in a great measure due to it. Huge mountain-masses, covered or flanked with thick envelopes of limestone, are often, to a depth quite unknown, made up almost exclusively of minerals and rocks of similar origin. They put on various shapes, and are known by many names. Our streets are paved with them, and some of the most enduring monuments of all ages are chiselled out of them when they have become crystallized into granites and porphyries. Our houses are roofed and partly furnished with them, and our schoolboys write upon them. Large tracts of country present them at the surface as the common vegetable soil. Our jewellers work them up into ornaments for the person, as garnets and emeralds, beryls and carbuncles. The real ultimate difference in composition in the case of all these minerals is wonderfully small, while the appearance and all the essential characteristics are as distinct as can well be imagined.

And so it is everywhere in Nature. She works generally on a large scale with few materials, modifying them and preventing monotony by the occasional introduction of small quantities of other substances having different properties. A little iron or manganese, a small proportion of some rare earths or alkalies, or a few grains of substances whose effect we cannot trace, suffice her for the production of a myriad of curious and useful modifications of sand, limestone, and clay; and thus it is that the essential ingredients of clay, slightly added to, form numerous important minerals and rocks that we should never think of comparing with clay, were we not obliged to admit the near relation that exists between them.

Clay, then, is one of the essential and abundant combinations with which Nature works. She works rarely on a large scale with the simplest forms of matter, and never with those substances that are exceedingly complicated. The great results are produced with a few mixtures of two, three, or four elements, and of these the mixture we call clay is one of the most frequently and largely used, and one that produces some of the most complicated and grand results.

## Chapter the Fourth.

### CHALK.

A RIDE over the fine breezy downs near Brighton, or a visit to the chalk hills north of London, is a pleasant treat to any one who can appreciate pure bracing air, and is able and willing to recognize the peculiar beauties and characteristics of English scenery. There is a soft swelling undulation about our chalk not elsewhere seen, a smooth outline of richest green through which the white rock constantly peeps, and at intervals a wide hollow sweep of that dead creamy white which we know by experience to mark the pit from whence chalk is being dug or has lately been removed. Let us go into one of these pits, or, if the reader prefers, let us place ourselves in imagination in a boat under the broad arch of some of those bays at the back of the Isle of Wight, with the picturesque Needles rising like ruined columns out of the blue waves. Everywhere the facts are the same,—a uniform mass of white soft rock, marked with lines more or less removed from the horizontal, and occasionally thin strings of black flint indicating these lines with surprising and picturesque regularity. If we travel round the English coast, or into the interior of the country, we find this same chalk very widely ranging. We ought to be proud of it, for one of our island's names, ALBION, is derived from its appearance. It forms the Shakspeare cliff at Dover, and the cliffs at Ramsgate and Margate. Beechy Head consists of it. It shows itself at Cromer, in Norfolk, and at Flamborough Head, and is seen in all its characteristic features, crossing the Isle of Wight, and standing out beyond it, as we have said, in isolated pinnacles of extreme beauty. We find it in Salisbury Plains, in the North and South Downs, in Berkshire, and in the Hertfordshire and Cambridgeshire hills. We pass through it in many of our railway-cuttings. We dig into and through it for water, and we quarry it for making lime, and other purposes. We write with it; we even occasionally build with it.

Let us examine it somewhat minutely. We all know its usual color, its soft texture, its purity when burnt for lime. Most of us know that numerous shells, fragments of star-fishes and corals, and even perfect skeletons of fish covered with scales, are occasionally found in it. It is very picturesque, very characteristic, very useful, and contains very curious things. The shells that we find in it are of many kinds,—some almost exactly like common shells of the sea-shore, some very unlike those, and evidently belonging to races extremely different. There are fishes in it not much like our sea-fishes; there are bones like birds' bones, which, however, on careful examination and comparison, turn out not to have belonged to birds, but to have supported in the air flying reptiles, some of them larger than the largest albatross; there are other bones that have not yet been found in England, proving that very large reptiles of other kinds lived when the chalk was formed.

But all these are comparatively rare; whereas, if we take up any fragment of chalk from any part of the mass, and make a careful examination of its particles under the microscope, our eyes are opened to a fact exceedingly remarkable,—namely, that all this large mass, often several hundred feet thick, and occupying so large a part of the surface of our island, seems to be one heap of very minute shells, either whole or broken, once belonging to many varieties of a very few species of small animals, such as those now found at all depths, but chiefly abounding in the deepest profundities of the Atlantic Ocean. Powdered chalk, or chalk mixed with water and reduced to a pulp, is also wonderfully like the mud from coral lagoons in the West Indies; but a large part of it seems absolutely identical, when examined under a powerful microscope, with what is called *oaze*,— the mud brought up, in a state almost tenacious and pasty, from the bed of the North Atlantic Ocean. Indeed, it would seem that after this *oaze* has had time to allow its particles, long compressed by the weight of the vast column of overlying water, to attain their natural state under the diminished pressure at the earth's surface, it is absolutely undistinguishable from powdered chalk.

Very unlike the other limestones in texture and some of its properties is this chalk, although it agrees almost accurately with fine marble in its chemical constitution. It is a nearly-pure carbonate of lime; the particles being minute, and only held together by adhesion, not cemented or crystallized in any degree whatever. This condition explains some of its peculiarities, such as its earthy texture, allowing us to use it for writing or drawing, and its extreme absorbency. In its driest state as a solid it contains a good deal of water, which cannot be removed by exposure to moderate heat, but when saturated a block measuring twelve inches every way will contain two gallons of water, very nearly one-third part of its total content, and about the same proportion that is contained by soft loose sand.

From its actual composition and its contents, there can be no doubt that chalk was formed at the bottom of water, and, in all probability, tolerably deep and smooth water. It has undergone little change since, for the particles of which it is built up lie side by side, apparently as they were originally placed. Here and there are threads of crystal or calc-spar, and occasionally bands of black flints,—sometimes touching each other, sometimes asunder; but these are not rolled like the flints found in the gravel, and the chalk that touches them is generally precisely similar to the rest of the deposit.

The position and form of the hard angular flints may also be accepted as proof that they were produced where they are, and have never been removed since their creation. The evidence of this is indeed quite as good as that by which we judge from the position and form of the rounded pebbles of the gravel-beds that they are due to the mechanical force of moving water. Gravel is a collection of rolled pebbles and sand, while the flints in chalk have never been rolled for a single instant. We have only to look at them to be sure of this. The whole mass of chalk is probably a deposit in deepish water but little disturbed, and the flints do not seem to have been deposited in the same sense as the chalk has been. They do not seem to have existed at any time as mud; and to understand them we must look for some other origin.

Making use once more of the microscope, we may learn something that will throw light on this inquiry. The examination of thin slices of flint reveals the same truth as that often indicated on a larger scale visible to the unassisted eye,—namely, that these curious black stones contain within their substance sponges or other marine bodies. Not unfrequently we find the spine of some old sea-urchin or sea-egg sticking out from an unworn and unremoved flint; occasionally a shell is there; very frequently there is a peculiar structure reminding us of the sea-anemone; and now and then are corals. Some flints are hollow in the middle, the hollow being partly filled with crystals of the same substance,— the crystallized flint (silica) projecting inwards, or some small detached stone, with a rough, spongy surface, being loose in the middle. Every thing seems to prove that the flints were formed by chemical agency, brought about during the temporary stoppage of a deposit of chalk-mud, and while the pause admitted of a multitude of sponges and other marine forms of life being accumulated on the ocean-floor. Perhaps some eruption of hot water, charged with silica, may have taken place from submarine volcanoes. The number of beds of flint is very variable in different places, many being often observable in a single cliff or quarry, while elsewhere a great thickness of chalk exists without any. The flints are generally lying on the ancient floor of chalk, but occasionally they occupy cracks and fissures in the completely-formed deposit.

The way in which this curious accumulation of flint was originally produced in the mass of the chalk remains, as we have already seen, a mystery; nor is it quite manifest why the beds of flint are sometimes regular, sometimes quite irregular, and sometimes altogether broken up. Whatever the reason may be, it would seem impossible to suppose that the whole process of the deposit of chalk-mud, chiefly by marine animals, and of flint hardening on sponges and soft animals, can have been completed without the lapse of a very long period of time.

But the fact that chalk is met with at such elevations as Dover, and Beechy Head, and the Surrey hills, is another startling fact. Originally deposited at the bottom of an ocean, the mud of former times is now a solid mass, several hundred feet thick, no longer near the sea, but composing the whole of the land, at various elevations, in many parts of England, as soft chalk, and, in a somewhat harder state, in Poland, Moldavia, and the Caucasus. Over all these countries then, at any rate, there was sea, and perhaps deep sea, when the chalk was deposited, although some of them are now in the centre of continental land. Of the land of those days we will not now speculate.

The bedding of chalk, marked very distinctly in many places, is by no means generally horizontal, as we know it must originally have been. Certainly, a deposit of fine mud at the bottom of water can only have been produced in parallel and horizontal planes; for whatever the form and irregularity of the ocean-floor, or the strength and direction of marine currents, an impalpable mud must certainly have been originally accumulated at a dead level,

—the mud first filling up the hollow places, and then covering all over with a succession of thin films. But now the beds, though parallel to each other, are no longer horizontal: generally, they are tilted up at an angle of several degrees. The chalk of the North Downs has a distinct tilt towards London, and that of the South Downs towards the coast of the British Channel; while in the Isle of Wight and the coast of Dorsetshire, not far off, the beds are either curved over in magnificent and lofty arches, as seen at Scratchell's Bay, near the Needles, or are absolutely vertical, as at Culver Cliffs, on the east side of the island, between White-cliff and Sandown Bays.

The white chalk-cliffs of the south coast of England are, as it were, repeated and reflected by an almost similar series on the opposite shores of the British Channel, between Calais and Havre; and there cannot be a doubt that the mineral deposit is continuous, and that the separation of England from the Continent by the waters of the Channel does not separate the chalk, which is only covered over and concealed, and not entirely eaten through. But chalk, though seen in abundance on the French coast, soon passes into a harder limestone in the interior of France, losing its peculiar texture towards the south, beyond the valley of the Seine. The actual composition of chalk and of the limestones that it passes into is, however, nearly the same; and there would seem not to be much change in the shells and other remains of animals with which it abounds, although the mineral peculiarities of the rock are quite lost. The fact is, that the passage of chalk into limestone is an event altogether modern compared with the deposit of the chalk-mud.

Chalk is not only sometimes covered up by other rocks,—such as clay, sand, and gravel,—but also by the waters of the ocean, which between England and France conceal it from observation. In either case, by very simple means, we can satisfy ourselves of its presence by the boring-tool, the dredge, or the diving-bell.

With regard to the solid accumulations, it is not difficult to prove that there are, in various places, small patches of such substances; but in the great valley of the Thames these entirely cover a triangular area, measuring nearly a hundred miles in its longer direction from Hungerford to the Essex coast,—the base of the triangle, between Ipswich and Sheppey, being fifty miles, and the area enclosing more than two thousand square miles of country. At various localities within this wide area, the chalk has actually been reached by boring-operations carried on for water; and the thickness of the deposits amounts, here and there, to more than a thousand feet. A somewhat similar, but less extensive, portion of the chalk is covered by similar deposits near Southampton.

On the other hand, there is a large area surrounded by chalk-hills clearly traceable from Dover, along the line of the North Downs, as far as Alton, in Hampshire, there rounding and connecting with the South Downs, which terminate in the sea at Beechy Head. On the opposite shores of France, the chalk-hills in like manner recede. Within this range of chalk-hills are sands and clays, but no chalk is found either on or beneath the surface. The area thus excluded and cut out from what would otherwise be (as it probably once was) a continuous bed, is not very different in extent from that concealed by the clays on which London is built.

Across the German Ocean, chalk is found at Faxoe, in Denmark; and a soft limestone, of the same kind, with the remains of similar animals, in a similar state, on the banks of the Meuse, in Belgium. But true soft chalk is here replaced by a crumbling mass, while in France, as already stated, it becomes harder. It is singular that, in its integrity, the chalk is almost confined to our own island, and, indeed, to the eastern side of it.

When holes are bored into it, or cuttings made through it, chalk is found to be throughout very uniform in texture. It is also extremely and uniformly absorbent of water.

In the interior of a large mass of chalk, after a wet season, if the whole becomes saturated, it is certain that any empty spaces or cavities that exist will be also quite full; and if these are pierced by bore-holes, and the water pumped out, a large supply may be procured. All the water that falls on the surface, either of the chalk itself or the rocks near it, will almost inevitably be conveyed into the rock, which, indeed, acts like a sponge, besides being everywhere open at the surface by many small cracks. The mass of the chalk thus acts as a kind of large reservoir,—receiving the rain that falls, retaining it for a time, distributing it in the earth's interior, and at length giving it out again for the benefit of men and animals, either from natural or artificial springs.

In its ordinary state, true chalk is of little or no value

as a building-stone, owing to its softness and the readiness with which it is reduced to powder by exposure to damp air and frost. Still, it has been used for interior ornamentation, owing to the great readiness with which it can be cut; and instances of its employment in this way may be found in many of our cathedrals in the East and South of England. Methods have been suggested by which the specimens in certain cases should be hardened, so as to be no longer subject to injury on exposure to the air. It can then be used for inside building and decoration with great advantage.

Most of the chalk is, as we all know, remarkable for its peculiar dead-white color, although occasionally there are tinted varieties. The chalk near Flamborough Head, in Yorkshire, is naturally red; but the colored chalks used for drawing are artificial productions.

The chief use of chalk is in the manufacture of lime, whether for mortar or for dressing land. For these purposes the consumption is very large, the chalk being usually burnt in kilns in the pit or quarry from whence it has been hewn, to avoid cartage.

The lime thus obtained is very pure, but this is not any particular advantage; as lime made from limestones having a little clay, or sand, or iron, makes a mortar which sets more rapidly and is harder than that made from pure carbonates of lime. Chalk is also used occasionally without burning to improve certain kinds of soil, and is the only kind of limestone of much value for such purposes.

When we seek for the origin of chalk and flint, and the circumstances that would seem necessary for their formation, the conclusions we are forced to accept are almost overwhelming. True it is that we are speaking of a rock very uniform in its texture, and comparatively limited in its range, though really much more widely spread than one might suppose from the hardening it has in some places undergone, which modifies its usual appearance. An inch cube of this substance would contain countless millions of fragments or of complete shells of one small tribe of animals, and would be almost identical in its contents with a corresponding cube of mud taken partly from the bottom of the Atlantic, anywhere between Valentia and Newfoundland, and partly from the *oaze* or mud at the mouth of the Thames. Since, however, the Atlantic floor, thus covered, measures at least a thousand miles from east to west, and probably several hundred miles from north to south,—its thickness, probably irregular, being quite unknown,—so the area of country occupied by chalk must be measured by hundreds of miles each way, and its thickness is known to amount to from six hundred to a thousand feet. Think of the number of individuals required for such vast accumulations! Truly, the sands on the sea-shore are as nothing in comparison, and might be taken as the unit in so marvellous an arithmetic! All ordinary descriptions of number fade into insignificance in comparison; and we must admit that Nature has not adapted our faculties even to conceive and comprehend such combinations of the most minute atoms into the largest mountain-masses. And yet it is clear that time alone is needed to render possible the results we see in the chalk, even assuming that its whole mass was formed as the bed of an open ocean of deep water

Rapidity of growth and accumulation correspond with minuteness of organization. The smaller the animal, the more efficacious does it seem in producing large and abiding results; so that for every bone of reptile there are thousands of visible shells, and for every shell millions of these little invisible habitations of the simplest of Nature's productions.

What thoughts crowd upon one, in thus contemplating so simple an object as a chalk-pit! Here we seem to possess unchanged, except by being lifted up into sight for the convenience of study, a section of an old ocean-floor. Here are the proofs of ever-busy, stirring life,—most busy, and most powerful and influential, when acting in its simplest mode, and producing an infinite repetition of similar objects. Not, indeed, that these are monotonous in their resemblance,—for here, as everywhere, the type or general plan is the same,—but each individual possesses its own personal existence, and some peculiarity that distinguishes it from its neighbor and brother-atom.

There seems nothing now going on strictly analogous to the formation of beds of flint alternating with the fine chalky mud on the Atlantic ocean-floor. In this the analogy fails, and we are forced to assume that the flint, in a pasty state, or having the consistence of a jelly (as is the case in certain combinations with potash), was only an occasional deposit, no example of it being at present known to us.

Very rarely indeed rolled pebbles of granite or other distant rock have been found buried with the chalk, and forming part of it. Out of the line of drifted icebergs, there would be but few stones and pebbles conveyed now into the Atlantic, a few hundreds of miles from the land: so that we need not be astonished that such an event was equally rare in former times. What goes on now is, probably, only a repetition, with small variations, of previous events; and in Geology, according to the best experience of scientific observers, we arrive at the conclusion, arrived at long ago by King Solomon, that " there is nothing new under the sun."

The chalk must be regarded as one deposit of a great multitude,—a mere unit in a host. But it abounds with interest and instruction; it illustrates a recent deposit of the most curious kind; it is itself very peculiar, and unlike most others, and it well deserves careful attention. Moreover, it is essentially an English rock, and produces a very distinct scenery in those parts of the country where it prevails. Being strongly marked and easily recognized, and also pretty widely spread, it forms an admirable starting-point for the young geologist, while its position in the great series of rocks adapts it still further for this educational use.

## Chapter the Fifth.

### LIMESTONES AND MARBLE.

CHALK is a very soft kind of limestone; but being rarely used as a stone for any purposes of construction, and generally burnt to turn it into lime, it is convenient to separate it from limestones, as we have done, by treating it in a chapter by itself. Limestones differ from chalk in being more consolidated and less earthy, having while buried in the earth become to a certain extent altered by a process which, if continued long enough, would turn them into crystalline minerals. Many of the limestones, indeed, are already partly crystalline, either here and there in the bulk of the rock, or else in cavities. Crystals are often seen shot out, as it were, from the walls of a cavity, although all around there is no apparent change in the mixed fragments of shells and fine particles of sand of which the stone was evidently made up. In proportion as limestones are of closer grain, of firmer texture, and more compact, they approach to the condition called semi-crystalline; and thus they pass, by successive stages, into marbles, which are true crystalline limestones.

Limestone is, as every one knows, a common mineral enough in England, very large parts of the country consisting of little else. Vast quantities are also found, not only in most parts of Europe, but generally throughout the world. There are, however, some large districts in which this rock is absent, and others where it is not to be obtained very near the surface; and as lime is wanted not only for building purposes, as stone or mortar, but for mixing with and forming part of soils, the places where limestones are rare generally suffer much from the absence of them. When it is remembered that all bone consists chiefly of lime, and that birds require it to form a hard coating for their eggs, the necessity of this mineral will be seen. It is useful to know how to recognize the varieties.

There are two or three very different minerals generally called limestones: one is the common carbonate of lime, such as Bath and Portland stones used for building. This kind passes by insensible gradations into marble, having the same composition with the addition of some impurities. Another kind is the magnesian limestone, or dolomite,—a mixed carbonate of lime and magnesia, also a building-stone, and unfortunately very notorious as being the stone of which the Houses of Parliament were built, concerning whose early decay there is so much discussion at present. Gypsum, or alabaster, much used in a burnt state in making plaster of Paris and other varieties of plaster, and occasionally sculptured as an ornamental stone, is a third kind; but this is a sulphate, not a carbonate, of lime, and has, therefore, a distinct chemical composition. The two first varieties, when burnt, yield a hardish, compact substance known as quicklime, but the last yields plaster of Paris, an extremely fine powdery material, having very different properties.

Quicklime, mixed with water, heats, swells, and falls to powder; but plaster of Paris absorbs water, and immediately sets and becomes permanently hard. The difference between the common and magnesian limestones and gypsum is, therefore, practically very essential.

Many of the limestones, such as those used for building, are of a grayish and dirty white or cream color, of very uniform texture and tolerably hard; some, like those found in Derbyshire and Devonshire, are compact enough to take a high polish, but being colored and veined are of no value for artistic purposes, though much used for furniture and decoration, for which they are well adapted. Others, again, such as the Carrara and Parian marbles, are used in sculpture, and are known as statuary marbles. These latter are of the most exquisite white tint, and show a texture like loaf-sugar, or even sometimes like virgin wax.

Of building-stones, again, there is an immense variety, —some of them being hard and others soft, some brittle and others tough, some full of shells, some made up of little round egg-shaped particles like the roe of a fish (*oolite* or *roe-stone*), some of sandy grains easily separated. Most of them absorb water very readily and in large quantity, and when exposed in building, where the weather affects them, or where they are subject to alternations of wet and dry, heat and cold, they are very apt to become rotten, the sculptured and ornamental parts breaking off.

In England it is rare to find limestones of a dead-white color like chalk and at the same time extremely hard and close-grained. Such limestones, however, are common enough in other countries, and are very valuable materials for construction, as they are handsome and durable, absorbing but little water. Each country possesses its own materials, and those of one district are by no means always, nor are they usually, identical with those of another.

Most of the common limestones lie in beds of moderate thickness, separated from each other by an intermediate bed of clay or rubbish, or of stone valueless for building purposes. Very often these beds lie horizontally, or nearly so, and they are almost always parallel to each other; but occasionally they are tilted at a high angle,—a position that must have been produced by some force lifting them up from below after they had been hardened,—and generally in such cases the beds are broken asunder and more or less rotten near the point where the elevation took effect. When limestones lie on the flanks of mountains, or form mountain-masses reaching to the clouds, it seems less difficult to see and understand the mode of action of the force, and we even judge of its magnitude; but when a large district is affected by moderate and very slow elevations, it is not easy to trace the cause.

All limestones when in the earth contain a good deal of water, and they are softer and more easily chiselled when just removed from the quarry than after a few months' exposure. When left exposed to dry air the stone dries, and a hard crust forms upon it which resists the action of weather; but if used at once, and subject to the pressure which must act upon all stones in a building, before the stone has had time to consolidate, the weather will generally have much more effect upon it.

Most of the stones in a quarry very near the top are more cracked and destroyed than those taken from some depth, so that many quarries now are completely under ground, the stone being worked out from the bed within the bowels of the earth just as coal is removed from the mine. One result of this method is that, with care, the best bed and the best part of a bed of stone may be secured; but it is necessary to take precautions that the stones thus brought out are properly dried before use, as they will have undergone no chance of weathering until removed into the open air.

An old quarry and a quarry where the stone is got in the open air is a picturesque object enough; the steep face,—the successive steps as one bed is worked in advance of another,—the vegetation bursting out from all the cracks and corners, and the half-decayed weathered look of the parts where no work has been going on for some time, are all objects on which the eye rests with pleasure. In one place a huge crane is lifting large blocks to a truck,—in another a puff of smoke marks where a recent blast has taken place; while the approaches to the quarry, with their rough roads and broken rails, form a contrast with the surrounding scenery which is eminently favorable to the picturesque.

Those quarries where the whole or most of the work is carried on under ground and out of sight are far less interesting. Opening often on the bank of a river or canal, nothing is to be seen but a small tunnel or entry, the wagons bringing out the stone, already reduced to convenient sizes, and ready to put on the boats lying alongside. Still, even here the eye rests with pleasure on a certain contrast of Nature with Art, which rarely fails to produce some effects pleasing to the lover of the picturesque.

In many limestone rocks of large extent, there are caverns or open spaces communicating with the outer world. Among such caverns, those of Adelsberg in Carinthia, on the road from Vienna to Triest, and the so-called Mammoth Cave of Kentucky in America, are the largest that have been described. The Peak cavern in Derbyshire, the caverns in Yorkshire, Somersetshire, and South Wales, those in Sicily, and Central France, and Bavaria, and others in the Rock of Gibraltar, are well known as objects of curiosity visited by strangers; and some of them afford very curious facts for consideration. These are of two kinds: one having reference to the mechanics of the cavern,—the way it was hollowed out, and has been partly filled up with those wonderful appearances called *stalactites*,—and the other to the curious remains of animals found frequently on and in the earthy floor of the cave.

The extent of caverns is sometimes very great, and is often quite incapable of being accurately determined. The more interesting of them consist of a multitude of passages, often narrow,—too small, indeed, to allow a human being to penetrate,—but connecting large open cavities lying far within the rock. They are often more or less full of water, which enters and gets out of the chain of caverns in a manner scarcely traceable. The open spaces are sometimes large and lofty and well ventilated, but sometimes they are smaller and nearly choked. Nothing, indeed, can be imagined more irregular than this chain of open cavities,—running, perhaps, for miles under the earth at various levels, with no reference to any place or system that we can at all trace. Almost all imestones are exceedingly liable to be penetrated with these irregular holes.

Within the cavern—the walls of which are generally worn and often smoothed, as if by the passage of water—there are often sheets, columns, and pinnacles of stone, which, when undimmed by the smoke of lamps and torches, are half transparent, and of the most brilliant yellowish-white appearance. These hang down from the roof, rise up from the floor, arrange themselves fantastically, as curtains, tables, or festoons, and even take the forms of animals and human beings. They are of precisely the same material as the limestone walls of the cavern, but are easily seen to be of different origin. By a little examination it may be found that all of them have been formed in connection with the drip of water; the water, while penetrating through innumerable small cavities in the limestone rock, takes up a part of the mineral and carries it along, eating away its course,—partly chemically by dissolving the rock, and partly mechanically by constant rubbing. When it reaches an open empty cavity, where is a current of air, the water is evaporated and the stone left behind. Such is the history of that variety of curious and beautiful appearances seen in caverns,—the magic fountains and organs, the cathedral aisles and vaulted roofs, the drooping trees, the crouching animals, the busts, and the apparent vegetation. All these are nothing more than fantastic forms slowly and gradually accumulated; and the wonderful things told about them are due quite as much to the fancy of the describer as to Nature herself.

The floors of such caverns are often nearly level and

hard, being repetitions of the same half-crystalline material, and produced in the same way. The sheets of limestone on the floor of the cavern are sometimes called *stalagmite*, to distinguish them from the *stalactites* that drop from the roof. In the limestone floor, in the mud under it, and often in heaps not yet covered with stalagmite, there have been found, in many caverns, numerous bones of animals. Some of these were no doubt wild animals, that had used the cavern as a den; some were certainly the prey of wolves, hyenas, and other savage tenants, which they had dragged into their lair, perhaps for the benefit of their young; some, again, seem to have been carried into the cave and buried there, when unusual floods of water had drifted river-deposits, mud, bones, and other material from a distance, leaving it behind in these sheltered places after the waters had retired. When the bones thus found are carefully examined and compared with those of known species, they are found to belong to races that are no longer common in the adjacent country. Thus, in England and Western Europe there are bones of hyenas and large bears, of a kind of tiger, and of many other fierce carnivorous creatures, only met with at present in Asia and Africa. In Brazil, under similar circumstances, are bones of wild animals equally different from the inhabitants of the neighboring tropical or temperate land; and in Australia there have been found remains of kangaroos and wombats, much larger than, and very distinct from, those of the present neighborhood. With the carnivorous monsters in our English caverns are numerous bones of the elephant and rhinoceros, and even of the hippopotamus, mixed with fragments of reindeer, and of a very large horned deer, long since lost sight of among existing races, as well as of large animals of the ox tribe. Every thing indicates great antiquity, and a different climate; and yet with these strange associates are seen chiselled flints,—evidently human weapons,—all buried at the same time. The condition of the bones, the great proportion of some one species in each cavern, the number of bones and teeth of young individuals not at all more injured than the harder bones near them, and the fact that many of the bones of the deer and oxen are much gnawed, as if by the teeth of hyenas in the hyena caverns, and not at all so when the cavern was apparently otherwise owned, all seem to prove that the caverns had long served as the dens of these wild and powerful animals.

Limestone presents itself in nature under very different aspects. Crossing England diagonally, and owing to various causes not much developed on the coast, the peculiar features of limestone cliffs are not much seen on our shores; but in the interior there are many fine and some noble specimens of limestone-cliff scenery. In the beautiful and wild valleys of the western part of Yorkshire, in the Peak district of Derbyshire, and some of the river-valleys of Derbyshire, especially near Matlock and along the course of the Dove, the bold vertical faces of compact limestone rock are grand and picturesque in the extreme. Something of a similar beauty characterizes the Chedder Rocks, and others adjacent, in the Mendips; and still more remarkable are the deep narrow gorges and richly-clothed ravines of Linton, in North

Devon. These specimens of scenery are well contrasted by the hilly parts of the middle of England, especially near Cheltenham and Bath, where a much softer rock of the same nature, but very different texture, presents a correspondingly different appearance. No one who did not carefully examine for himself would suppose that the hills of Gloucestershire and Derbyshire were composed of the same mineral; for it is difficult for two minerals to be more distinct from one another than are the limestones in these localities, in respect to color, hardness, compactness, and mode of resisting or yielding to the action of weather.

Almost all limestones may be found, on a little investigation, to be made up of beds of various thickness. Between the beds there is often a thin plate of some other material, or of the same material in a different form. All, without exception, of the limestone rocks are also more or less cracked, so that water has access to the interior; and thus it is not to be wondered at that numerous springs of water come out wherever these beds are cut off abruptly, on a hill-side or cliff, and that in all limestone districts the surface is dry, while water may generally be had by digging.

The minerals found between beds of limestone, or cemented with broken blocks in former cavities, and sometimes crystallized in cracks of the limestone, are of great value. Almost all the lead and zinc used in commerce are found in the shape of ores or stony minerals under these circumstances; and often, at first sight, it would be difficult for any one not familiar with minerals to distinguish some of the most valuable of these from valueless stones. Even iron is found sometimes, in enormous quantities, mixed up with limestone, and looking so much like it that for a long time it has been regarded as a mere variety. Tens of thousands of tons of iron-ore are now obtained from beds that, a few years ago, were looked upon only as poor and worthless limestones.

While chalk is made up almost entirely of the very small shells of animals, of which thousands would be required to bury a pin's head, most of the harder limestones are equally remarkable for fragments of shells and corals and other hard coatings of animals, which are for the most part of much larger size. Such common shells as are cast up on every sea-beach will in time, and by long accumulation, occupy an important place even among rocks; for, with water constantly running through them, they become at last firmly cemented together. But it is chiefly by the work of the coral animal that large mountain-masses of limestone have been obtained. Coral, especially certain varieties abounding in some tropical and warm seas, consists of a curious mass of individuals, with one common jelly-like living substance connecting them. The whole mode of growth is more like that of a plant than an animal, the individuals resembling the leaves and flowers, while **the common** central mass is the stem or trunk. These curious animals are able, with great facility, to separate from the salt water about them those few grains of limestone they require; and these are immediately replaced, because the sea washes over limestone, and quickly sucks up as much as it needs when deprived of any part by animals. There is thus a never-failing supply of lime in the ocean, and the little creatures we refer to have been pilfering in safety from the very creation of the world till now. What they take, however, they at once use, building up with it a stony and almost imperishable framework, which, so long as it is coated with living matter, does not become worn or wasted. When myriads of these individuals collect together in a mass and secrete limestone, they construct walls which rise to the lowest level of low-water, commencing at the bottom of the sea at some moderate depth. If every thing remains in the same state, a fringe of coral soon forms round every part of an island, or along the whole of a coast, that has once been reached by the animals,—except, indeed, where an interruption exists, such as a river or stream of fresh water of some magnitude entering the sea, or some extraordinary and abrupt submarine ravine prevents the advance of the coral, by depriving it of a support to build upon. Such fringes of coral are well known in some parts of the world, especially within the tropics, and in the warmer waters both of the Atlantic and Pacific Oceans.

But besides these fringes of coral—which, when the animal dies, may, if not washed away, become coral limestone—there are other equally well-known districts, where the coral extends to a very much greater depth than the larger kinds are thought able to work in,—the extreme depth of coral having been found to amount to many hundreds of fathoms, whereas the larger corals are believed to die if removed even twenty fathoms deep. In some way or other, it certainly seems that coral-beds can even now be prepared, of great thickness, as well as covering a wide surface-extent; and if this is the case at present, there is no reason why a similar result should not have been obtained formerly.

Many of these remarkable and extensive limestones, to which we are indebted for much of the picturesque in English scenery, were beyond doubt the composition of little animals, just such as those now building coral in warm latitudes. The results may be seen and compared together, and, in many cases, the whole form of construction and the peculiarities of the animals may be identified. We are thus bound to admit the close resemblance between the present manufactures of the coral animal, and those ancient and crystalline limestones that are now quarried for building-stone, or those which are carefully selected and set aside as furnishing marble for some of the most elegant manufactures or the noblest works of genius.

Limestones form the staple material of the flanks of the Alps, and extend in still greater abundance eastwards into Asia, scarcely any thing else being seen in the Carpathians and the Caucasus. A large part of Italy and Greece is also made of or covered with similar rock. In these latter countries, marble often replaces common limestone; and this seems owing to the vicinity of the great disturbing forces exemplified in the elevation of the mountain-chains to the North, and the frequent eruption of melted rock and hot vapors from the important volcanoes of the South, of Europe. Spain is not less remarkable for its marbles and limestone rocks than France and Italy; but they are less known, owing to the rarity (till lately) of any commercial or industrial activity in that country.

The second kind of limestone mentioned at the beginning of this article—that kind which is known to mineralogists under the names *gypsum* and *alabaster*—is very different in many respects from the stones just described. It is not often in regular beds of great extent, being far more commonly found in large detached lumps. It is very much softer than any of the building-stones, and is either of a dead-white appearance, like chalk (but not soiling a black surface), or else nearly transparent. It is more frequently found with sandstones than limestones. Large quantities of it are obtained from Derbyshire and Nottinghamshire in England, and from deposits around Paris, and in Italy near Florence. Egypt also abounds with it. When pure, whether white or transparent, it is often cut into vases, lamps, figures, and other ornaments, some of which are of great beauty and value; but for the most part it is burnt, and in that state sold to make plaster of Paris and other plasters by various treatment.

There is another kind of limestone, quite different from either of the two described, and often so hard as to be mistaken for flint. It is found in pebbles in large quantity in the gravels of Suffolk, and in beds in some other parts of England. It consists of rolled bones and other remains of animals, and is called by chemists a *phosphate of lime*. When properly prepared, this stone serves as an admirable mineral manure or dressing for land for agricultural purposes. The pebbles thus used were at one time called *coprolites* (abbreviated to *cops*), owing to an idea entertained that they were petrified dung. Among them, however, we often meet with such things as ear-bones of whales, parts of the backbone of whales and sharks, bones of quadrupeds, and other things, that point to them as being for the most part, like the common limestones, due to animal life in its more complete form.

Such is an outline of some of the principal facts known about limestones. We may sum up the account in a few words, by saying that they are a group of stones of great usefulness to man in almost all their varied forms, both directly and indirectly; they are widely spread, they form very picturesque and characteristic scenery, and they contain mineral wealth. Most of them are directly due to the influence of animal life at some period or other, often very remote; but they have since undergone a good deal of change, and hardly now resemble what they once must have been. Some, no doubt, are still soft and little altered; but most kinds have been converted into a substance which, though greatly altered, still shows its origin very clearly, or into a curious half-crystallized mass, which gives no clue at all, by its appearance, to the history of its formation.

# Chapter the Sixth.

### SAND AND SANDSTONE.

EVERY kind of rock when ground and rubbed to a fine powder becomes sand, and accumulates in heaps or is drifted about on land, or else is carried into the sea by every wind that blows. In addition, however, to loose sands thus driven by the wind, there are many places where we find beds of sand, of great thickness, buried deep within the earth. Such are the dark-red irony sands of Bedfordshire, the paler red sands of Reigate, the white sands of Cornwall and elsewhere (valuable for glass-making), and the black sands of Australia, loaded with tin and gold. These sands are sometimes barren and mischievous, sometimes abounding with metallic wealth, and sometimes used as manure. There are few parts of the world where sands do not appear in some form or other, and a few words about them will be useful and perhaps amusing.

There is an old Greek story of Midas, who, when he found that his faculty of turning into gold every thing that he touched proved inconvenient, was enabled to part with so dangerous a power by washing in the river Pactolus. The fable states that the sands of that river have ever since contained golden particles; and if the story be true as to the general origin of similar phenomena, it may be supposed that the representatives of Midas must have been pretty widely spread over the earth in early times, —since most other rivers are provided with similar rich sands. The Rhine is one of these, the Tagus is another; many of the smaller rivers, not only of Europe, but of all parts of the world, might be enumerated as other examples; and, in point of fact, there are very few streams proceeding from mountain countries in whose beds particles of this precious metal have not been found. Golden sands are thus not rarities; but the difficulty with most of them is, that it costs at least twenty-five shillings, in labor and machinery, to obtain gold enough to make a sovereign. Such deposits are not, therefore, of necessity sources of wealth, and picking up gold from the gutter may be a far less profitable occupation than tilling the soil and obtaining the precious metal by selling the crops grown from it.

Still there are parts of the world where sands are well worth washing and separating in order to collect the valuable substances they contain. For a long time Brazil, then Siberia, afterwards California, and more recently Australia and British Columbia, have been very remarkable for their rich yield of various precious metals, of which gold is the most valuable and abundant. In all or almost all these cases, the sand in which the largest quantity has been found has been largely associated with pebbles and gravel.

Although it is true that all rocks except soft clay yield sand, while even the crystalline varieties of clay itself, and pure alumina in the form of emery, afford a similar powder, we generally understand by sand the powder of siliceous or calcareous rocks; and the latter, though not very uncommon, are more conveniently regarded in their chemical nature as varieties of limestone. We will, therefore, limit the expression in this chapter to the fragments of rock that have been chiefly or entirely derived from flint or silica.

As in the last chapter we spoke of clays as silicates of alumina, considering these deposits as distinct from all others, owing to their composition, so here we propose to take into account another distinct class of materials, forming numerous mineral varieties and extensive rocks, but all of which consist chiefly of *silica* not combined with alumina. Since we are not here treating Geology as if it were a branch of Mineralogy or Chemistry, we have not hesitated to take the substances in this order, because there seemed a certain convenience in describing the clays before the sandstones. We must now, however, go back a little, and explain what is meant by *silica* and the relation it bears to the element from which it is derived, and the substance (*alumina*) with which it is so largely associated.

Silica, like alumina, is derived from a kind of metal, but the metal silicium has never been obtained for any purpose of utility. In this respect silicium cannot be compared with aluminium, and, indeed, its essential properties as a metal are hardly known. On the other hand, the mineral silica is even more abundant than alumina, and is, in fact, almost everywhere present in all soils and rocks. Silica is a combination of the metal silicium with the gas oxygen, just as alumina is a combination of the metal aluminium with the same gas. The combination in both cases produces an earth capable of being crystallized; but in the one case (silica) the crystalline form is very common,—in the other (alumina) very rare. Silica is, in fact, as much more common than alumina as aluminium is more common and easier obtained than silicium.

The further combination of silica with alumina we have spoken of in the last chapter, and need not now further allude to it; for there is quite enough to describe in reference to silica, and the various forms in which it is generally presented on the earth.

In the first place, there is rock-crystal, in its various forms of Brazil pebble or Cornish diamond, amethyst and cairngorm, quartzite and sandstone; then there are the agates, chalcedonies, cornelians and cherts, onyxes, bloodstones, and a number of others; after them the flints and jasper, and lastly the opals,—a long list of beautiful minerals, many of which are used and valued as gems or precious stones; but, as we purpose to devote a special chapter to such objects, we may pass them by for the present. Those we now wish to direct attention to are the sandstones and flints, the humbler members of this large and decorated fraternity.

Flint is a substance so common in certain localities as to be used for making and mending roads, and occasionally for building walls and houses. Elsewhere it is entirely absent, and almost entirely unknown; and as the only real and characteristic flints belong to the chalk, either being found in that rock now or having been washed out of it at some former time, wherever the chalk is at hand the flints may fairly be looked for at no great distance. But they are not always found, for large tracts of country where chalk exists in abundance have no flints, so that their distribution is still further limited. Most parts of England, however, can show them either as belonging to the district, or brought there accidentally or by intention: so that we need not describe at any length these dark, half-transparent, brittle stones, always having the same appearance, and showing the same clean wax-like surface when broken, whether we have removed them from the chalk in which they have been long buried, or taken them from the heap of gravel a hundred miles away from the chalk, or picked them up, rounded and shapeless, from the beach at Brighton or some other part of the coast.

Flints are curious stones enough in their way. Under the microscope they always show some fragment of sponge or the shell of a small animal, or some other proof that they were not always what they are now. Not unfrequently we pick them up after they have been broken in half, and may see that there has been a hollow space in the middle, sometimes partly occupied, sometimes empty. Here and there is a flint with part of a shell or a portion of a sea-urchin or sea-egg sticking far into its substance. More frequently there is unmistakable evidence of a sponge, round which the flint seems to have formed, and altogether it is always a puzzle how it was that the flint and its contents became associated. It seems quite impossible to conceive any other way than by the flint having been at one time soft like a jelly, a substance in which the most delicate and most minute objects might be caught, and where they might be preserved until the jelly became converted into hard stone.

Flint is one of the purest forms of silica, although, from the dark color it generally has, we see that the transparent rock-crystal is not exactly repeated. Its condition is also peculiar, as it is more brittle than other varieties of silica, and is more readily dissolved, and, when mixed with alkali, converted more readily into glass than the rest. One of the great uses of flint now is in the manufacture of glass and porcelain; for although, formerly, myriads were required for our muskets, and they were used with steel for obtaining fire, these uses are now quite superseded. Made red-hot, and in that state thrown into cold water, they very readily break up, and may be pounded into a very fine powder; or, placed in a boiler in high-pressure steam, exposed to the action of potash or soda, they dissolve completely, the result becoming afterwards soluble even in cold water. But though the state of a jelly may thus be obtained artificially, the flint cannot be reproduced.

Though chalk is the principal nursery for and nest of flints, many other limestones contain lumps of silica more or less resembling them. Such lumps are more frequently of a dead-white color than half transparent, and are then called chert. They are tougher also than flint, and differ slightly from it in other ways.

By far the most common form in which silica is found in the earth is that of sandstone. Rocks under this name are found in most countries; and though they differ a good deal from each other in minor points, there are many elements of resemblance. Sandstones are generally made up of particles either of fine sand or very small rolled pebbles, these particles being in some way or other cemented together. Certainly in some rocks there is no foreign substance cementing them, and they either simply adhere by close contact, which is possible, or are fastened by a siliceous paste. More usually, the grains are cemented by something like mortar, obtained naturally, or by the action of water containing lime and iron. The ordinary sandstones are of the latter kind, and vary much in appearance, hardness, and compactness. There are many in which the grains are of different sizes; but when some are so large as to form detached pebbles of the size of a pea or walnut, the whole mass has a different appearance from that of a common sandstone, and is called a conglomerate or pudding-stone. In Hertfordshire and elsewhere there are large blocks of this kind, in which the pebbles are cemented so strongly that it is easier to break the flint pebble across than to separate the cement.

The colors of sandstones vary chiefly according to the quantity of iron and marl they contain. All varieties of yellow and red are met with, and frequently the best and hardest kinds are of a pure white and pale gray. Such are the stones of which Edinburgh is chiefly built,—stones which seem to be unchangeable by any amount of exposure.

In Yorkshire are some admirable beds of sandstone, of very fine grain, which split readily into slabs, and are used for foot-pavement. There are others, equally hard and indestructible, of very coarse grain, and useful for making millstones. In the South of England, at Blackdown, is a particular kind of rather coarse-grained stone, valuable for sharpening scythes, and sold for this purpose; while in the North of Scotland, and in Wales, are huge masses of the purest and most compact fine-grained stone, almost too compact and massive to be practically available.

While there is thus a great variety of sandstones, all equally pure and useful for various purposes, the middle of England, and several counties in the west, especially Devonshire, Warwickshire, and Cheshire, abound with a much softer kind, easily cut and very cheap, but soon falling to pieces when exposed to damp air. Near Liverpool there are large quarries of such stone, and the great salt deposits of Cheshire and Worcestershire are among them. The alternate mud and sand of these deposits has been the cause of some of the most curious and interesting discoveries of modern times.

To understand clearly the nature and value of these discoveries, let the reader watch for a while some gently-shelving beach, where there are moving sands and occasional mud. In consequence of the variable height of the tides, which are not only periodically high and low, according to the moon's age, but which are also greatly affected by prevailing winds, there are always large patches on such a beach which the water occasionally but rarely reaches; there are others, reached perhaps every fortnight at spring tides, and the rest covered almost every tide. Rills of fresh water often wash fine mud over such flat sands, leaving the mud on the surface, and filling up hollows with it. Almost the whole surface, whenever it is wetted, will be covered with worm-casts, or scratched with the trail of marine insects and crabs, indented by the footprints of birds and small quadrupeds, or spotted over with little pits made by heavy driving rain. After being wetted, the sun shining on the surface will dry and crack it. If in this state the mud is deposited in a thin film over every thing, and another deposit of sand happens to be drifted by the wind so as to cover up and conceal the previous marks, it is quite possible that all of them may be permanently preserved. They are as it were stereotyped, and will remain as long as the sands remain, whether they continue soft or are hardened into stone. Now, precisely what might thus happen at any time has happened in former times; and we have in some of the stone-quarries near Liverpool, and others in Warwickshire, many beds of stone, of which the surface is marked all over with footprints and other indentations.

And this is the case not in England only, but in Germany, in various parts of North America, and elsewhere,—generally in particular kinds of sandstone, adapted to retain the impression. Here are to be found, then, the footprints of scores of animals that lived on the shores of islands or continents at the very distant time when the great series of rocks that now form the dry land in the interior of the country had not even begun to exist. All such animals, and all like them, have long since ceased to live. The conditions of existence have changed, and the animals have changed with them.

Examining these curious markings, we are, however, in a condition to judge in some measure of the inhabitants of the land and sea at the time they were produced. Among a number of round pits, where rain once fell, are numerous little irregular heaps, thrown up by ancient worms, multitudes of lines such as are made by small crabs working their sidelong way to the water, and not a few broad thick lines, crossing, nearly at right angles, the marks of ancient cracks in the mud and sand. All these are easily seen and understood. But besides them are others less familiar. Triangular footprints, as of birds, are mixed with marks of the step of some small but heavy animal,—perhaps an ancient turtle; and here and there are huge clumsy indentations, more like the effect of a large hand than a foot pressing on the sand. These hand-like marks are in sets of two, not four,—the corresponding two being not only much smaller, but generally obliterated. It would seem that the animal must have resembled in its proportions those living kinds which, like the kangaroo among quadrupeds and the frog among reptiles, have two large hind-feet and two very small fore-feet. But no animal now lives, of either class, capable of producing such a footmark; and, until some bones of the animal could be found, it was hopeless to speculate on its nature. At last, in rocks not far off, and of the same kind, bones and teeth were found, which proved that a reptile had lived whose proportions correspond with those of the frog, but whose dimensions exceed those of the largest kangaroo. Thus have the rough marks left in sand, and filled up with mud, on some ancient seashore, introduced us to the knowledge of an animal so entirely unlike any living creature, that the wildest imagination could not previously have imagined the possibility of its existence.

Sandstones in which such markings are common, being for the most part alternations of perishable and imperishable material, are not very valuable for building purposes, though used to some extent, when at hand, on account of their cheapness. Much of the town of Liverpool is built of them. They are very absorbent of water, holding large quantities in ordinary seasons, though in time of great drought they cannot be depended on. The water they contain, when exhausted by continual pumping, is apt to become salt, especially when the place is not distant from the sea.

Large quantities of common salt, often in crystals, are found in some of the sandstones, and in that case the salt may be got away by mining. There are not many known localities where this kind of salt-mining can be carried on, as it is far more common to find brine springs than solid salt. So large is the quantity of water filtering constantly through the earth, and so few the cases where it does not pass through porous rocks, however far they may be from the surface of the ground or from the sea, that it is rare to meet with large and important deposits of rock-salt. The gypsum, or plaster-stone, which is another accompanying mineral, is much more commonly found.

Neither salt nor gypsum is, however, found in those hard compact gray sandstones, free from clay and iron, that are common in Derbyshire, Yorkshire, and elsewhere, where the sandstone is simple in its composition, and tends apparently to turn into a yet more compact and even crystalline mass. Of such a nature is the beautiful white quartz-rock of the Stiper Stones near Shrewsbury. A large quantity of similar rock exists in Scotland. It is too hard and works too irregularly to be available for any useful purpose, except indeed for road material; and its sharp-cutting edges and want of toughness do not well fit it even for that purpose.

Lumps and even larger deposits of bitumen are found in rock of this kind, but they are of no value generally, owing to the difficulty of obtaining the mineral. Some loose sandstones, however, especially those in the South of France and the Pyrenees, abound so much with pitchy matter that it is found profitable to export them. They form the basis of the asphalte pavement, more used in France than England, and perhaps better adapted to a moderate than excessive amount of wear. Asphalte is, however, a useful and valuable material.

Sandstones are better fitted for conveying water through the earth, for yielding it in natural springs at a hill-side, or for retaining large stores under ground, than any other rock. But for this purpose the sandstone must be open and porous, and must rest on a bed of stiff clay or hard compact rock.

Few remains of animals are preserved in rocks of this kind. When the particles of sand have been much rolled about before forming the stone, it is natural that most of the fragments of bone and shell, being softer than the sand, should be ground to fine powder. When a deposit is rapid, the state in which the stones and sand are accumulated is unfavorable for the preservation of animal remains. Still, there are some districts where exceptional causes have acted, and fossils occur. In such cases fragments of vegetation are more common than animal remains, and large quantities of wood, now formed into coal and accumulated as stores of mineral fuel, alternate with sandstones in which are the remains of ancient forests in various states of preservation. Leaves of ferns, trunks of trees, and even sometimes very delicate and destructible parts of plants, have been thus handed down in sand-rocks for our examination.

In some places gigantic trees, thus buried, have not been destroyed, although, doubtless, they were lost sight of from the earth for scores of thousands of years. Fruits of such trees, as well as the trunks and leaves, remain to speak to their nature, and they point out to us the peculiarities of the forests that supplied the coal which we use and waste without thought of its origin.

Minerals are not rare in sandstones. The whole large family of those that are strictly varieties and modifications of quartz or rock crystal, and that have some value and interest as gems, we leave to another chapter. Others, incidental and not essential, are present in the crevices and veins that abound in the hardest and most compact varieties of sandstone-rocks. The most precious of all metals, gold, often occupies the little interstices in the half-crystalline quartz that forms reefs or ledges,—the local name for veins and bands of quartz in sandstone rock. It is true that most of the gold obtained for commerce has been hitherto got from the sands already broken off from these ledges, but a very important quantity is now worked from the solid vein, both in Australia and California. This work is hardly less speculative than the ordinary mode of washing sands, and is not more frequently successful.

Diamonds in India and Brazil, topazes in Australia, and other valuable gems elsewhere, are, in nature, associated with quartz, and are often found in sands and gravel. Tin is obtained from sands, just in the same way that gold is, and there is a remarkable instance in Australia of both these heavy metals being found together in large quantities, in a peculiar black sand, that was for a long time regarded as without value.

Under the name of quartz and quartzite, crystalline sandstones are in some places developed either into projecting veins, penetrating other rocks, and forming picturesque objects jutting into the air, or they occupy important positions in mountain countries, remarkable alike for their picturesqueness and absolute barrenness. The Stiper Stones, a singularly striking group of rocks in Shropshire, are not less favorable illustrations of the one condition than are the rocks in some parts of Scotland of the other. Pure white in color, jagged and broken in outline, unmixed with other mineral, untouched by decay, uncolored by moss or lichen, these singular examples of the uselessness of those forms of matter that resist change stand out in relief, and tell a lesson of no small importance to human nature.

It is, indeed, by no means the simple minerals in a crystalline state that are useful and available. For rich soils a mixture of a large number of minerals is essential, and even for a soil to provide any sustenance except for grasses, something more than rock is needed. No doubt, if the quartz is in a fine state of division, and thus acts as a sponge, it will, by retaining a certain quantity of moisture, admit of certain growth; but there are some natural cases of finely honeycombed quartz absolutely barren, proving that without the actual breaking up of the mineral into the finest grains, so as to allow of capillary action, there is no means of supplying what plants require. Water has no effect in decomposing quartz, nor is it affected by any of the ordinary acids.

While therefore silica, in its combined form, is one of the most useful and important of minerals, and is present in almost every part of every mass of matter upon earth, yet in its pure state it is, though occasionally met with, of comparatively small interest and value. It is then almost a curiosity, or might be so if less common; and, except for its picturesqueness when in a mountain district, it would be regarded only as a worthless material, interfering with vegetable growth.

## Chapter the Seventh.

### GRANITE, GRANITIC ROCKS, AND LAVA.

There are stones of a kind different from any of those we have been describing in the last four chapters. There are superb but intractable granites, whose crystals are of substances not affected by water, of which the adjacent rocks are altered as if by heat, and whose structure is so close and firm that no trace of water-action can be seen. There are black cindery-looking heaps, the results of an outpouring of molten rock that has taken place within the memory of the children who sport about the still hot ashes. There are other equally black columns of stone that are not modern, but that are quite as plainly the results of some great conflagration within the earth. All these are stones that have passed through the fire. These are the materials we have to describe and consider in the present chapter.

And first for the granites. To understand them we must study them first where they run out in sharp reefs and rocks, apparently detached beyond the extremity of some land, and where they lie in wait for unhappy ships, which too often drift upon them and are wrecked in sight of home. Such granite forms the Scilly Islands and Rocks beyond Land's End, in Cornwall; it forms the rocks that render the navigation of the Channel Islands so dangerous; it recurs at intervals all along the western coast of Europe, chiefly when the land terminates in long promontories. The delight of the artist and lover of the picturesque, it is more dreaded than admired by the sailor and the ship-owner. It is one of the natural guardians of our island home, but, like other guards, it exacts its payment.

Granite must next be seen and examined in the cliff. Bold, grand, naked, and terrible, the granite cliff reveals the source of the danger arising from the detached rocks of the same material. There are fine specimens in Norway and Scotland, almost equally fine in Cornwall and Brittany, and others more accessible and quite as grand and characteristic in the islands of Jersey, Guernsey, and Sark. To every one who has an eye and taste for scenery—to every one who can appreciate bold, noble, and picturesque outlines, and loves to see Nature in her wildest moods—there are no spots within reach more instructive and finer than the coasts of these little islands. There the granite may be studied in all varieties of form and color. Black and frowning cliffs, where the intense but soft darkness of hornblende crystals gives a distinct character to the coast,—broad lines of white quartz or pink felspar intersecting the mass,—other narrower lines of white and pink or gray color crossing these at right angles,—these are the ordinary conditions. Often covered with sea-weed near the water-line, and with tufts of grass or trees jutting out from the higher parts, these cliffs exhibit a certain amount of vegetation, but this is rarely sufficient to conceal the structure of the rock. Varieties of color are common, but granite, commonly so called, is rather pink than dark-green in its general tint.

It is not only color that is seen in granite cliffs, and that distinguishes this rock from others. Form is equally remarkable. There is a bold, rugged wildness in the naked rocks and peaks of granite that cannot easily be mistaken. There is also a general want of vegetation, not universal, but affecting most parts of the rock not decomposed or broken by veins. The veins themselves are characteristic in the highest degree. They are as beautiful as they are useful. Some are white, vertical, narrow, and of a zigzag broken shape, like lightning-forks. Some are broad, regular, and monotonous. Some are threads darting into and penetrating the solid rock in the most singular manner. Some are wide fissures of the rock, filled up with crystalline material, not extremely unlike the rock itself.

There are other forms of granite,—broad, large rounded mountains, as well as needles, rising out of perpetual snow and shooting into the sky, far above the clouds that conceal the sun from the plains below. The rounded masses are not unfrequently covered with stunted vegetation or with peat-bog. Smooth surfaces of granite often, however, terminate seaward with picturesque cliffs; for granite, as well as the softest chalk and loose sand, can be undermined and eaten away by water, and often presents appearances of strength and permanence which are by no means justified by the event.

We may study granite under other aspects. The traveller crosses the sands of Egypt and the mud-banks of the Nile to look at the great Pyramids and the Temples of Thebes, the results of labor carried on four thousand years ago, and may there see how far in a dry climate the most delicate sculptures on the surface of quarried stones may be preserved without injury. He may study the same result in the British Museum, where are more such specimens to be seen in a day than in many weeks' travel in Egypt; but he must then lose the impression made upon the mind when all the senses as well as the eye combine to tell the same tale.

But we need not travel so far to learn how enduring a material granite is under favorable circumstances. We cannot, indeed, afford in England to construct the exterior of our buildings of polished granite; but it is not uncommon as an ornamental stone for internal work. Under such conditions it may seem, indeed, imperishable; but a little examination will show that it is even then subject to a certain corrosion from the air, and one can well understand that when sun and rain and frost combine they effect a change in course of time.

Still the preservation of this stone in the air in our climate is almost perfect, especially when the surface is not broken by little cracks, into which the rootlets of plants and moisture can enter. In such cases, the surface once covered with lichens,—a leathery vegetation which, like a stout pair of boots, is a great preservative from damp and injury,—there is little change perceptible from century to century, and we call the rock imperishable.

To understand how far this apparently imperishable condition differs from the real state of the case on an exposed coast, it is only necessary to watch carefully for a short time in such localities as those indicated above.

Sark, a little island nearly torn to shreds, but still resisting the final stroke of fate, is full of illustrations of this kind. Every cliff, every cavern, all the curious natural holes, and the natural causeway that connects the two parts of the island together, help to illustrate this destruction of granite.

The construction of granite is peculiar. According to the definition of geologists, it is a mass of crystals bedded in a crystalline mass. The crystals are generally of two kinds, the mass being a third kind of mineral. The oblong, flesh-colored crystals in common granite are called *felspar*. The little, bright flaky crystals are *mica*, and the mass in which they occur, often white or gray, is *quartz*. Often the flaky crystals are not there, but in their stead are dark-green crystals, so abundant as to color the mass. The granite is then called Syenite. There are many other varieties, and the minerals are very differently arranged in different places. Geologists give different names to each principal variety, but it is not necessary to trouble ourselves with these names.

The veins of the granite mass have already been alluded to. They are often crevices of some width, more or less open, and full of beautiful crystals, partly of the minerals of which the granite is made up, partly of foreign minerals valuable as yielding metals. Silver, copper, lead, and a multitude of other less common metals are found, either as metals, or as stones yielding metals, in these crevices. They are then called mineral veins, and are the object of search to the miner. They are by no means confined to granite, but are so frequent in that rock (though not always valuable) as to be characteristic.

Granite peeps out in almost every part of the earth, when for some reason the great underlying mass, often called the skeleton of the earth, is made to show itself at the surface. Thus it forms the extremities of land as on the west coast of Europe and in the European islands. In the Alps and other great and lofty mountain-chains it forms either the central or some important parallel range. It is seen where the oldest and last of the limestones, sandstones, and clays is past, and where their changed conditions have also been passed by. It is thus a rock belonging to the earth's interior, and all that is known about it tends to prove that it has been formed at great depth, under great pressure, and even where there was very great heat. Not that it bears marks generally of having been a molten rock in the ordinary sense of the word. It is not like lava, which we shall speak of presently. It has none of the slag-like appearance or structure of substances melted near the air. In its most intimate substance among the very crystals of which it is composed, it contains water clearly discoverable by the aid of the microscope, and recognized even sometimes by the naked eye.

Such is granite. Porphyry is another name for it. There are porphyries of various kinds, and granite is one of them. They are all crystals in a crystalline mass. All are hard; some are among the hardest substances known,—so tough that they can scarcely be worked into shape with any tool. In the great exhibitions of wonderful works of art and manufacture we see vases and ornaments of various kinds, chiefly from Russia, constructed of such material, and they mark the employment of enormous labor, with the aid of all that modern ingenuity can supply in the way of machinery. Even under these circumstances years are required for their completion. In other museums where are collected the curious implements of our forefathers—of those human beings who dwelt in these and other lands, long before the historic period, before the Romans, before the Kelts, before all those peoples who have had definite names assigned to them—we may find from time to time, among the axes and spear-heads and stones of curious shape and doubtful use, specimens of such hard porphyries, or of stones equally hard, and not known as rocks nearer than Asia, worked and smoothed and even polished, in spite of their hardness and of all the difficulties involved. These, it is true, are facts that only belong to Geology in a limited sense, but they deserve mention when speaking of the porphyries, of which granite is an example.

Occupying a very different position in the earth,—often resting upon limestones, or sandstones, or clays,—unevenly and irregularly deposited, and manifestly intrusive in every sense, there is another class of rocks that we must consider in this chapter. These are known as lava and basalt,—lava, if found to have been erupted recently in a melted state; basalt, if forming part of the earth's crust in places where there has been no volcanic disturbance within human experience.

Lava is a very characteristic mineral. It is a kind of glass, produced by the melting of all the common minerals and rocks near the earth's surface, assisted by those alkaline earths which act as fluxes, the whole having been exposed to a great heat at a moderate depth in the earth, and brought to the surface by one of those volcanic disturbances connected with earthquakes, which from time to time produce such destruction in particular localities. Etna, Vesuvius, and Hecla, in Europe, and a multitude of similar mountains in Asia, South America, and elsewhere, are familiar examples. In all these, after the earthquake, and the eruption of gas and steam, a flood of lava generally follows, and this lower part, cooling slowly under some pressure, becomes a compact stone, while the upper part, mixed with air, and cooling rapidly, is spongy, and converted into a kind of slag. The magnitude and extent of these floods of melted rock will be alluded to in another chapter.

Basalt is the lava that has been erupted from volcanoes, probably at the bottom of the sea. It is often spread horizontally in sheets over large tracks, and not unfrequently there are many successive sheets overlying each other in the same district. Many varieties of this rock occur: they are generally of various shades of gray and green, passing into black. Some are full of crystals, others compact and fine-grained. The most usual character, however, is that they are grouped in columns so regular, and on so large a scale, as to present all kinds of grotesque appearances.

Among the best known of these groups of basaltic columns may be mentioned the Giants' Causeway, on the coast of Antrim, in Ireland; Fingal's Cave, in the Isle of Staffa, nearly opposite; some very fine specimens on the Rhine, near Bonn, and others a little higher up the same river; and some in the Eifel. Few things are more striking in their way than these basaltic columns when shown in a cliff or cavern. The uniformity, which seems almost complete when one column is compared with that adjoining, is not continued over a large area, but amply fills the space which the eye can reach. Rising straight or curved from the ground, there is an appearance of myriads of six-sided columns touching each other, and only made manifest by weathering or quarrying. Generally of a black color, the effect is gloomy and grand. If the columns run out towards the sea, they are of course broken off and form a causeway, or are partly eaten out and leave caverns. If in a quarry, they are like the pipes of a gigantic organ. For miles, in a cultivated country, their existence is shown by milestones, gateposts, and all other vertical stone supports, constructed of these convenient and natural columns. Often they are carried to great distances for these purposes, and for road-material, as they do not readily injure by exposure, and are among the toughest substances known. All varieties of lava and basalt are not indeed alike in this respect, but most of the rocks of the kind described in this chapter are both hard and tough.

Returning to the granites, we must now notice a rock extremely abundant in Scotland and elsewhere, often seen on the flanks of granite mountains, and presenting almost the same mineral group as granite itself, but splitting readily into slabs,—more or less thin and regular in different places. This mechanical arrangement is not met with in the granite, and the rock that exhibits them is called *gneiss*. It is one of a class of rocks, some of which are *schists*. The young geologist may easily be puzzled in endeavoring to draw a line of demarcation between the granites and these other rocks, as such line does not always exist, and, when it does, is not well defined. Gneiss and granite may be looked on as quite sufficiently similar to be classed together as minerals, though distinct in their mechanical arrangement.

Rotten granite is a condition of the rock so different from that with which most people are familiar, that it may seem almost an absurdity. Nevertheless, there are very extensive tracts where the granite falls so easily to powder, on exposure to the air, as to affect the scenery. There is a curious example of this in Bavaria, near the mountains that separate Bavaria from Bohemia. It is a considerable hill, where the granite is eaten away at the surface; and the following description of it is accurate and picturesque. The hill is called the Louisenberg :—

" The road to the Louisenberg lies along the slopes of a hill, copiously strewn with loose masses of granite, increasing in size and quantity as you advance, until at length the hill seems to consist of nothing else but disjointed fragments, piled in heaps one over another. Such a vast pyramid of loose rock might have furnished the Titans with ammunition when storming Jupiter in Olympus. If you begin at the bottom of the hill, and climb to the top, or compass it round, you will find nothing but rocks in pieces, tumbled about in all directions; and the result is a kind of labyrinth, in which one may wander about for hours, sometimes creeping, for many hours together, through caves, dark or barely admitting a few gleams of light between the interstices of the huge superincumbent masses which form their roof, at others threading narrow clefts, or scrambling over projecting masses to the summit of the hill, which is itself a detached block."—*Murray's Handbook for Southern Germany*, 3d ed. p. 88.

Many other remarkable points of scenery are produced in the same way, but chiefly in sea-cliffs and by the coast on bleak moors. It is not often that the decomposed rock is so favorable to vegetable growth as in the case above described. The number of trees growing on the hill give, indeed, the appearance of a wood, and "the peculiar luxuriance of the dark-green moss, covering the rocky walls with a continuous tapestry," imparts an air of soft beauty almost peculiar to the Louisenberg. The whole neighborhood consists of sand and gravel, derived from decomposed granite.

# PART III:
## THE PLACEMENT & DISPLACEMENT OF THE STONES IN THE GREAT STONE BOOK.

# THE GREAT STONE BOOK.

## Part III.

## Chapter the Eighth.

### IN THE BRICK-FIELD AND THE GRAVEL-PIT.

We have now seen the way in which a river removes and deposits stones and mud, the effect of the tide and the storm-waves of the sea in destroying a cliff and producing a shoal, and the mode in which a glacier removes and an iceberg distributes the accumulated fragments of the mountain-side on which it is formed. We have also seen what are the clays and limestones and sandstones with which the water and the ice have generally to deal; how these are, for the most part, water-formed and water-worn, though since hardened, and often much changed. But there is a connecting link between these relics of a time long past and the mud and sand left by the river in its recent course, or now moved by the sea; and this link we must next endeavor to make out. It is a very interesting and important one. It is the most direct, and perhaps the most instructive, of all the early lessons in Geology. It introduces the subject of Geology, and all its peculiarities and characteristics, as distinguished from what is called Physical Geography, a science which relates only to the present.

There are many ways of making this step in our science, and each place will, generally speaking, have in its neighborhood some particular locality better for it than another. In many parts of the country, the only means at hand will be the examination of the spots where, by some road-cutting or the passage of a small stream, the common vegetable soil has been removed and its gradual change laid bare. This change is generally as follows:—first into a coarser soil, then into a mass not worth calling soil, and then, at last, into some uniform mineral mass that we may call a rock. Whatever this rock may be, it is sure to serve our purpose, and mark the difference between the soil in which plants are nourished and the great body of the earth.

In many parts of England, however,—and, indeed, in most parts of Northern Europe,—there is, near the surface, a considerable heap of rounded stones and sand, that we call gravel, and often a good deal of stiff clay, working into a paste with water, and very tenacious. Of such clay bricks are often made, and thus it is known as brick-clay. The mixture of rounded stones and sand, called gravel, is often very thick. It is found both in hollows and on hill-tops. It is made up of stones of all kinds, many of them quite unlike those of the rocks at hand. These are mixed irregularly, and the whole mass seems as if placed on the surface without any order, the clays in one place and the stones in another. Occasionally there are thin beds of white sand, but these are rare. Sometimes there are bones of animals mixed with the stones. These are not always broken, and were apparently brought or left with the heap of stones in which they are found. It is evident that some reason must exist for the occurrence of all these heaps where we find them; and people's ideas were first, and for a long while, directed to the probability of their being proofs of a great deluge that once swept the human race from the earth. A closer examination proves that this is not the case; but these heaps remain, and to them we now request the young geologist's attention.

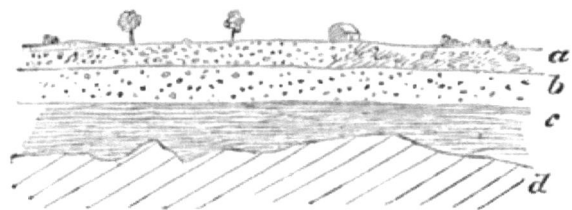

SECTION SHOWING THE HEAD OF EARTH, THE SAND, AND THE CLAYS IN A BRICK-PIT.

*a*. The *head* of soil.   *b*. Sands above the clay.   *c*. The clay.
*d*. The rock below the clay (not *conformable*).

To understand more clearly the facts of the case, let the reader, if possible, repair to a brick-field or gravel-pit, and examine the cutting made to get at the clay or gravel. Near the top, but below the vegetable soil, there is probably a quantity of earth which the workmen call a *head*, consisting of rubbish; and through this, though not real soil, many of the roots of trees and plants have penetrated. The rubbish is not everywhere of the same kind or of equal thickness: some parts of it probably contain good soil mixed with it, while other parts, close by, only show a thin coating of a few inches. Below the good soil will, perhaps, be found poor, hungry, worthless clays, broken stones, and sands, until at last one particular bed of clay is reached that is fit for making into bricks.

Just so with the gravel-pit. The gravel is in streaks or beds below the vegetable soil; and of these beds one lies above another, not very regularly, but still with some approach to order. Particular beds show all the stones well rounded, and nearly of the same size; while other beds or parcels of the gravel are more sandy, or made up of stones less completely sorted. In all cases, wherever you look at any cuttings such as are seen in gravel-pits, you will find that there is a good deal of order in the way the different materials are arranged, although they are by no means built up with perfect uniformity.

Now, how do you suppose the clays, and sands, and pebbles were placed where you find them? A little careful search will generally discover, buried in the earth at the top, some snail-shells, and bones of horses, cows, dogs, rats, or sheep, hidden among the roots and buried vegetation. You will probably find none of these, nor any thing like them, below, but, in their place, some of the common fresh-water shells, such as belong to the inhabitants of adjacent rivers or ponds, mixed with the clay and sand; or perhaps there may be a few bones of animals not common in the neighborhood, or some shells which have certainly come from the sea. These latter are often heaped in considerable numbers, and must have come in originally as part of the gravel or clay deposit.

With these marine shells, which are familiar enough on the nearest sea-shore, but seem strangely placed in the brick-pit, and still more strangely mixed up with fine sand and mud between two beds of gravel or flint-pebbles, there is generally no mixture of bones of land-animals, and no plants, although these are common enough elsewhere, and equally well preserved; neither are there pond-shells. When, in comparatively rare instances, bones are found, they are worn and rolled, as if by water, but they are not the bones of domesticated animals.

Knowing, as we do, what water can effect in the way of collecting, removing, and arranging such things, we cannot help feeling that all the clay, and mud, and sand, and pebbles must have been placed where they are by water. True, there is no water now near them,—true, the sea is not only far off, but at a lower level; all this may make it very difficult to understand how the matter was arranged, but it need not alter the conclusion that as water now does precisely similar things in a way we see and know, so water must have done this thing. We can only believe that the accumulation, whatever it was and whenever it took place, occurred under water which has since departed from the surface.

All beds of gravel and sand mixed with mud, whether containing shells and bones or not, must, doubtless, have been brought together under water; and most parts of our island are covered with such beds here and there. All or nearly all the plains of Europe are of the same kind, and were certainly under water when their present coating of gravel, clay, &c. was brought together. "What!" it may be exclaimed; "has all England, and almost all Europe, been under water so recently?" There cannot be a doubt that such is the case.

In the sacred history, with which all are acquainted, there is an account of a great deluge which covered the land with water, destroying almost all the living inhabitants.

The precise meaning of the sacred history in respect to that deluge, or its exact date, are subjects that we need not here discuss; but one thing in regard to it is certain,—namely, that a large part, perhaps the whole, of the earth's surface has been under water since man was among its inhabitants; and it is possible that many similar and partial deluges have taken place at different times during the earth's history.

A deluge, however, does by no means assume that water was miraculously added to the quantity previously existing and forming part of the earth's surface. It means, no doubt, that the relative levels of land and water were changed, and that what had once been land became buried under water. It may also mean that, in places long covered by the sea, the sea-bottom was lifted up and became dry land. All land, probably, has been in turn the bottom of a sea, and while under water it became covered with mud and marine animals. The bottom or bed of the sea has often been converted into land, and the land has become buried and lost sight of. The new lands were of different shape and had a very different climate from the old which had previously existed in the same neighborhood.

But neither is it necessary to suppose that every deluge, or great rush of water, was accompanied by a violent breaking up of the land. This may sometimes have been the case; and earthquakes have often produced wonderful and very mischievous commotions, in different parts of the world, tending to this result. But the change of level may sometimes have been very gradual, and need not have been attended by a breaking up of the surface. There may, in other words, be destructive and change-producing causes that take even thousands of years to complete; and during such slow and unnoticed revolutions the clays of our brick-field and the stones of our gravel-pit may have been placed in their present position.

When rapid changes such as those of earthquakes happen on the earth, the effect, although it excites more attention, is not so great as that brought about by the slow alterations which many hundred years are needed to complete. It has taken a long time for frosts and ice to bring together such a heap as is to be found in any of the principal gravel-beds near London,—a time far longer than could be supposed; longer, indeed, than can be calculated; longer, even, than we have been accustomed to think the world has existed. What, then, must have been the time required to build up the world, if there are many of these gravel-beds heaped one upon another, all of different ages, the lowest being the oldest? This is one of the difficult questions of Geology, and one that can never be exactly answered. All we can do is to examine and compare facts, and judge by comparison when we have fully considered the facts.

But let us look more closely at the beds of gravel, separated from each other sometimes by sand, sometimes by gravel of a different kind. In a thickness of twenty or thirty feet there will generally be a good many varieties, and we shall see any particular bed that is worked vary here and there. Pick out a few of the pebbles, and look at them.

Here is a well-rounded black pebble, about the size of

an egg, very smooth and almost polished, but the surface is scratched all over with fine marks, showing clearly how the stone became round and smooth. Next to it is a broken fragment, the edges rounded and worn and a clean broken face presented. Both are flints, and both exactly resemble other flints, whether in the gravel, on the sea-beach, or in the chalk-cliff. It takes a long while to roll so hard a stone as a flint into the shape of an egg and carry it with others into a great heap far away from the sea. It takes considerable force to break a flint pebble in half.

We have next to see what a flint is, and where it comes from, in order to know what is the relation of this gravel-pit with the various rocks in its neighborhood. Let us break it in half with a hammer and try if any thing is to be learnt by looking at the inside. It is not unlikely that when broken there will be a small empty space in the middle, partly occupied with little crystals. Perhaps there is no empty space, but a distinct shape resembling some more or less known part of an animal, as if the flint had once been pasty and had entangled a sponge, a shell, or sea-anemone, just as in jellies the cook will enclose fresh strawberries or cherries, or as flies are caught in resin. At any rate, we are almost sure to find, if we look closely enough, using that wonderful contrivance the microscope, that little white or gray spots in the clear flint once belonged either to sponges, or to shells, or to some other creature formerly inhabiting the sea.

The flints generally found in gravel are very different from most other stones we meet with. The former all seem similar, and, though mixed with other very different stones, they, no doubt, have all come from the chalk. The only places where such material is at all abundant are the various chalk-hills, many of them at considerable distance. Beds of flint, unbroken and undisturbed, often alternate with the beds of chalk, and it is supposed that the pebbles once formed part of other chalk-hills now washed away.

Must we, then, believe that all our gravel and brick-clay consists of the remains of older deposits broken up? Such is, indeed, the geological conclusion; and thus it is that these pebbles, so useful and so common, carry us back to rocks of much older date than themselves and serve as connecting links not only between the sea-beach and the heaps of boulders far removed from the sea, but also between the gravel-bed and the chalk-cliff.

There was a time when our gravel-beds did not exist as gravel, but when the raw material, the unrounded stones, were buried in the chalk-hills, which were then entirely under water. As gravel covers not only a large proportion of England, but also much of Northern Europe, there must have been a larger quantity of chalk then than there is now, and probably it extended much more widely and to places where we can at present find no appearance of it. By the washing of the sea the chalk was worn away in many places and the flints separated from the fine chalk mud. Being hard stones, they were then rolled about till most of them were rounded, and they were collected in heaps, those of the same size keeping together, and the mud and sand forming bands between them.

Looking at the flints in gravel merely as stones, they

thus mark a great change and the lapse of a long time; but when we find shells sticking in them, or sponge-like bodies buried in them, like flies in amber, they offer other subjects for thought. Of all things, flint is one of the most solid and hardest. If people build walls with it, or expose it in other ways to weather, it never seems to alter or decay. It is true that, if put in a hot fire, it gets very brittle, but still it never melts; and no process of nature that we know of could soften it into a paste, so that one could stick a shell upon it, or make it to enclose the delicate little sponges so often seen within it.

But though neither fire nor water will soften flint unassisted, there are means not only of making it soft, but even of dissolving it in water. When put in open iron cages, and held for some time in a steam-boiler, with caustic potash or soda, such as is obtained plentifully from chemical works, it becomes at last completely sucked up by the water, like a lump of sugar, and the water itself looks like a thick syrup, in which you might easily put the most delicate little coral without injury. Exposed to the air, this syrup thickens and at last hardens, but it does not turn into flint again quite so easily. It long remains white, and is greatly affected by damp air. Still, we see how a soft condition of flint may be produced; and some day we may discover the way in which, the potash and soda being quite got rid of, a flint can really be re-made.

But there are no steam-boilers and stores of caustic potash and soda at the bottom of the sea, where chalk was made. This is merely a way in which shells and sea-weed might now be buried, as it shows that the change of hardness is not quite impossible. Nature's way was rather different, and perhaps much slower, but not less complete in the end.

We return now to the completely-formed gravel. Mixed with the pebbles, and above or below them, are found sometimes bones, and occasionally, though not often, pieces of flint, looking as if they had been split and chipped into their shape by savages. No bones of men have been found, but there are remains of such animals as horses, horned cattle, wolves, foxes, and bears, mixed up with the leg-bones, backbones, and teeth of the elephant, the rhinoceros, and the hippopotamus.

A strange and unexpected discovery was this mixture of flint weapons, sculptured by man, with the bones of domestic animals and the bones of such animals as the elephant and hippopotamus. One's first idea is, that either the one or the other set has been introduced accidentally at a different period, or that all have been removed together by some recent torrent, the older being mixed with the newer. We feel inclined to look upon the deluge of Noah as a probable cause of such a mixture, and to speculate on the races of men that lived before the Flood as having indeed covered the whole earth, and been all inhabitants of a world whose climates were little varied, and in which the elephant and the lion of the tropics, the horse, ox, deer, dog, and beaver of the temperate regions, and the great polar bear and seals of the icy seas, could live together in the climate of England.

But a little further knowledge and examination into what Geology teaches will show that this way of explaining appearances is not the right one. The elephants, and other large animals of that family (the rhinoceros and hippopotamus), were not exactly like those living now in India and Africa. The elephant was covered with thick and long hair, the rhinoceros and hippopotamus were differently proportioned from those we are now familiar with. Their bones, also, are in far too perfect a state to allow us to suppose that they have been rolled about on the sea-shore; and the harder bones and teeth are too abundant to allow us to imagine for a moment that they have been drifted a long distance, from places where the climate more resembles that of their present habitations.

Some sixty years ago, a complete elephant was found buried in frozen gravel in Siberia, and similar frozen cliffs elsewhere have been found to contain complete carcases of other large animals. The flesh on these carcases was preserved as we preserve meat in ice-chests, but still more perfectly and for a longer time. When thawed, so that foxes and dogs could get at it, these animals soon showed that they had not before had such a chance, by devouring the flesh as rapidly as possible. These large quadrupeds must have lived in the neighborhood, and had been unexpectedly caught up in the water, —perhaps carried to a distance after being drowned,— till they entered within the region of perpetual frost, where they were built up as part of a frozen mass of water, mud, sand, stones, and carcases, to remain unchanged for centuries, owing to the preservative power of ice.

Frozen water has, no doubt, had much to do with the distribution of gravel, as well as with the burying and preserving these curious remains of a former world. In the upper valleys of the Alps, and in other mountain-districts, under favorable circumstances, where water that would otherwise have fallen on the plains in rain is deposited as snow, and the snow, instead of melting, hardens into ice, and then, by its weight, slides gently down into the lower valleys, are formed the *glaciers*, already described in a former chapter. These rivers of ice continue to descend, until they become converted into rivers of water in temperate climates; but far away on the vast and little-visited shores of the polar seas, every nook and mountain-gorge is loaded with such masses, which fill the valleys and project far into the sea, and, when large enough, break away and float off in the form of ice-islands. Owing to currents in the ocean moving always from the poles towards the equator, the ice is drifted in very large quantities, coming down towards the south from the north pole and towards the north from the south pole, until the whole of the ice is melted. But so long as the ice is attached to the glacier and the land, it is constantly receiving fresh supplies of broken rock, split off at every change of weather from the mountain-side, so that each floating island, or iceberg, becomes loaded with thousands of tons of mud and stones, which of course reach the bottom of the sea when the ice melts. Thus there must be a constant accumulation on the bottom of the ocean of such stones brought from a great distance; and, as they are rolled over and over one another on shores and shallow places, they become at last converted into fine mud and rounded pebbles.

But there are some other things to be considered, for it must not be concluded that all the ice continues floating till it is melted. Owing to the fact—a very curious and important one—that ice is rather lighter than water, the ice floats at or near the surface, with only a small part visible in proportion to the whole mass. This proportion is smaller as the weight of the load, the freight of stones and mud it conveys, is greater. If the ice is eighty or ninety feet high above the water—and this is no uncommon height—it may be very safely assumed that it is six or eight hundred feet or more in depth, and correspondingly larger; and if it passes over a sea not so deep as this, the whole mass will be stranded and prevented from further advance. When this happens, the momentum or impetus possessed by so large a mass of matter in motion cannot be suddenly stopped; and the ice-island, like a ship when it takes the ground, will be partly lifted over the mud or stone-bank on which it has struck, and in this operation will grind and be ground with extreme energy, and remain firmly buried in its place till it becomes sufficiently lightened of its load by melting above to float off again. Wonderful effects of this great force of grinding are sometimes seen on rocks that have been exposed to it.

Besides the ice and the load of stones it conveys, there are other important means in nature by which broken rocks are turned into pebbles more or less rounded, and into mud more or less fine. Every coast is inevitably exposed to the action of running water, and materials are removed with a rapidity proportioned to the softness of the rock and the violence of the waves.

Cliffs are thus torn away and destroyed, and every bed of shingle and sand is rolled over and over by the ceaseless rise and fall of the tide, and disturbed by the occasional dash of the tempest, till it is in time ground into mud. There is, however, constantly a fresh supply of raw material, consisting of fragments of worn and fallen rock; and after the first angles of the broken stones have been knocked away, pebbles are soon formed. The formation of beds of gravel and clay is probably going on constantly in many seas, and ample provision is being made for future lands in this respect.

But if pebble-beds and thick clay were heaped together under water, as all the facts concerning them seem to show, it cannot be wondered at that they contain now and then the shells and bones of the inhabitants of the water and adjacent land, nor, on the other hand, need we be surprised if in most cases these delicate organizations are bruised and injured, and a large proportion of them totally destroyed, by the rude conflict of the waves, and the rubbing and grinding they have undergone. Where simply drifted without being much rolled, the fossils may remain; but where drifted and long exposed, we may be sure there will be little indication of life.

When we consider the wide extent of country that is covered with thick beds of brick-clay, and the innumerable patches of gravel, some of them not small, distributed over the surface even of our own country, we shall see how wide-spread must have been the causes at work. And when we look, too, at the thickness of fine soil often lying undisturbed over the clay and gravel, and the long time that things must have remained nearly as they now are to account for this accumulation of soil and growth of vegetation, it will be evident that the changes by which our island was brought into its present position and height above the water were no affairs of yesterday, but must date back far, very far beyond our records. In the beds of gravel below the vegetable soil, and among the remains of large elephants and rhinoceroses, are buried those curious flint weapons that have been already alluded to, now generally admitted to be of human manufacture. When and how could these our ancestors have existed, and what must have been the state of our island when they were its only inhabitants? These, again, are among the queries to which we cannot expect to receive satisfactory replies, and it is better not to puzzle or confuse ourselves at present by discussing them.

## Chapter the Ninth.

### IN THE QUARRY AND THE MINE.

EXCEPT to those—who, however, are numbered by millions—buried for the greater part of their lives in the streets of large towns, there are few who have not access to some kind of quarry. Even the townsman, however, can generally find within moderate distance a good bare face of railway-cutting, if he cannot reach a spot where stone is being removed for building purposes or road-making. To the young geologist every quarry, of whatever material, is full of instruction of many kinds.

All kinds of stone are quarried. From the hardest and toughest granite, or from the tough or soft sandstones and grits, to the merest sand in a pit,—from fine white statuary marble, through all varieties of limestone, to chalk,—from magnificent sheets of slate to poor shale, there are places to be found where it is worth while to pare away the vegetable soil and subsoil, to cut the hard rock into a series of steps such as giants might climb, to split away the stone with blasts of gunpowder, to pile the waste stone or let it fall down some steep slope to the sea, and thus to exhibit the skeleton of the earth for convenient observation and experiment.

Very large and magnificent are some of these illustrations of Nature, and often the contents of such large quarries are of absorbing interest. Others are much smaller, and in many cases the whole interest is concentrated in the present works, the surface soon becoming weathered by the action of damp air, rain, and frost.

The points of chief interest in quarries are these: (1.) They show us the mineral crust of the earth, sands converted into sandstones, muds into limestone or slate, materials of which we know very little into granite. (2.) They show us the peculiar changes in position by which these materials, once at the bottom of deep water, have been placed in the order we now find them; or, in other words, they illustrate the nature of the forces that have lifted the earth's crust. (3.) They show us very often, in a perfectly distinct manner, that the original accumulation, now stone, was a succession of shelly beds, or an alternation of shelly and impalpable mud, or a heap of sand followed by mud with shells. (4.) They tell us whether the original material was deposited in water, and whether the water was deep or shallow. (5.) They enable us to measure, in a rough and approximate way, the relative time required for the original deposit. (6.) They inform us of the changes that have taken place in the arrangements of the animal and vegetable world since the present hard rock was deposited as soft mud.

In the present chapter we will only consider a few of these numerous and valuable sources of information. It is in quarries that we can most easily learn how the stones in the book are built into their places; how they have passed from one state to another; how they are connected with remains indicating life; how in undergoing one kind of change—hardening to become stone—they have undergone another,—splitting up by the general contraction of the mass; how in some cases the animal or vegetable has been embalmed in a perfect state, while in others we find only its broken shell, a few fragments of bone, the impression of a leaf, or the impress where an organic substance has once lain.

In all these respects quarries are so varied that no two teach precisely the same lesson. Each has its own special fact, and each material has behaved so differently, under apparently similar circumstances, that no monotony need be feared. We may consider quarries as either of granite, basalt, slate, sandstone, or limestone. Chalk, although so soft, is a variety of limestone, and tells the same tale. Marble is a hard variety.

In granite quarries there is always much grandeur of effect. The rock itself is so hard and tough and heavy, that if it were not for the natural lines of cracks with which it abounds, it would be hardly worth while to quarry it at all. These lines are wonderfully systematic, and they break up the rock into masses of similar shape, large or small, according to circumstances. Much of the value of granite depends on these joints, as they either assist or prevent the obtaining of large slabs or blocks. The great quarries at Peterhead, near Aberdeen, the Cheesewring Quarries in Cornwall, and some others in the British Islands, are remarkable instances of this. The granite in a quarry is not all favorable for working. There will be portions, called veins, exceedingly hard and durable, but by their side will be other veins equally rotten and poor. The grain will be different, the arrangement of the particles of the stone will vary, and a thousand little local peculiarities will exist. It is these that are so instructive. By the study of these the history of granite will have to be learnt; and the direction, number, and magnitude of the different veins will be found to lead to curious generalizations. It is thus that the structure is discovered, and the varieties of structure are so great that no two quarries are exactly alike.

It often happens that a very wide district will be governed by similar laws with reference to the direction of the principal joints and systems of crevices. There will be an apparent system in all the sides and backs of the rock, a fact which (naturally enough) is known practically to every good quarryman. But these systematic joints, which by the quarryman are only thought of as assisting him in his work of destruction, are recognized and theorized upon by the geologist in reference to the nature of granite itself.

But no granite is without veins of another kind of rock penetrating its mass. These, indeed, are sometimes so large and so numerous as to be intimately mixed up with the rock, but at other times are so small as to resemble mere threads. Narrow strings of quartz and broader stripes of porphyry, rotten films of granite and oval blisters, as well as other surer indications of great change, and that of a chemical nature, abound. A rough and doubtful appearance of existing in layers or strata is not unusual, but the vein-structure chiefly prevails. If at the sea-side, the waves will have helped to render this very clear. Sometimes the vein, sometimes the rock, is the hardest; and whichever may be so is sure to be found jutting out, while the softer portions are worn and eaten away into caverns and recesses.

Granite generally improves in quality on being followed to some depth below the surface. It has not escaped the effect of weathering, and the stone is often split into fragments too small to be of much use where it has long been exposed to the air. Not unfrequently it is altogether rotten close to the surface, and is converted into a mixed mass of rounded fragments and fine sand. However this may be, there is always something to show to the experienced eye the real nature of the case.

If the chief mechanical lesson that can be learnt in a granite quarry is the curious tendency to split only in certain directions and break up into regular solids, sometimes roughly bedded, there is much more to be seen, and even greater difficulties are to be surmounted, if we would understand the structure of slate. Here the whole rock presents material for study. In a large quarry there will be only certain portions that contain the best slate, and many times more of the material quarried is thrown away than can be sent away for sale. But all is characterized by the same peculiarity of splitting, carried to an extent almost inconceivable. Throughout not only the whole of a quarry, but often in a large district scores of square miles in extent, is seen everywhere a general tendency of all the rock to split in one direction. That this is not the direction in which the beds were thrown down from water is often quite clear, from the position of shells found lying in natural order, and indicating a very different arrangement. But this is not all. Besides the cleavage, as the former tendency is called,—being that according to which the mass can be cleaved or split up into thin plates, adapted for roofing and other purposes,—and the bedding, as the latter arrangement indicates, there is also, as in granite, a splitting of another kind, by joints or "backs," often helping the quarryman, and pointing out to him the direction in which his blast will be most efficacious. These joints, too, are in sets parallel to each other and making definite angles, so that we have in the slate quarry all there is in the granite quarry, and another and more perfect system of splitting in addition to that. Occasional wide fissures in the rock, filled up with a different material, clearly show that all this has not been accomplished without great exertion of force, the nature of which we shall have to consider afterwards. It is clear that slate quarries, even in the simple matter of the structure of the rock, are likely to afford much instruction.

Limestone quarries are more varied than those of granite or slate. In the first place, the rock is sometimes marble, when the original accumulation by beds or strata is lost; while, most frequently, the bedding is an essential and characteristic feature, replacing, after a clumsy and imperfect fashion, the cleavage of slates. The joints remain,—the mass is split into many masses, small near the surface, and gradually more brittle, massive, and compact as we go deeper. But, again, there are differences in this respect. Some of the limestones are carbonates of lime; some carbonates of lime and magnesia; some are quite crystalline, some half crystalline, some not crystalline at all. Almost all are cracked and broken near the surface; but, while some are pierced through and through by crevices and caverns, others seem to have very little of this porous constitution. The joints in limestones are very numerous, and often extremely systematic, being in sets parallel to each other, and making a uniform angle over very wide areas. The hard and most compact and brittle limestones, approaching marbles, are sometimes not at all bedded, or rather, perhaps, this structure is obliterated. The softer and less altered rocks abound generally in fossils, and split easily in the natural beds,—some of these serving as good stone, others very poor, and others powdery and bad. In all these cases the crevices are still systematic.

Sandstones are very generally bedded, but the beds are often thick, and only separated one from another by thin films of iron, sand, or dirt. The harder kinds of sand-rock are always jointed, and the rock breaks according to this structure. The bedding is often marked by indications of animals or vegetables, but these are sometimes mere impressions made by stems of sea-weed drifted upon the sand, or the trails of animals that have passed over the mud while the rock was being formed.

Quarries in basalt are often in the highest degree picturesque, for they exhibit a curious columnar appearance, the result of the somewhat rapid cooling, under peculiar circumstances, of the lava of which the rock consists. That melted rock does cool in these forms is well known by actual experiment, and the magnitude of the mass does not seem to produce any change. Some of the most striking quarry phenomena in existence are derived from huge masses of this kind of material, black and frowning, but of marvellous and systematic regularity; the masses breaking up very readily into short six-sided columns, well adapted for certain purposes of construction. On the banks of the Rhine there are many fine instances of the kind; and other places, where there have been volcanoes in former times, are similarly circumstanced.

But there is absolutely no resemblance between their appearances and those of rock deposited from water. They clearly show their origin, and this is in all details of structure as well as in general aspect. At a distance, indeed, there is a marked flatness where such material is spread over the earth on a large scale; for all is rock once fluid from heat, and often it has been poured forth at the bottom of the sea beneath a great pressure of water.

Quarries, then, each one in its own way, may be regarded as illustrative of the state of rocks after they have been placed, and when they are so far altered as is involved in their being now near the surface:—altered by those slow processes that go on out of sight, and deep in the earth, or under the waves,—altered by being lifted up, and thus exposed to enormous squeezing,—altered, lastly, by exposure to rain and sun, cold and heat, precisely in the way in which these causes of change are most efficacious.

To obtain good stone, many methods are resorted to, besides merely paring away the surface, and working the hill-side or cliff into convenient steps. Near the city of Caen, whence comes stone that has been used for the last thousand years in the construction of buildings both in France and England, a very beautiful cream-colored limestone is obtained by long tunnels, run into the earth at the foot of a low cliff by a river. The stone thus reached has not been exposed to weathering, and is much finer and less injured than from parts of the same bed near the surface. Since, also, particular beds are more valuable than others, these must be followed out of sight, since the mass above them could never be removed. Thus the fact of the beds or strata that come out to the surface at one place being continued out of sight in another, is shown by actual experiment. In thus working it is often necessary, for the sake of air, to sink a deep hole or shaft, to meet this gallery run in for the stone, and thus we have the first illustration of mining operations as distinct from quarrying. In one sense, indeed, mining is only quarrying under ground out of sight of day; and when the object of mining is to get coal, this is really all that is needed mechanically.

Mines, however, generally lay bare other peculiarities of structure, and even of composition, of rocks than those seen in ordinary quarries. In the first place, mines, when not for coal, are generally in districts where the many open spaces in rocks are now filled up, partly or altogether, with foreign minerals. Mining is carried on for ores,—or those stones from which metal is obtained; and most of them actually occupy the crevices formed long ago in such rocks, as granite, slate, sandstone, or limestone. Such crevices are then called *veins*.

We have seen how systematic the cracks in these rocks are, and now, in reference to mining, this correspondence in direction of the chief systems will be found to extend far and characterize large districts. If we take Cornwall, our own great mining district, and look at the Ordnance Map, geologically colored to show the rocks and their condition, we shall see a number of gilt lines parallel or nearly parallel to each other, ranging nearly east and west, but crossed by others running more nearly north and south. On looking more closely, the former will be seen to mark the places where the great copper and tin mines are placed; while the latter, if they show mines, are chiefly lead and silver. Miners call the former, or east and west veins or crevices, by the name of lodes or right-running veins. The others are called cross-courses, and are less valuable. Something of the same kind marks every great mining district. The object of the miner is to discover and reach the deposits of valuable mineral in these veins, and every point of geological knowledge concerning the structure of the rocks is useful to him, in as far as it assists in this.

Under ground in mines, therefore, as well as above ground in quarries, the geologist must pursue his studies, —must compare, and examine, and decide, to the best of his ability, how far the veins affect the rock, or are affected by it,—what are the conditions favorable for ore, and what appearances are deceptive and unfavorable. In these dark recesses he learns many important lessons; he sees under what conditions rocks yield valuable minerals, or refuse them; and he learns other lessons, more valuable and instructive, inasmuch as they are less marked and confused with surface-action.

Thus, then, there are means available in most countries,

and often in many parts of a country,—in most rocks, and often in the same rock, under very different conditions,— for making out Nature's work, in preparing rocks for their ultimate destiny. Originally the river-bed and the ocean-floor, covered up with other deposits or pressed down by a steady weight of water, exposed to such uniform temperature as exists in the depths to which they are carried, they gradually lose their first state and acquire some other, according to the causes that act. Drying and hardening, they occupy less space, and crack. Elevated or depressed, they occupy a different space, greater or smaller; they are squeezed, and bent, and altered. Then come those systematic cracks which terminate in veins, originally open crevices, but, as time goes on, filled up with various minerals and metals. Ultimately brought near the surface, they are, each time a movement takes place, gradually more and more split, and the original crevices become more and more defined, larger, and more systematic. At length the whole rock is left high and dry, as a part of land,—a leaf in our Great Stone Book, having its writing and its illustrations, telling its story, and helping to clear up the earth's history.

Such are some of the lessons to be learnt in the quarry and mine. They are lessons of importance, though not perhaps those that the young geologist would first direct his attention to. Every crevice and joint,—every bed,— every disturbance indicated by a fracture or heave of the beds,—every obscure marking,—every portion of the stone, whether selected for superior excellence or set aside as flawed and faulty, affords good material for study. It is here that the plan and course of Nature must be learnt; and it is well sometimes to neglect the fossils, interesting as they may be, for the sake of the laws that have governed the whole deposit.

## Chapter the Tenth.

### VOLCANOES AND EARTHQUAKES.

IN various parts of the earth there are mountains of a sugar-loaf form, having at the top a cup-shaped hollow, instead of rising to a point; and from within this cup, or from cracks in the side of the mountain, there issue from time to time large quantities of steam, and various stifling sulphurous and other poisonous gases. Showers of fine ashes and lumps of stone are shot out into the air from the same vent with extreme force, accompanied by peculiar sounds proceeding from the very depths of the earth; while floods of melted rock, called lava, pour forth over the land, sweeping away trees and whole villages in their course, filling up the deep beds of rivers, and only terminating when the sluggish stream of boiling lava accumulates to such a thickness at the vent as to overbalance the pressure acting from beneath, and thus close the safety-valve for a time.

Of all phenomena, these outbursts of fire from the earth are among the most alarming and mischievous. In former times, tens of thousands of victims have been sacrificed to them; and recently, within a few years, there have been many terrible eruptions recorded, proving that the cause that produced them is still at work, and is as capable now as it ever was of overwhelming a city or devastating the richest plains. About fifty years after the death of our Saviour, two important cities in South Italy, Herculaneum and Pompeii, were overwhelmed by loose ashes and melted rock erupted from Vesuvius, one of these mountains; and it has since continued, from time to time, to repeat similar eruptions up to the present day. Etna, another far loftier mountain, in the island of Sicily, has poured forth a burning flood within a few years, and is described, as it appeared some 2300 years ago, by Pindar, one of the earliest poets of Greece, in the following sentence :—"The snowy Etna, the pillar of heaven, the nurse of everlasting frost, in whose deep caverns lie concealed the fountains of unapproachable fire; a stream of eddying smoke by day, a bright and ruddy flame by night, and burning rocks rolled down with loud uproar into the sea."

Volcanoes are of all elevations. In the year 1831, an eruption took place in the Mediterranean, between Sicily and the site of ancient Carthage, where upwards of a hundred fathoms of water had been proved by soundings; and, after this eruption had gone on for some time, an island was formed, which ultimately was upwards of 200 feet high and three miles in circumference, entirely composed of incoherent ashes thrown up out of the earth. Other similar eruptions have taken place in the Atlantic in still deeper water. At the level of the surface, in many parts of the world, distinct volcanic appearances have often been reported,—in Sicily, in India, and in Persia. In India, not very far from the mouth of the Indus, there is a tract of a thousand square miles of country covered with low cones erupted at various times. At Stromboli, one of the Lipari Islands, between Naples and Sicily, is a constant eruption at an elevation of about 2300 feet. Vesuvius itself is 4000 feet; Etna is 11,000 feet. In the Sandwich Islands, a few years ago, a copious stream of lava, two miles broad and twenty-five miles long, proceeded from an opening 13,000 feet above the sea; while Cotopaxi, one of the loftiest mountains of the Andes, has its cone and crater more than 20,000 feet above the sea. At all elevations there is this mysterious power in the earth's interior exerted, and apparently with little difference at different heights.

Very widely, too, are volcanoes distributed. There are several in Europe,—five of them active; for Etna, Vesuvius, and Stromboli, Santorin in the Grecian Archipelago, and Hecla in Iceland, seem to have been for more than twenty centuries continually in readiness to burst forth, although they are not always throwing out a sufficient quantity of matter to do serious injury. Of these the three first are in the South of Italy and adjoining islands, and are close together; the fourth is some distance towards Asiatic land; but Hecla is far removed, touching the Arctic Circle. In Asia there are two principal groups,—one near the shores of the Mediterranean, the other in the central part of the continent; but the Asiatic islands, between the Burmese peninsula and Australia, are everywhere dotted over with active volcanoes, no less than 115 of which have been named. Others are known in the Pacific Ocean; while the Pacific coast of America, and the whole of Central America, abound with them.

But we must not measure volcanic agency by the number of volcanoes that have been seen in activity in recent times. Wherever there are peculiar cone-shaped mountains, made up of piles of ashes and molten rock, and even where the materials are present but the cone is no longer there, we may be sure that the same cause has been at work. There is, as far as we know, no other possible way by which heaps of volcanic ash and lava can have been produced but that of eruption from the earth; and thus the presence of the ashes marks the existence at one time of the volcano.

Regarded in this light, there is proof of this reaction of the interior of the earth on the surface—this pouring forth volumes of matter, either melted or the result of heat—in many places where there are no volcanoes. Even in the British Islands such proof is not wanting; for the northeast coast of Ireland, at the celebrated Giants' Causeway, and the opposite islands of Scotland, Staffa and others, are remarkable for rocks entirely identical with the lavas of Vesuvius and Hecla. In parts of Europe where no one has seen eruptions there are real volcanoes, as in Central France, and on the Rhine not far from Bonn, in Hungary and in Northern Italy. The East of Europe, the peninsula of Spain and Portugal, Syria and the Holy Land, the east coast of Africa, many large tracts in Central and Southern Asia, many parts of America, and several of the West India Islands, all present similar appearances; while many islands rising out of the Atlantic and Pacific Oceans are evidently due to the same agency. Volcanoes recently active, or indicated by the unmistakable results of their former activity, are thus proved to exist, or to have existed, over a very large proportion of all the land that has yet been visited by man. Whether the interior of Africa and Australia—countries that are as yet very little known—will prove to have been in like manner visited by volcanic eruption, remains to be seen; but, certainly, all that is known at present would lead us to doubt whether they are not rather freer in this respect than other tracts of the same dimensions. On the other hand, the bottom of the Atlantic is, beyond a doubt, subject to very serious and, in some places, frequent eruptions; while parts of the Indian Ocean are yet more remarkable in this respect.

When, in addition to these proofs of the existence of some wide-spread source of heat in the interior of the earth, quite independent of the warmth obtained from the sun at the surface, we take into account the multitude of springs of hot water that rise out of the earth at various places, and the high temperature that is soon reached in all mines, particularly in those of great depth, we shall be obliged to admit that volcanoes are only vents or outlets to heated matter far below out of sight. That such heated matter is everywhere present, could we open a communication with the rocks a few thousand yards under our feet, there can be no doubt; and perhaps the occasional descent of water, soon turned into steam at very high pressure, and bursting out with resistless force through the weakest and thinnest part of the covering that presses upon it, may serve as a convenient, if not an accurate, explanation of the cause. Certainly most of the active volcanoes are not far from the sea; and those now extinct may be so only for a time, because there is no longer a way for the quantity of water to reach them that is necessary to lift the rocks above.

Volcanoes are frequently in groups, several within a comparatively small area; and it has often been remarked that a great eruption happening in one of a group is generally a sign that the others will be still and undemonstrative. In these cases they no doubt communicate, at a certain depth, with some common cavity. There are, however, exceptions to this; for sometimes eruptions have taken place, at no long interval, from craters not far from each other.

The history of an eruption is the next thing that requires to be told. First of all, there are frequently loud noises,—so loud as to be heard hundreds of miles from the part of the earth where they are produced. In the year 1835, a noise preceded an eruption from one of the great volcanoes of the Andes, which was heard to a vast distance in every direction. Nor is this a solitary instance; for there was a case in 1812, in the West Indies, when the noise was heard over a tract of land and sea about as large as all Europe. Noises are not, however, always heard, and such thunderings as these are comparatively rare.

After the noise, and sometimes without much previous intimation, there issues out of cracks in the ground, or from the cup-like depression near the top of the volcano, a strange mixture of several gases and steam, in a rapid succession of puffs. The gases include much sulphur, which is deposited like soot on the walls of the chimney through which the eruption passes. The steam that rushes out is soon changed into water, which falls in abundant showers of rain, and runs off the surface, carrying with it the sulphur and fine ashes thrown up at the same time.

Very numerous slight shocks, causing the ground near the place of eruption to tremble, have been next observed; and in some cases two or three hundred such shocks have been counted, at pretty regular intervals, within an hour. They seem to be the precursors of the great outburst which follows. This consists of an inconceivable quantity of the very finest dust that can be conceived, thrown into the air, sometimes dry, sometimes with steam, but with such enormous force as to be projected quite into the upper part of the atmosphere, where it comes under the influence of steady and strong currents of air, and is sometimes carried for two or three hundred miles, —gradually falling, of course, but, owing to its extreme lightness, not previously able to reach the ground. There are cases on record in which this dust has been carried for a thousand miles, covering the ground, even at that distance, to a thickness of two feet. This is about what would happen in London if a similar eruption were to take place in Vesuvius; but there is no doubt that the upper currents of air are both more powerful and steadier near the equator, where such vast distances are travelled by the dust, than in our latitudes; and, in fact, all the remarkable instances of the kind occur in the West Indian and South American volcanoes. Very large stones—stones as large as an ox—have been described as thrown into the air, and shot to a distance of a mile or two, from the Italian and Sicilian volcanoes;

but the dust does not reach so far as in the cases mentioned.

The fine dust of volcanoes is not less remarkable for the quantity that is thrown out, than for the distance it is carried. Cities have been buried and lost in it, and the sea has been rendered almost unnavigable for a time. This dust is the result of a process not much unlike that of blowing off the salt that is sometimes deposited in a steam-boiler at sea; and the ash was originally thin bubbles of lava; the boiling over of the great sea of molten rock, mixed with steam in place of common air, —the bubbles exploding with violence as soon as the pressure is removed.

After the ashes have been ejected, the next event, in a complete eruption, is the rending open of the side of the mountain, and the slow, majestic pouring forth of a river of melted stone, called *lava*, which is forced out in a semi-fluid or pasty state, and, after a while, cools and bridges over at the surface. This does not prevent the gradual issue of more and more of the same material, which creeps on, adapting itself to the irregularities of the ground,—carrying away every obstacle,—filling up great depressions, such as river-channels,—engulfing villages or towns, and quite altering the face of the country along its course,—burning every thing inflammable,—enclosing within itself every thing that cannot be destroyed, and not in any way to be turned from its course. In 1822, two streams of lava were poured out from Vesuvius, the total width of the two being about two miles, and the length of each of them about six miles. In 1852, Etna poured forth a similar flood, which in the first twenty-four hours advanced two miles and a half (about ten feet in a minute on an average), and then continued to move on more slowly for many days. In Iceland, floods of lava have had a depth or thickness of from four to six hundred feet; and wherever these outpourings have taken place, whether recently or in times long since past, they have spread uniformly over wide tracts of country,— and the same phenomena have been from time to time repeated.

In all parts of the world, and probably at all periods of the earth's history, the material thrown out from volcanoes has been alike. Slight differences in appearance and perhaps, here and there, peculiar mineral combinations have been observed; but, essentially, all lava and all volcanic ash is the same. The ash is, indeed, improperly so called, being merely pumice in a very fine state of division, the pumice itself being only the froth of the melted lava. It is, however, curious enough that mixed with the dust, or forming an essential part of it, the minute flinty cases of the simplest forms of vegetation (*Diatomaceæ*) have sometimes been found.

Volcanoes, then, are the vents or outlets by which the matter beneath the earth's surface—when, from any cause, obliged to expand and become relieved from some excess of force or newly-added force—is enabled to open communication to the day. They are the safety-valves of the fires glowing far beneath our feet, choked and foul, and only available in case of absolute need, but then yielding and preventing greater injury and irremediable mischief. They indicate, in some measure, where these fires are most active, and show that they form belts or zones in various parts of the earth, not always and at all times the same, but shifting in the course of ages, and apparently never very far from positions where water can have occasional access. They show, also, that the matter in the earth's interior is singularly alike in all places, and, moreover, that it has always been so.

The slight shocks that often immediately, and in quick succession, precede a volcanic eruption, occasionally take place on a far grander scale, and at a greater distance from the scene of ultimate outburst. They then act on a larger part of the earth's surface, and produce results which, however terrible, are not difficult to imagine, when the conditions of producing and transmitting an undulation or wave are considered. The earth's external shell—that coating of earth and rock which covers up and conceals all the mysteries of Nature's great laboratory —is in a general sense elastic. When, therefore, by some means, a convulsive throe takes place, and a certain portion of the surface is lifted up by a force which fails to burst through and rend it asunder, the result is, on a more limited scale, the same as would be the case if a sudden wave were formed in water. The motion, once produced, would be communicated to a distance, and thus the convulsive upheaval at a single point would be distributed through a space large in proportion to the magnitude and depth of the original disturbance and the degree of elasticity of the rocks.

But movements are not passed through rocks without some results that are heard and felt by those who inhabit the surface above. Each one involves a shock alike injurious to mechanical constructions, as houses and churches, and alarming to men and animals. Loud rolling, rumbling sounds are heard; the earth not only rocks, but wide yawning cracks appear,—not, indeed, opening into the interior, but sufficient to be dangerous and terrible. Tough rocks are strained and shaken, brittle rocks are broken, soft rocks are squeezed, and thus a general derangement is felt.

The duration of each earthquake is measured generally only by seconds, or even parts of a second; and as the operation is so brief, and generally quite unexpected, it is by no means easy to obtain observations of time that can be depended on. If the accounts of two or three intelligent witnesses to an earthquake-shock are compared, they will generally vary so much as to remove all confidence as to the actual correctness of either.

Earthquakes have, generally, a distinct course over the earth, and the area within which they are felt, however large, is always limited. By comparing the observations in different places, it is generally possible to mark the range and limits of each shock; and they vary exceedingly. There are many small shocks that range only for a few scores of miles, the breadth of the zone affected being only a few miles. A great earthquake will be felt across a continent, or even across the whole breadth of the Atlantic,—affecting, in the course of a short time, the coast of Spain, the interior of Scandinavia, Eastern Russia, and Canada, with all intermediate spots, and, almost at the same time, the West Indies and the coast of Africa.

The proportion of the earth's surface liable to be shaken in this way—judging only by the actual experience of the last few centuries as recorded in authentic statements—would seem to be very much larger than could at first be thought. So completely, indeed, does it include all the land with which we are most familiar, that we can hardly resist the conclusion that no district is free. Earthquakes are very frequent in the British Islands, upwards of a hundred having been recorded within the first half of the present century,—this being at the rate of one every six months during the time. In the same half-century about the same number of shocks are described as having been felt in Scandinavia; but these were not mere continuations of those felt in the British Islands. So, also, of 300 that took place in France, Belgium, and Holland, 170 in the basin of the Rhine and Switzerland, and 150 in the basin of the Danube, by far the larger proportion were limited to the particular district, taking the course of the river-basins and not traceable beyond. In the Italian peninsula there have been nearly 500 within the first half of the century, and in the eastern part of the Mediterranean as many as 200. But throughout Russia, unless the absence of any record is to be accounted for by the apathy and want of habit of recording natural events common with uncivilized and half-civilized people, the earthquakes have been very few; and the same may be said of the interior of Africa. It may be regarded as clearly proved that the whole of the western part of European land is now, and has been for some time, subject to earthquake vibrations, occurring very frequently. Each separate vibration is generally small, few extending beyond the districts in which they seem to have originated.

Asia and America are subdivided naturally, like Europe, into earthquake regions; and only the larger disturbances seem to cross the line of demarcation that surrounds each area, which seems generally sufficient to enclose the ordinary and small disturbances. In both countries, and indeed in Europe also, there are at intervals catastrophes which are more terrible as the interval between them is greater. About once in each century there has generally been such a catastrophe in some part of the world; and during the hundred years intervening between great earthquakes the intermediate pulsations have made up in number what they want in intensity and range of action.

There are very curious facts made out by a careful comparison of known earthquakes and the circumstances that preceded and followed them. Out of nearly six thousand that have been so far described as to have their dates mentioned, considerably more than half occurred during the colder six months of the year; and this general result is rendered more interesting when we find that in each separate earthquake district, taken separately, the result is the same; while if we only take the disturbances of the present century the result is even more strongly marked. Grouping the earthquakes in months, we find that the greatest number have taken place in the month of January and the smallest number in July, the proportion being about three to two. So, again, if we divide the year into quarters, we find January, February, and March to be the months in which the greater number have taken place, and May, June, and July the smallest. Thus, in the three first months of the year 1669 are recorded, and in the three early summer months only 1281 There seems no way of escaping from the odd conclusion that earthquakes are more likely to take place in cold than in warm weather.

If, then, volcanoes are safety-valves heavily loaded, which occasionally admit the pent-up vapors from the earth's interior not only to escape, but to carry with them millions of tons' weight of solid matter to the surface, and if earthquakes afford ample proof that convulsive movements, affecting large but variable tracts of land, are also extremely common, and cannot but affect in a marked degree the countries subjected to them, there appears ground for believing that the ordinary course of Nature provides means for making those alterations of level which we spoke of in the last chapter, and modifying the condition and position of rocks at the earth's surface to the extent described by geologists. It remains only to see whether the mere undulation or vibration of the earthquake is accompanied, habitually or occasionally, by a positive and definite change of level of the part of the country in which it occurs.

The recorded instances are very numerous of permanent change of level accompaning disturbances in volcanic or earthquake districts. In the neighborhood of Vesuvius there is proof of both elevations and depressions to the extent of twenty or thirty feet along an extended line of coast and to some distance inland, and this so gradually as not to destroy buildings, but simply submerge them when close to the shore. The rate a few years ago was estimated at an inch every four years, but is now different.

So lately as in 1835 an earthquake was felt in Chili, between Copiapo and Chiloe, and for some distance out at sea. After the earthquake, ships that had been riding at anchor in upwards of forty feet of water were found to have grounded, and many shoals became quite dry; while the shore became one mass of recently-killed mussels, chitons, limpets, and seaweeds, still adhering to the rocks on which they had before lived, the sea not rising to within four or five feet of its former level. The ground afterwards sunk slightly, leaving, however, a permanent elevation over an area of some thousands of square miles. A similar result had been produced by an earthquake in 1822, on a still grander scale, over a tract of country nearly as large as Great Britain and Ireland.

In 1819, after a celebrated earthquake near Bombay, a large district sunk down and became permanently covered with water, while at the same time an adjacent district was raised above its former level. The newly-raised country measures fifty miles from east to west, and is sixteen miles broad.

It is not necessary to multiply instances of this kind, all tending to prove that the violent shake and disturbance noticed during earthquakes may be, and often is, the result of some deep subterranean force lifting up the whole mass of solid matter in its convulsive effort to expand. Sometimes this is followed by a collapse, the rocks afterwards sinking into some vast cavern.

But we have further proof that even where volcanic eruptions do not extend, there are still upheavals and depressions going on, calculated to alter, in time, the form of the land and the proportion of land and water in certain districts. In that closed sea the Baltic, where the tides hardly penetrate, and especially in some of the long inlets and gulfs by means of which it penetrates the land, it has long been known that the land is undergoing a slow upheaval. This was spoken of in 1807 by the celebrated German traveller Von Buch, and it has since been proved that there is no doubt of the fact of the rising of the land. Marks were put at various places, natural objects were noticed, and every precaution taken against inaccuracy. The result is a conviction, in the minds of careful observers, that the whole of the land on the upper part of the Gulf of Bothnia is really undergoing a steady elevation, while south of that the movement, if any, is rather one of depression.

In many parts not only of the coast of Scandinavia but of our own shores, and indeed all along the Atlantic coast, there are seen at intervals ancient sea-beaches at levels greatly above the highest which the sea now reaches. These show that elevation has taken place to an extent amounting in some cases to sixteen hundred feet, while it happens occasionally that we find at no great distance equally good proof of local depression. While the shells and pebbles that once formed a sea-beach are lifted high in the air, the trees and other objects before above the sea, including even buildings, are occasionally buried many feet deep, and occupy positions quite incompatible with their growth or with their existence as human constructions.

Thus, then, it appears that by natural causes still in action, more marked in some parts of the earth than in others, but traceable over a large surface, there are changes taking place whose tendency must be to break asunder, compress, and tilt up the various rocks between the seat of disturbance and the surface. However small the result may seem at one operation, still, as it goes on at intervals without limit of time, it must at length produce large and important consequences. By such means, indeed, all the appearances alluded to in the last chapter can be produced, and all the fractures, elevations, and depressions accounted for. The only element required is time; and if it be admitted that the earth as a planet has been in existence long enough to account in a reasonable way for the production of the rocks themselves and their contents, there is nothing more required to account for other movements and changes in position. Some of these have always been going on, contemporaneously with the deposit of fresh rocks derived from the destruction of the old ones.

Of the cause of earthquakes and other upheavals of the outer crust of the earth, it is easy to theorize, but difficult to try experiments. They seem, as we have said, to be more common at certain seasons than at others, and they seem also to have some mysterious relation to the moon and sun. How far they are governed by those forces of electricity and earth-magnetism that are ever passing through and round the earth, observation has not yet shown; but that they are parts of a great system not limited to our earth, but influenced greatly by our relations with the sun as the centre of our system, recent observation would show to be at least probable.

We learn by these considerations how little, in any sense, men can claim independent existence. As inhabitants of the earth we are mutually dependent on each other and on all that lives above, around, or beneath us; but we are not less dependent on the various conditions of matter and on the laws that govern matter.

Our earth also with its attendant moon mutually influence each other, and much of the change necessary for our well-being is due to the presence of that satellite whose light is the smallest part of its value. Our earth and moon, as one group, form part of a large system of bodies by no means all similarly constituted or comparable one with another, but all dependent on a central sun. This sun, with its following, is itself subordinate, and forms a mere unit in a larger system. We know not how, or how far, we have relation with this infinity of bodies in space, but we certainly are influenced by them; and it is by such influences and by forces thus widely acting that the earthquake and the volcanic outburst, the storm within the earth, the storm in the air, and the auroral storm far above out of our knowledge, are all governed, and their times and seasons fixed. The laws on which these depend are as definite, and act as completely and freely, as those which are exemplified in the bursting of the leaves in springtide or the ripening of fruit in autumn.

## Chapter the Eleventh.

### THE DISTURBANCE OF ROCKS.

LIMESTONES, sandstones, and clays make up a large proportion of those rocks that are commonly met with in England; and when we add to them the varieties of slaty and quartzy rocks, there are only left granite and porphyritic rocks and basaltic rocks to complete the series. But how is it that we can find opportunity of examining all these rocks in so small a country as England? Do they always appear at the surface in small patches? Do they succeed each other in regular order? Is there any order at all observable with regard to them? These are questions that the young geologist may be expected to ask, and he must be able to answer them if he is to learn his subject and face its difficulties. Let us in this chapter devote ourselves to questions of this kind, and try to make out how and why it is that many rocks, which appear at the same level in traversing a small country, are so often described as overlying one another. Let us add to this an inquiry as to how we are to identify rocks in distant parts of a country.

Geologists, in speaking of rocks, describe them as lying one over another, like a parcel of books heaped upon a table. In one place you see the back of one book, in another a part of the side of a second. None of the books reach much above the level of the table, but with a little care you might make out the titles of a good many without moving them, or at least you could recognize the bindings if these were different one from another. Fifty books thus heaped on a table might occupy but a small space and no great height; but it would depend entirely on the way they were heaped as to whether we could make out what they were without moving them.

Rocks are really found lying one over another in very irregular positions, in a way not much unlike those in which books would be placed on a counter in a bookseller's shop. In such a case there would be in one place half a dozen in a heap, and of these we should only see one side of the uppermost. Elsewhere there are a number placed on edge; but in rocks this is rather an exceptional position, while in the bookseller's shop it would be the most usual.

Of a number of books carelessly placed on their edges on a table, the last one will probably have fallen so as to be horizontal, while others of this group will be more or less slanted as they are nearer to or farther from the end. Of the rocks, also, by far the greater number are thus slanted, and this notwithstanding that they have originally been horizontal and are now more or less tilted; whereas the books were originally vertical and are now more or less fallen. Bearing in mind this comparison and the differences, let us study some sea-cliff or railway-cutting, especially seeking for simple and instructive illustrations.

The journey from London to Brighton is one so very frequently and easily made that comparatively few readers will be unacquainted with it. It affords numerous instances of the way in which rocks are arranged, and one in which several can be seen by travelling over a comparatively small distance.

SECTION FROM LONDON TO BRIGHTON.

| Rocks. | Places. |
|---|---|
| a. London clay. | 1. London. |
| b. Chalk. | 2. The North Downs above Merstham. |
| c. Upper green-sand and gault. | 3. Reigate. |
| d. Lower green-sand. | 4. Horsham. |
| e. Weald clay. | 5. The South Downs at Brighton. |
| f. Hastings sands. | 6. The Sea at Brighton. |

The above Diagram illustrates several important geological points. It is a section across beds tilted in opposite directions, and across what is called a valley of elevation.

Passing from London, and leaving the slippery clays of New Cross and the clays covered with gravel at Sydenham well behind, we see near Croydon symptoms of the chalk, which is there not far from the surface. As the chalk is easily reached by boring, not only at and near Croydon but at various points between that and London, there is not a shadow of doubt about the relative position of the clays, the gravel, and the chalk in this district; and when, near the long tunnel at Merstham, the railway passes through a deep cutting, it is easy to see that the beds of chalk there incline towards London. This is seen again when we emerge from the tunnel at Merstham; but not far off the chalk is replaced by the sand hills of Redhill, near Reigate. Now, these sands come out from under the chalk, they are tilted in the same direction and nearly to the same amount, and they are further from London. They must, beyond all doubt, have been deposited below, and therefore before the chalk, and yet they now form hills (Leith Hill, &c.) nearly as high as the top of the chalk-downs. But the parts of the chalk itself that are seen on coming out of the tunnel must originally have been some hundred feet below those seen at its entry; for all the way through we have been going across tilted beds as shown in the diagram, and the beds we first saw have come out at the top of the downs. This, too, corresponds exactly with what we have said about the sands. Advancing farther south, it is soon seen that a bed of clay comes out from under the sands, and at length the sandstones of Tunbridge Wells form hills which were certainly once below the clays, and therefore, it must be supposed, far below the chalk.

But from about midway between London and Brighton the beds of sandstone, instead of continuing to point towards London, change their direction, and are seen quite as clearly inclining towards Brighton. When we approach Brighton, clays cover up and conceal the sandstones, sands cover the clays, and soon the chalk once more appears, covering up the sands just as it does on the other side.

To come back to our illustration of books on a table, it is easy to arrange them so that the appearances we have described should be given in a general way. To do this, we should have to put two books to represent each of the beds, and the middle two must be supported on one which is concealed. Are we, then, to regard the chalk of Merstham and that at Brighton as altogether different deposits, always separated as we now see them, or are we to look further for information before deciding? If we examine for ourselves, we shall find that we can actually walk on continuous chalk, always the same kind of rock in every respect, from Beechy Head past Brighton and Worthing into Hampshire, and thence back into Sussex and Surrey, till we come to Merstham Tunnel; and we may then, if we will, follow it to Dover. Thus it appears that our chalk represents a broken book which may once have covered up all the sands, clays, and sandstones between the North and South Downs, but whose larger and central part has been removed out of sight. So, in the same way, the sands and clays represent other broken books of smaller size. It is not difficult to see that if we wish to account rationally for these appearances we must suppose that all the upper beds have been carried away, after having once been lifted up and broken asunder by some slow upheaving force. In this operation of lifting, all that was brittle has of course cracked, and the tough beds have broken after much straining; while the middle tract of country represents a saddle or a ridge having the sides inclining different ways, like the roof of a house. The lowest beds are thus lifted up into the highest position.

There is clearly nothing unreasonable, still less impossible, in this explanation of a series of facts observed in one short trip. We have, while keeping nearly on a horizontal line, made our way over or through, first the gravel and then the clays near London,—afterwards the chalk, then a bed of clay, and then again some thick beds of red sand. After this we have crossed some tough clay, different from the first kind, and have come out into the sandstones of what is known as the *Weald*, or wooded part formerly (in Saxon times it was all covered with forest) of the county of Sussex. But when we reach a certain point in our journey we find that the beds we had crossed and lost sight of reappear, inclining from instead of towards us; and lastly, going on still farther, we repeat all we have done before, until at Brighton the sea stops our progress.

This simple example of tilted rocks might be very much complicated if we turned our steps to Wales, or visited Scotland. In those countries, where mountain-masses rise out of the earth, the extent and variety of beds that we cross over is much greater; and we must be prepared for long and complicated series of limestones, sandstones, and clays of very different kinds, with occasional interruptions by such rocks as granite and slate. There also the beds are twisted into very peculiar shapes: they are sometimes vertical, and are put into all sorts of strange attitudes, and they are often so changed as not to be recognizable, unless we actually trace them from some point at the surface where they have their usual characteristics, and thus fully identify them.

On the whole, it is found that by traversing our island from east to west, we gradually pass to rocks which lie under those we have lately visited. Lower and therefore older rocks gradually become the surface rocks as we get on towards Wales, and the newer or upper rocks disappear. No doubt there are some exceptions to this, but it is a good and fair general statement. The chalk is the most easterly, and also the newest, of the great series of lime-rocks of our island; the Portland-stone, which comes next in order, is the next older; the Bath-stones are much older; and the limestones of Clifton and South Wales, which pass into marble, are of yet more ancient date. So it is with the clays and sandstones, speaking always in a general sense; but, as is the case with the Weald of Sussex, there are many local exceptions.

But are we to suppose that, because the chalk is the uppermost and newest rock and is not found in Wales, it has once been there and since removed? By no means is this necessary; and the pile of books, our first illustration, will still help us out with a suggestion and comparison. The books all end somewhere, and generally soon and abruptly. Similar beds, whatever they are, were not formed at the same time all over the earth. They form patches, sometimes very small, sometimes much larger, but they are never exactly the same in all respects for a very great distance. Often they disappear entirely and suddenly at a particular place, and in some cases never extended beyond their present limits.

The beds, or strata, or by whatever other name we call the heaps of one kind of rock found in a certain district, are, beyond all doubt, exceedingly variable in surface, thickness, and form, as well as in material. One is a long stretch of a particular kind of clay, ranging for hundreds of miles, but of very small breadth. Such a bed might have been formed on an ancient coast. Another is a uniform and widely-extended mass of sand, here and there mixed with beds of clay, sometimes full of salt, not unfrequently hardened into distinct layers of stone, but always so far the same that we can easily prove the identity. This might have been a sea-bottom, since lifted and dried up. A third, and many besides it, may have been composed of limestone separated by animals; some of it by animalcules at the sea-bottom; some by heaps of solid coral pushing out and rising up against the whole force of the waves of an open sea; some of it, again, may be the *débris* of innumerable shells drifted into a bank by some local current. Every one of these was originally at the bottom of the sea, and owed its origin as well as its form to some local cause which we can now only guess at; but since then all have been moved from their original position,—have been covered up in part by other deposits,—have become hardened or altered, and have been at length partly pared away while being lifted into the upper air and exposed to the action of weather and water.

What has happened in England has happened elsewhere, but by no means always in the same proportion. In some countries, as in the great plain-country of the North and East of Europe, the deposits remain extended uniformly over hundreds of thousands of square miles hardly altered at all from the horizontal position in which they were formed under water. The same is the case, to some extent, in America, where the modern deposits are on a large scale compared with any we have. The interior of Africa, and perhaps much of the interior of Australia, will be found marked with another peculiarity: —they are extensive areas covered with similar and little-altered rocks.

On the other hand, in the great chain of the Alps, which runs like a broad lofty wall across the middle of Europe, the appearances of the various rocks are in the highest degree complicated and difficult to unravel and explain. Not only are the rocks tilted, but they are entirely altered. Limestones and chalk are converted into marble, and all mark of the method of formation entirely lost; sandstones are changed into compact rocks of quartz, abounding with large groups of crystal and many varieties of minerals, which owe their origin to very base and common materials, but which are now so brilliant and rich as to be sought for as stones of great value.

So, again, the clays are turned into slates, and altered as much in position as in appearance. On the flanks of these mountains the beds are greatly tilted, particularly on one side; while on the other side there has been abrupt fracture, and the rocks, broken short off, have been lifted up high in the air, till they now rest against others whose date of formation was far more recent. There is no amount or variety of twisting and breaking and displacement which rocks in such localities do not show; and some of the most striking and noble appearances of Alpine scenery are due to the fantastic and irregular lines into which beds originally horizontal have been thrown.

Vast gaps are not unfrequently observable, the marks of bedding on rocks of the opposite sides clearly corresponding, though now there is a wide interval yawning between them. Jagged peaks rise, and broken ridges extend for long distances, all connected at some ancient period, but rent asunder by the vast force that has elevated the mountain-mass and lifted the continent out of which it rises.

The great mountain-chains of the globe—the Alps,

continued from the Himalayan chain, and the Andes—each with important links and spurs—being the loftiest, are the youngest of all. Others of more ancient date chiefly affect older rocks, and their axes have a different direction from that of the main chain in the neighborhood. There can hardly be difficulty in understanding that the forces sufficient to upheave to the height of tens of thousands of feet these lines of rock, may also have lifted at the same time, but to a smaller extent, wide tracts of flatter country. It is beyond a doubt that the lifting-up of the various continental masses of the earth must be regarded as due to, and of the same date as, the production of the great mountain-chains that form, as it were, a backbone to the land. Thus the chain of the Himalaya Mountains in Asia, stretching into Europe by the mountains of Persia, Arabia, and Turkey, are continuous with the Alps in Europe and the Atlas Mountains in Africa. The former chain, uniting with the Pyrenees, reaches quite into the Atlantic on the north of the Mediterranean; while the Atlas Mountains, stretching across Northern Africa, are also continued beyond Morocco, and are lost under the same great ocean. In America there is but one chain, which reaches from the islands of Tierra del Fuego in the south quite into the Arctic Circle,—the two great portions of the continent being connected by the mountains and having the same direction. But there are other directions in which land has been elevated, and these no doubt belong to different periods and different mountain-systems. We must not here enter on difficult and disputed geological problems; but it is safe to point out the direction of English rocks and their manifest relations to mountain-chains ranging through Cornwall, Wales, and Scotland, as illustrations of the fact we now allude to.

Very numerous and important results may be traced, in all mountainous districts, of the force that has acted to bring the mountains to their position. The various beds, once so regular and clear in their arrangement, are now confused and broken. The fracture that has taken place has often rendered it almost impossible to follow the part of a rock that has undergone removal and connect this part with the rest. Intervals of many yards filled with rubbish, broken away from the rock or transported from a distance, are seen to exist between the walls of a crevice. Rocks are apparently annihilated, though really they have undergone only a removal or a rearrangement of their particles. New rocks are created out of old materials, and, in a word, the whole aspect of deposits is so altered that it becomes impossible to identify any one of them by its mineral character, or by following it mechanically from one place to another. All that is most picturesque and most pleasing to the eye, as well as stimulating to the imagination, in mountain-scenery, is due to mixed mechanical and chemical action consequent on the great change incurred in lifting the rocks from the bottom of the sea and placing the fractured edges in the upper regions of the atmosphere.

In speaking of the results of such movements, geologists have become accustomed to employ a special language. The tilt or inclination of the beds they call the *dip;* the direction of the line on which the elevation has taken place is the *strike:* and by observing and recording the dip and the strike they decide on the extent and direction of the original disturbing force of the beds presumed to act from below. The fracture, when a bed has been broken asunder during elevation and a part of it protruded above the rest, is called a *fault* or *dike* (see diagram); and the ridge or saddle, from which beds incline in opposite directions, is an *anticlinal axis* (see p. 195).

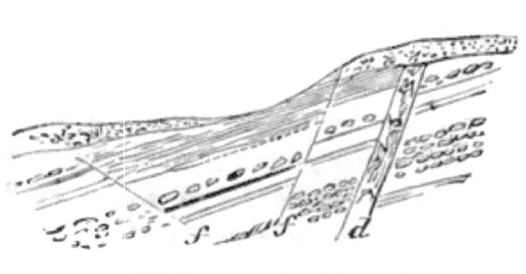

SECTION ILLUSTRATING FAULTS.
*d.* A dike.   *f.* A fault.

Besides these, there are some other terms in common use. Thus, the regular arrangement of beds in deposits parallel to each other is *conformable stratification;* and when disturbances have acted after part of a series is deposited and before the remaining part is completed, so that the upper series is not parallel to the lower, we have *unconformable stratification.* It will readily be seen that these technical terms are simple expressions of certain facts determined by observation, and neither involve theory nor pretend to give any reason for the appearances they allude to.

It is not unusual to find as the central rock in a mountain-chain, or projecting from the flanks as a subordinate range, very large quantities of that peculiar mixed rock, made up of hard crystals imbedded in a hard matrix, to which the name of *granite* is popularly applied. Such rock appears to have been formed at great depth, under a heavy pressure of overlying earth or water, and at a temperature high compared with that of the earth's surface, though not necessarily high compared with molten rock such as is poured out from volcanoes. Great chemical changes were needed to convert any mixture of limestone, sandstone, or clay into this material, although the ultimate elements are not different; and it is quite consistent with all that we know of the origin of granites that they should have been produced far down below the earth's surface, and that a very long time should have been occupied in preparing them.

The very great amount of expansion and contraction that must have taken place while these rocks were in preparation and when they were afterwards elevated, and the pressure thus exerted on all adjacent matter, will account for some of the most singular and otherwise inexplicable appearances presented by the clays and limestones near them. In this way the slates and marbles grew out of the simpler and more mechanical deposits, and while this was being done those numerous cracks and open fissures were produced, which, being afterwards filled up, became mineral veins. The systematic nature of these veins is due, no doubt, to the regularity of the condition under which the whole change was effected. The filling up with mineral wealth is a later operation, and one requiring much attention and study to comprehend.

The reader may see that, in thus speaking of rocks originally placed at the bottom of the sea and now lifted up to occupy positions in upper air so far removed from their origin, it has been taken for granted that certain movements have occurred upon the earth; and it may seem almost necessary to assume that these must have been on a far grander scale, and therefore more destructive, than any that living men can either have experienced or imagined. It may be thought that catastrophes are indicated involving the destruction of all that was living upon the earth at the time,—that the whole world groaned and was troubled at these upheavals, and that each one of them must have involved a special and manifest interposition of the Creator who has so wisely and so well ordered terrestrial affairs.

I believe that there is no greater or more mischievous error than this. I say no greater error, because it assumes the Law of Nature to involve a system of interferences,—not of adaptations; and to intelligent human beings, endowed with divine intellect, interferences, if not manifestly called for to answer a special moral purpose, denote weakness and partial knowledge. On the other hand, a system so contrived as to involve, in its very nature, a complete and continuous growth and adaptation, indicates perfect foreknowledge and wisdom. I say, also, no more mischievous error; for by habituating the mind to look for an escape from all difficulty by miraculous intervention, the student of Nature would not only become accustomed to a comparatively low view of Almighty Power, but would cease to search, in the right way and the right spirit, for those hidden Laws of Nature which can alone assist him in comprehending and expounding the great universal history which it is the province of Science to lay open before men.

It must never be forgotten that the study of every

# THE DISTURBANCE OF ROCKS.

department of Science and Natural History—the effort to acquire every knowledge useful to or attainable by man—is but one of many ways of exercising those powers with which man has been endowed; and that the due exercise and cultivation of all his powers, whatever they may be, is the clear and obvious duty of every human being.

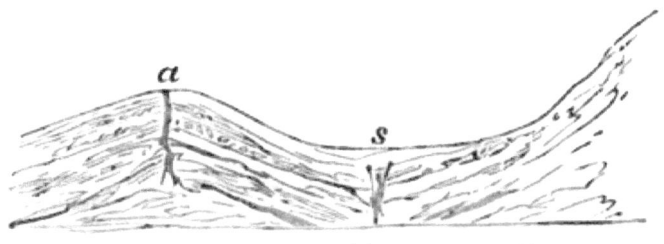

(*a*) ANTICLINAL AND (*s*) SYNCLINAL AXES.
See page 192.

# THE GREAT STONE BOOK.

Part IV.

## Chapter the Twelfth.

WHAT THE PICTURES ARE, AND WHAT THEY MEAN.

In the last chapter we arrived at the conclusion that, provided time enough were allowed, the changes in position that have brought to the flanks and summits of lofty mountains various beds of rock, formed originally at the bottom of the sea, might be well accounted for without assuming violent and sudden disturbances to have taken place. The disturbances and movements of land, whether of elevation or depression, have indeed been so small at any one time within human experience, that one's first impression is that they must be insufficient; and it is only by careful and continued observation that we recognize them as possible. But when we examine carefully the rocks themselves, and those remains of animal and vegetable existence they generally contain, we find time as necessary here as elsewhere.

When speaking of limestones, sandstones, and clays, the fact that the former rocks almost consist of, and the others generally contain, remains of living things, was alluded to, and some results stated. These remains were once called *petrifactions*, or things turned into stone; they are now often called *fossils*, or things dug up; and, considering that they must necessarily be dug out of the earth before we can examine them, the change of name does not seem of much importance. At first it may appear strange that any thing that has once formed part of a living substance should be petrified or turned into stone. Still more strange will it seem if (as is the case) the details of structure are preserved in the stone; so that, without much difficulty, the most minute and complicated peculiarities, whether of shell, bone, or wood, can be examined under the microscope in the fossil state, after the conversion into stone, quite as well as if recently obtained from a living specimen. This is effected in a manner not very easy to understand, since the original substance must be removed, and the new one supplied particle by particle; and this must have taken place not unfrequently while lying on the ground, or scarcely buried more than a few feet in the earth. There can be no doubt, however, as to the fact; inasmuch as both wood and coral, and occasionally shells and bone, are found in the transition-state, consisting partly of the original and partly of the replacing mineral. It is something like those curious metamorphoses we read of in the ancient poets; and we occasionally so far penetrate the mystery of Nature's laboratory as to be able to see the change partly effected, if not in actual progress.

*Organic Remains* is another name given to these proofs of former life; and it is the most accurate term of all. Whatever we choose to call them, they are very widely spread, occupying a part of every rock originally formed in water, though often injured or almost obliterated. Nor is this very wonderful. The mud and gravel accumulated at the bottom of water is likely to have retained, mixed up with its particles, fragments of the shells, bones, or other animal substances accidentally introduced, and belonging originally either to the inhabitants of the water or adjacent land; while, if these fragments should happen to be long rolled about with sand and pebbles, it is equally clear that little would remain to denote their origin, or at least little that could be distinguished by the unassisted eye. Such remains of animals and vegetables, when met with, may be regarded as the Pictures in the Great Stone Book of Nature, illustrating the story told in other language in the text of the book itself.

There is hardly a river that now enters a lake or the sea,—there is not a coast-line in any part of the world,— and it would seem that there is hardly a spot buried under tens of thousands of feet of salt water between England and America, that has not, resting on, buried beneath, or drifting along its bottom, a multitude—"which no man can number"—of the shells, the encrusted cases, the external or internal skeletons, the teeth, and other remains of animals living near. These are the illustrations vividly representing the conditions of existence. Of the myriads of animals that pass along, carried by the water, the greater number serve as food to other animals of larger proportions, and thus become immediately reconverted into organic structure. Many more, when dead, become the prey of minute creatures, which soon reduce them to their parent dust, with no trace left of their former existence. Some decay and fall to pieces, and are thus altogether lost; while of the rest the harder parts may be buried under favorable conditions. Of these last only it can be that a few, in the course of time, undergo the change which fits them to serve as permanent records of the age in which they flourished. How few this is in proportion to the whole number—how partial and imperfect is the record of former times thus handed down to posterity—may be imagined by those who will take the trouble to search for themselves, in recent formations, for evidences of the life of the district. But the real poverty of the record can hardly be thus appreciated; because it is quite impossible for us to know how much, or rather how little, is preserved in the larger deposits, owing to there being no means of looking forward in time, and anticipating the amount and extent of the destruction that will follow the decay that now goes on, and that conceals the real nature of organic substances during their conversion into new minerals.

It is, indeed, wonderful in the highest degree that, in spite of all causes of destruction and all changes of material, so great a variety of remains as those already described should have been preserved and discovered by geologists. A few centuries ago, the very existence of fossils was hardly known as a fact on which an argument could be based. For a long time the fact of their having really belonged to animals and vegetables was doubted. Afterwards, many rocks were considered as being quite without fossils which now are known to contain them in infinite abundance; and although each year still adds to the number and variety of the different species, and introduces us either to new localities for known species or new species from the known localities, there are yet many naturalists and geologists who are unable to recognize the probability that our knowledge of the subject is still very imperfect, and ought not to be assumed as complete in any department.

Remembering what has been said of the resemblance of the strata in the earth to a heap of books on a table, we may carry on the illustration a little further in reference to the subject of Fossils. We have called our earth the Great Stone Book, the leaves of the book being represented by the various strata or beds of stone. We might, indeed, for some reasons, have called it the Stone Library; but it is a library in great confusion; for the books, which in this illustration represent the beds, are piled irregularly on the floor. Each book tells its own story, and describes a history in some measure independent. It is true that many stories are too long to be told in a single volume, and require a complete series; and we must further assume that the Stone Books have been accumulated on the floor of the World-Library as they have been thrown off from the press. If the original order of precedence has been disturbed, it is by some accident from without, and very rarely indeed have any been shuffled in between others previously placed. In this sense, the fossils are the literary contents of the book. Some are very distinct, and mark an important epoch; some are very commonplace, and record facts which may have happened at any time. Many are so obscure in the language and dialect in which they were written, or so injured by time and damp, that they are hardly legible. Some are in black-letter,—some in bold, large type; some are very minute, requiring assistance to read them. A vast number of the series are absent, not perhaps altogether, but, at any rate, in the parts of the library we are allowed to examine; for we may assist the comparison by supposing that we are only able to reach the surface of the books, after removing an accumulated dust and rubbish like that which has buried the ancient city of Pompeii.

This illustration by no means exaggerates the difficulties that have to be overcome in endeavoring to obtain a knowledge of the ancient natural history of the world by a careful examination of the fossils. A large mass of evidence exists, but it is often, and indeed generally, abundant only in reference to particular deposits, or certain kinds of animals and vegetables,—never complete, even for a single period.

It is very important that the imperfection of the series of rocks and fossils should be clearly understood; for without it the real value of this kind of evidence cannot be estimated. As far as it goes, it is sound and thoroughly to be depended on; for if the books that form the collection were thrown into the library as they successively got ready, the general sequence must be perfect. In other words, a book at the bottom or in the middle must belong to an earlier date than a book at the top. But, just as the work of printing may have gone on more rapidly in one country or at one period than at another, while sometimes, owing to revolutions or disturbances, an interval may have elapsed when literature was dormant, so we find among the fossils that the conditions under which they were accumulated were sometimes favorable and sometimes the contrary. Sometimes the accumulation was rapid for a time in one country, and altogether stopped in another; sometimes long intervals would take place, when Nature seems to have been idle over a large area; and not unfrequently accumulations of enormous extent and thickness belong to one not very long period.

Without tiring the reader with further continuance of this comparison, let us now consider what kind of remains of animals and vegetables are found fossil, and how far they characterize particular periods or deposits.

Beginning with the most simple forms of life, we find the vegetable and animal so nearly alike that it is scarcely possible to decide clearly the real difference that separates them. Each is a single cell or small closed bag, often coated or defended with flint or limestone. Every part may absorb, separate, grow, divide, and decay,—all with extreme rapidity; and each new offspring generally retains at first some sort of connection with the original parent. Often we find a compound animal or vegetable made up of tens of thousands of the simple individual, and possessing a kind of independent existence. The whole solid structure produced by the compound being may, however, be so minute as to require a microscope to see it; and millions of such specimens of existence make up a bed of mud such as is found at the bottom of deep water in the Atlantic and in other oceans.

It may be supposed that such mud, some of which is flinty and some calcareous, will remain unaltered, except indeed by hardening and drying, for a very long time. Some of it, perhaps, is as old as any thing that has been made by living beings in the whole earth. And such kinds of life vary wonderfully little, whether found in deep or in shallow water,—whether existing in hot water at or near the Equator, or in freezing water in the Arctic or Antarctic Circles. They serve as indications of the fact that "there was life:"—the command of the Almighty had gone forth, and had been obeyed. Such life, however, being in itself the simplest, can hardly exhibit change, and is repeated from generation to generation as Time advances towards Eternity. Such life existed at the beginning, and the exact analogue exists now.

Sponges are familiar, because often they are large-sized representatives of this great class of beings whose existence is almost as much vegetable as it is animal, inasmuch as the characteristic and essential peculiarities of animals and vegetables have not yet appeared in their structure and habits. Sponges are found fossil in a great variety of rocks,—some with a kind of simple skeleton of limestone, others with flint, and some merely horny, without much mineral. Certain forms of sponge belong apparently to one period or one set of strata rather than to another, but they can rarely be regarded as distinctive.

Remains of trees abound in coal, and in the sandstones and half-slaty beds among which coal is found. Not only the trunks but the leaves, and in some rare cases the fruits and flowers, are well preserved; but they are almost always insufficient to give such an idea of the plant that it can be identified. One remarkable fact, however, is clearly made out by these discoveries,—namely, that plants and trees allied to ferns, not only small but of the very largest dimensions, were extremely common, and contributed more than any other kind of vegetation to the formation of coal, and to supply the more common fossils of the coal measures.

Of animals, almost all kinds have left some indication of their existence, but chiefly, as might be expected, those provided with hard and indestructible parts. Thus, corals, both the more delicate horny varieties and the hard-plated kinds such as build reefs, are very common,—indeed, among the most common of all fossils. Nor is this wonderful. The animal that separates the coral from sea-water, and builds up a living wall against which the waves can make no impression,—a wall extending for thousands of miles, rising to the water's edge from a depth of a thousand feet,—has been in many cases assisted by Nature in a wonderful manner in producing an abiding monument. There are many parts of the Pacific in which such works are being constructed, and there are others in which, having been built, they are being preserved from destruction. A reference to almost any limestone or clay rock will show their presence in some form or other, and thus, being among the things easily and well preserved now, and found in most rocks whatever their age may be, they are doubly useful; for they not only afford opportunities of comparing the varieties common at different periods, as marked by rocks higher or lower in the series, but they enable us to obtain a continued series or chain of forms, and thus to learn that at all times similar causes seem to have produced like results. It is also extremely convenient, as well as a striking proof of the vast changes that have come over this part of the world, that we are thus able to study the structure of coral-banks in the lofty limestone-cliffs of Cheddar and in the wave-worn shores of Lough Earne, as well as in the upheaved coral-islands of the Southern

Seas. In the fields about Steeple Ashton, every stone turned up by the plough is a coral; and our inland quarries and chalk-pits afford materials for the study of a class of animals almost wholly wanting on the present shores of Europe.

A marked peculiarity of structure has been noticed in the corals found in the lowest deposits, most of these having their small cups or stars in rays numbering four, eight, or twelve (or other multiples of four), while the more modern kinds are in groups of six. It has not been found possible at present to suggest a reason for this; but so it is. It is one of the differences produced in the course of time, having reference, perhaps, to some cause of which other indication is lost. It is one of many similar differences unaccounted for and apparently arbitrary, but not the less real, and often of great value as guides in comparing and identifying the contents of different rocks.

Star-fishes and sea-urchins are members of a family of stone-plated animals, having structure and habits exceedingly curious, but still having more or less of that compound life that is so remarkable in the coral animal as well as in many small inhabitants of the deep.

The stony parts of these animals are as widely spread and as common in all rocks as the corals; but they never form such large masses, and indeed are very seldom accumulated in heaps,—being rather distributed through the deposit, and mixed up with other fossils. When complete, nothing can be more exquisitely beautiful or ingenious in their arrangement and fitting than the myriads of little stones that build up stars, lily-shaped cups growing from long stems, grotesque round boxes covered with warty projections, strange sweeping netlike branches, serpent-like forms radiating from a central point, and a hundred indescribable shapes assumed by these fossils. They are most of them represented by species not very uncommon in various seas. The serpent-like stars (*Ophiuridæ*) have been dredged up alive, in mid-Atlantic, from more than a thousand feet of water: the star-fishes and sea-urchins are common enough on our own shores as well as elsewhere. We know their curious habits, feeding for the most part on offal, moving in some strange way by a thousand little suckers,—their stone jackets pierced with minute pores, through which the animal imprisoned communicates with the outer world. We know also the risk they are subject to, and the shelter they generally obtain by concealing themselves under stones or in mud; and we recognize their peculiar habits, and the half-compound nature of their life, when we see them jerk off important portions of the body if interfered with, or fall to pieces (some of them, at least) when thrown suddenly into water. All these habits also belonged to similar animals whose remains are found fossil; and the abundance of the fragments, compared with the comparative scarcity of the complete shell, is proof that the old habits were identical with the modern ones.

Multitudes of peculiar forms of these curious animals are found fossil, some totally different from, others very nearly resembling, those now found and belonging to living animals. Now that we know them to be able to live in very deep water, we may account for their wide occurrence in most rocks. The oldest rocks contain the least familiar forms.

It is a curious thing to notice the division into five parts of most of these animals found living, and to find that in many of those whose remains are in the lower deposits this tendency is not so evident.

Worms and such-like animals would naturally be rare in a fossil state, as being seldom provided with any solid framework. Still there are indications, even of the soft kinds, preserved permanently in numerous worm-tracks that were left on the muddy shores of ancient seas. It is also a habit with many of these creatures to coat themselves with sand or little pebbles for protection; and as the cases thus made do not die with the animal, if not exposed to violence they will remain buried in the mud. Such worm-cases have been met with in some rocks, and a kind of natural armor with which a few of the same class of animals is provided also remains without change. The tubes which such animals have bored are also sometimes recognizable.

Insects, though they have horny cases, are not likely to be much mixed up with river-mud; still less can they be carried out to sea in large quantities and buried in deposits at the bottom of deep water. No wonder, then, that it is a rare event to discover such creatures. Buried occasionally by some accident, and caught up from time to time in the resinous fluids oozing out of trees and hardening in the air, there is a possibility that a few might be found; and perhaps, on the whole, the number actually discovered is more rather than less than could have been expected.

On the other hand, crabs and lobsters and other marine animals, coated in a thick shell of limestone, which they from time to time throw off, are much more likely to be common. Under favorable circumstances, very considerable numbers of them have been met with, and they fully justify the expectation. Such animals are common on rocky shores, where there are occasional beds of mud and sand in holes, and they are not found on all shores. Neither are their remains in all rocks; but enough have been detected in the older as well as newer rocks to render it certain that the old seas and shores resembled the modern in the existence of creatures of this kind.

There are some shells belonging to very minute crustaceans (as this group of animals is called) that would hardly be recognized as of the same family as crabs except by the naturalist. Some of these are exceedingly small and simple, resembling in shape the pod of a bean, and the two shells together not unlike a bean, but smaller than a small pin's head. Myriads of such little shells are found in certain clays, and they even help to build up some clays and limestones. Some of them mark the presence of fresh water, or, at least, seem to show that where they were accumulated fresh and salt water were mixed,—or, in other words, that the bed of clay or limestone in which they are found was deposited near the mouth of a large river. Such conclusions may be the more depended on when other remains of animals also indicate the presence of land not far off, and when fragments of the vegetable kingdom are well preserved.

In some beds near the bottom of the series are found

crustacean shells of the most curious form (*Trilobites*), belonging to kinds not now known in a living state. These are also exceedingly abundant, and with them are fragments of a kind of lobster, that must have attained a length of as much as seven feet.

In all seas there are found some specimens of a curious kind of bivalve tough shell, pierced through the extremity of one valve with a hole, through which is a bundle of silky fibres attaching the animal to the rock. The modern kinds are called lamp-shells, and within the shell there is, generally, a delicate loop or screw of stone. Most of those now obtained are from rocky bottoms and in deepish water; and, though found in almost all seas, they are nowhere very common. Of such shells there are specimens in almost all rocks, showing extreme differences of form and many singular peculiarities of structure. There is hardly a single group of deposits that we can examine, from the lowest to the most recently formed, that has not some of them. There are specimens of all dimensions:—some covered with long spines, some perfectly smooth; some thin, others enormously thick and heavy; some quite simple, others extremely complicated; and many of these, that have been buried for ages, could with difficulty be distinguished from shells taken from a living animal.

While there is this vast variety and abundance of the lamp-shells, now very rare, there are also many deposits of limestone almost made up of other shells. More than a third part of all known fossils are bivalve shells, and another third univalves, leaving only the remaining third for all other species of animals. There is, however, a curious difference with regard to them. Of the species of bivalves, or double shells, such as the oyster and cockle, whose habitations consist of two shelly or strong cases enclosing the animal, there are twice as many varieties found in rocks as are now found in the sea; while of the univalves or single shells, such as the snail, the whelk, and others, there are one-third more from the modern sea-shore than from all rocks.

The variety as well as the absolute number of individuals in the remains of these animals is exceedingly great; nor need this be a matter of surprise, when it is considered how easily they form part of any deposit rapidly brought together, and how slowly they decay and alter if not at once crushed. Formed of limestone, they are sufficiently liable to injury to be quickly broken when rolled about on a sea-shore, though even under such circumstances the number of fragments could not fail to be very manifest; but once buried, they are hardly exposed to other danger. For a long time they retain their color, —for a much longer time all those distinctive marks by which shells are recognized and known one from another; and even when, as sometimes happens, they are turned into crystal, whether of limestone or flint, they still retain their exact shapes, and can often be known as well as if they had undergone no change.

Very beautiful and very curious are the shells that are found in various rocks. Those from the chalk differ exceedingly from those we are familiar with on our own or other shores; those from the limestone below the chalk differ from the chalk varieties; and those from limestones lower still in the series are again quite different. Shells found in deposits of clay differ greatly from those found in limestones, and singular changes of appearance are observable even in very similar deposits, provided specimens are taken in different parts of a great series. Among modern shells the nautilus is one of the most curious; and as the animal that constructs it much resembles the common cuttle-fish,—whose skeleton, or bone (as it is called), is constantly found washed up by the waves on a sandy shore,—there is a good deal of interest in all that relates to it. Rare as the nautilus now is, and confined to the Southern hemisphere (the *Argonaut* of the Mediterranean being a different animal), it is remarkable that there should exist in England numerous beds containing millions of shells having similar structure, and certainly once belonging to creatures of similar habits. These almost build up some of the limestones, and are also found in some of the clays. Together with the lamp-shells (the *Terebratula* is a familiar group), the *Ammonites* (twisted shells divided into many chambers) make up a large proportion of the whole number of fossil shells.

Remains of fishes, often very small and not readily distinguished, but sufficiently determined to leave no doubt as to their true nature, are found, as might be expected, in deposits from water. Not only teeth and occasional bones, but scales, are easily preserved; and it seems that the scales are the parts by which the nature of some fish is best known. Sharks very often have spines sticking from the back, to which fins are attached; and such spines, being excessively hard and indestructible, are among the parts of fish found in the oldest rocks. The skin of sharks is likewise very durable. From those that live now we obtain shagreen, and small bits of similar substances are buried in many rocks. Some kinds of fishes, very rare now and known to inhabit only a few rivers and lakes, are enclosed in a kind of box of bone, and coated with the hardest enamel. Complete or partial coats of mail, evidently belonging to similar fishes, have been obtained among fossils for comparison with them. The teeth of some fishes are like pavements, excessively hard, flat, and all connected together; other fishes have numerous rows of sharp hooks, others teeth like brushes, and others delicate teeth like the finest needles. Specimens of all kinds are found in the earth in beds of all ages; but the scaled fishes we are now most familiar with must either have been rare in former times, or the others must have been much more favorably placed for being kept buried in rocks for many ages.

Of all land-animals, certain reptiles are those which have the most chance of their remains being preserved. Wrapped up in a bony coat, which prevents injury while alive, the whole framework of the creature holds together long after death; and as the reptiles thus armed live chiefly near water, and are often buried in deep mud for a long time during dry weather, they must constantly be exposed to be covered up permanently and retained in deposits under course of formation. The scales, teeth, and bones of such reptiles (crocodiles, alligators, &c.) are naturally to be expected, therefore; but no one could be prepared to expect the singular richness of many masses of clay and limestone in such fossils, for we know of nothing in existing creation that could afford a standard of comparison. Not only remains of common kinds, but numerous complete skeletons of others not now known, point to the fact that such animals were once plentiful and lived in multitudes in these latitudes.

Serpents and frogs are, of course, much less liable to be retained, even if buried in water and mud. A few of them have been found, but they are rarities.

Birds would seem hardly more likely to be buried in mud than land-animals; but as some of them make the sea their chief resort, and many others inhabit land close to water, it is not surprising that a few remains of them are from time to time discovered. Still, the bones of these creatures that have been obtained from the different rocks, except those of the very latest date, are, with one or two rare exceptions, few and not very instructive.

Mammalia, with the exception of whales and dugongs and such marine monsters, can only live on land, and most of them seem to require considerable tracts of land. Islands even of large size are often almost without such animals at the present time, and this must always have been the case in the world's history. And although large tracts of land may always have had numerous quadrupeds, and have been crossed and drained by rivers, which carry down mud in large quantities to the sea, and with the mud remains of all that dwelt on the river-banks, there are so many chances of accident to these that they can only rarely have been preserved. Even when they reach the sea it will be found that, before being in a state fit for handing down to future times, they have for the most part suffered so much from decomposition, and from rubbing about among stones and against each other, as to be hardly recognized. Thus there is no likelihood of large quantities of such remains being found under any circumstances, and their total absence might indicate much rather the absence of large continents than the absence of all land. It is quite possible that there might be large deposits going on, in which remains of shells and corals should be very common and remains of fish and reptiles by no means rare, but in which were no remains of land-animals. Such deposits might even be greatly influenced by the vicinity of a large group of moderate-sized islands, and yet, until man should visit these islands, no quadruped larger than a rat might exist in them. Such would be the case now in some of the islands of the Pacific on a small scale, and may have happened elsewhere on a larger scale. We must not conclude that, because no bones of quadrupeds or birds were buried with the reptiles and fishes, or with innumerable shells and corals, there were no birds or quadrupeds near; still less are we justified in saying that there were none anywhere at the date of the deposit.

From this account it will be seen that, whatever there is living upon the earth, in the air, or in the water, indications of such life may be met with buried in the mud at the bottom of the sea, or built up with the lime stones and other rocks, as illustrations of the state of life when such rocks were formed. We also see that very imperfect knowledge would be obtained from these accumulations as to the relative abundance or importance of the animals. The point really decided is, which of them have been best able to resist the causes of decay and destruction, and which were most conveniently at hand to be caught up in the deposit.

## Chapter the Thirteenth.

**ANCIENT FORESTS AND MODERN FUEL.**

ANY one travelling a few hundred miles through England, on one of our great lines of railway, north or west of London, can hardly fail to be reminded of the magnitude and importance of the coal interests, some part or other of which he must traverse. Somersetshire, South Wales, Warwickshire, Staffordshire, Lancashire, Yorkshire, Durham, and Northumberland, exhibit portions of a vast chain of mineral fuel, of which the under-ground links reach from the fertile valleys of the west to the storm-beaten shores of the northeast of England; and if the journey is farther extended, Scotland will be found to comprise a second and outer line equally manifest, and in its way not less valuable.

Through this wide extent of British lands, it is true that coal is rarely seen at the surface, except when brought there by the active industry of man. From various depths, varying from a few yards to a third of a mile,—up pits and shafts, sometimes simple enough in their structure, sometimes exceedingly elaborate and costly, but almost always lifted by the aid of steam-power,—the coal is brought to the surface, and, when there, is distributed and conveyed to its destination. The thousands of men and boys, the numerous horses employed, and much of the machinery,—all these are out of sight, and we see only the result; our eyes are, perhaps, offended with the interruption and injury to fine scenery by the unpicturesque surface works and heaps, or we are annoyed by the smoke vomited forth from the chimneys of the numerous steam-engines; and we throw ourselves back in the railway-carriage, indifferent and wearied, caring nothing and thinking nothing of those vast mines of wealth we are passing over, compared with which, the gold of California and Australia, and the diamonds of Golconda, may be regarded as unimportant.

Or should we pause, and endeavor to make ourselves familiar with coal as it exists in the earth, and compare its appearance there with its aspect on our fires or in our cellars, the effort, which is one involving no trifling amount of fatigue to those not accustomed to underground travelling, might result in a notion more confused than useful; and if we had previously any book-knowledge of the subject, we should, perhaps, come away with the conviction that written and published descriptions of such matters were far more interesting than the reality.

A visit to a coal-mine is not, however, without meaning, especially to any one who has some little idea of mining operations. The descent through hot air, foggy with floating particles of coal, the darkness and gloom but very imperfectly revealed by candles or lamps, the crowd of trucks, horses, and men at the bottom, and the incessant clanking of the machinery,—all these prepare the visitor for his work. Once landed below, he is led past vast furnaces, burning day and night to create a draught of air, on which the very life of all those employed under ground depends; he is told that air close to him, passing into the chimney a little above his head over these fires, is highly explosive, so that a spark entering it would involve destruction; he is introduced first through broad and then into narrower paths, where the roof has once come down, or the floor squeezed up; he sees men working with difficulty, picking a deep groove in a black wall, and he hears, when away from the work going on, a dull singing noise of escaping gas always oozing through the coal. At one place he is shown where tons of roof have recently fallen, and at another cracks, whence hogsheads of fiery gas are issuing with rapidity, poisoning and rendering dangerous all the air of the mine. He is taken along miles of a vast black tunnel, cut through the mineral, and the road is to him a perfect labyrinth, though really designed and executed on an admirable system. At last he is brought, somehow or other, to a pit-bottom, whence he is lifted, greatly to his satisfaction, to the outer world, and finally he makes his way to a warm bath and pure air, and endeavors to remove, as far as possible, the marks of his visit from his skin and lungs.

We have said that the impression made on an intelligent person by such a visit is not without some good result. He learns at least to estimate the nature and extent of the deposit; he sees some of the peculiarities connected with its position in the earth; he feels some of the difficulties and recognizes some of the dangers of under-ground engineering; and he wonders that men can be found who, for moderate wages, will undertake mining as a regular employment, and give up so much of the satisfaction that all human beings must have in seeing the light of day and breathing the fresh air.

But while looking at the black mineral, cut through with a pick, or blasted with gunpowder under ground, it may occur to him to look back to the period when this material was first formed or deposited, and consider the circumstances under which it became coal.

The floor of the coal—in other words, the earth on which we tread in a coal-mine—is generally a bed of bluish clay; and if a specimen of this clay is brought up and examined, it will perhaps be found loaded with innumerable black stringy markings, crossing each other in every direction. These were once the rootlets of plants, that either grew in this clay as a vegetable soil, or were matted up with it into a tough mass before the plants had decayed. Overhead there is generally sandstone, and on the roof, where the sandstone and coal were once in contact, we may often see long flat markings, the stems of ancient trees that had not entirely decayed when the sands buried the whole mass. Thus the coal lies upon a clay on which plants grew, and is covered with a material that contains innumerable marks of similar vegetation. Whatever the thickness of the coal in the regular coal deposits in England, these conditions of the rocks above and below are singularly uniform. In France, especially in the small coal districts in the west and south, such is not the case; but the coal is there generally of different quality, and has been accumulated in a different way.

The first thing that is learnt on examining coal deposits in England is, that they are generally pretty uniform in character and thickness over several square miles of country. In some countries, especially in the Northern States of America, near the Ohio, where the extent of coal is enormously greater than in England, this regularity is far more striking than with us; but it is always observable. Beds of coal, varying in thickness, but each retaining its own thickness, or nearly so, are found lying one above another, and form a long series. Many are thick enough to be worth working, and each of these is known by some local name; others are only just thick enough to be recognized as coal, forming a thin black ribbon among the rocks; but all are generally so circumstanced, with reference to the clay below and sand above, as to be easily known to those accustomed to look for them. The clay below, with its rootlets (the *under-clay*), and the sandstone or other rock above, with leaves, twigs, and trunks of trees,—these are almost but not quite invariable accompaniments.

It is impossible not to conclude, from all the circumstances connected with coal deposits, that this mineral is the remains of an ancient vegetation, growing on or near the place where we now find it. Even the coal itself, black and opaque as it seems, yields under the searching power of the microscope some evidence as to its own origin. When ground down to the thinnest possible slice, and carefully examined under a high power, traces are seen here and there of spiral vessels, such as belong to woody fibre, and of some other marks proving a complicated vegetable structure.

Fruits, such as nuts of strange forms, and even delicate flowers, have also been detected. Examples of each of the two principal divisions of vegetable structure, derived from the mode of growth, have been identified. Insects, and other animals, have been found, and proof exists in abundance that all coal was formed near land, if it did not actually grow on the soil with which it is now buried.

It is worth while to look back into Nature's history, and endeavor to reproduce a chapter of the Stone Book, in reference to this subject. There is a good deal written, and the illustrations are ample.

From a pile of rubbish near the shaft of a coal-mine it would be difficult to take up a dozen specimens of the peculiar hardened blue clay, called *shale*, so abundant in such places, without finding in some of them impressions of leaves; and a very little examination and comparison would suffice to enable any one accustomed to plants to refer these to some kind of fern. Why these fossils should be so invariably fern-leaves, instead of leaves of the forest-trees (which one might have expected to form at least some part of the deposit), is perhaps the first question that would suggest itself to any one who was desirous of obtaining information concerning the remains of a former world.

A more thorough examination, and a visit to local museums, where such things are collected, arranged, and exhibited, would, however, show that, though not entirely absent, leaf-fragments of other plants than ferns are so exceedingly rare that they may practically be disregarded in considering the important contributories to coal.

Either of two causes may have brought about this result. The other plants may have been absent altogether, or they may have been less easily preserved, when buried—perhaps under water—in the conditions favorable for making coal out of wood. Experiment has shown that the leaves of our forest-trees decay much more rapidly than fern-leaves, and thus there may have been large accumulations of the former that have disappeared, although they have helped to make coal; but the vast multitude of ferns seems, of itself, to show that these were really predominant, and a further study of the trunks of the trees points to the same conclusion.

Remains of the trunks of trees are sometimes very numerous and very large in the sandstones near coal, and numerous fine specimens have also been found in the shales or clayey beds, especially when these, instead of sandstones, rest upon the coal, forming a roof. In fact, it would seem generally that the greater number of recognizable fossil plants occur in this position, heaped as it were on the top of the vegetable mass that has been converted into mineral fuel.

Let us now endeavor to reproduce an ancient forest such as existed in and near our island at the time when the great mass of our coal was in preparation; and, as far as the materials will justify, let us also people this forest with animal life. In the half-title to this part of the book will be found an art representation that will help the reader in forming an opinion.

Such a forest certainly abounded with lofty plants of ferns, like those we now call tree-ferns, and to such an extent that in many places it probably contained little else. As, however, in Norfolk Island and other parts of the Antipodes, where such vegetation now prevails, the outskirts of the thick forests may have exhibited a considerable admixture of other trees, and here and there groups where the ferns were absent. Pines of large dimensions were certainly among these occasional trees.

Let us look a little more closely at the trees which seem to have been the chief agents in supplying material for coal. There are many portions of large trunks, many markings of the bark, many casts of the interior, and not a few fragments, which show the texture of the wood, the springing of the branches, and the attachment of the roots. Occasionally the structure of the wood can be examined under the microscope; but this is a rare exception, for the stone is generally not in a state to admit of this minute examination.

There are three kinds of trees exceedingly unlike one another that appear to have combined to form a very large proportion of the actual coal. Each of these may have been represented by a great variety of species; but as, on the whole, it is the habit of plants, when they grow freely and abundantly, to exclude strangers, so there may have been then but little admixture in the depths of the forest. We can in a general way understand the appearance and nature of these three kinds of ancient forest-trees.

Crowds of lofty trunks (*Sigillaria*), not scaled like pines, but fluted like the columns of a temple, rise before us in groups, each trunk terminating in a magnificent crest of fronds, some drooping over, some curling in curious contortions towards the light. Whether of the dark green of some of our ferns, or of the bright metallic tint of others, these ferns, forming the capitals of natural columns, must have presented a strange appearance. Thickly grouped, they must almost have excluded light from the ground, and thus there was, perhaps, only a small amount of other vegetation, except where an opening occurred. Rapid growth and equally rapid decay, in a moist atmosphere, and under a clouded sky, would accumulate a vast amount of vegetable matter in such forests in a short time, and it would be left to the insects to destroy the fallen wood. Should it happen that the land was swampy and insects not abundant, the trees might accumulate and form a thick mass of half-rotten matter.

The trunks of these trees would not seem to have been very solid, or at least the interior was liable to decay more rapidly than the bark. Flattened stems that have belonged to trees three or four feet in diameter, and from forty to fifty feet high, are not uncommon. Others have been found larger, and some that were, perhaps, double the height mentioned. At regular intervals the channelled stem is deeply marked by curious scars,—the places on which leaves or fronds have formed and grown, and from which they have fallen. Within the thick bark there was woody tissue, growing, like that of ferns, by additions above and not around. Thus, a young fern now will shoot up and become a tree by degrees, and even assume the proportions of a lofty tree; but all this time it does not enlarge its bulk, and is rarely branched. Trees of this kind continue to grow in height as long as they live, and break off near the root when once dead.

The roots (called *Stigmariæ*) of these singular trees were not at all less remarkable than the trunk. Large circular roots passed off in every direction from the base of the trunk, like the spokes of a wheel. Each main root had its offsets of smaller size, and each one of these its leaf-like, long rootlets, spreading in every direction, and producing that complicated mass of tendrils found in the beds of under-clay that serve as floors to the coal. Thus, this tree, instead of seeking food from the air by a complicated apparatus of branches, twigs, and true leaves, obtained what nourishment it required from the earth, and passed this food, by circulation, through the lofty vertical trunk to the fronds at the top. The roots and rootlets remain in the clay, little changed even when the trunk and fronds have been converted into coal, and have lost all traces of their original form as well as of their texture.

Such would seem to have been the condition of one of the principal trees of the coal period. How long it continued, how often it was repeated, why these particular trees rather than others were so frequently accumulated in thick masses on the ground, we cannot tell. These speculations we must leave for the present.

Another very different tree demands our attention. Lofty, and having the proportions of firs, such trees (*Lepidodendron*) shot up into the clouds on a mountain-side, and yet they present the peculiarities of leaf-vegetation of the club-mosses. New Zealand and other moist insular climates present us with club-mosses, not unlike dwarf trees; but these are only a few inches high: the coal seems to show us these magnified into forest vegetation. There are trunks twenty to fifty feet high, branching and forking in a peculiar manner, and scarred like pines. The stems of such trees were like those of ferns, and must have grown by additions to the extremity; the leaves, or whatever they may be called,—delicate feathery filaments, pointed at the end,—shot out from the stem; and there were no twigs. The fruit grew at the extremity of the branches, and resembled the very long cone of a fir. Trees such as these are not rare, but they do not seem to have been so numerous as the other kind we have attempted to describe. Their remains are found in similar localities.

A third singular form of vegetation is before us,—a gigantic reed, made up, like a bamboo, of numerous joints, hollow and cylindrical, now only to be seen crushed and flattened, and often only known by the markings it has left on stone. This tree (the *Calamite*) was limited to swampy places, and was there exceedingly common. It is met with wherever coal is found, and the varieties of detail are very great. Some naturalists have thought that it resembled those marsh plants called *mare's-tail* (Equisetum), so common in our own country. Some have referred to it as a variety of plants with true woody structure, increasing by an annual thickening of the wood under the bark. Leaves seem to have proceeded in a fringe-like form from each joint, and branches were given off at intervals. Nothing is known of the fruit. These trees were sometimes thirty or forty feet in height, and two or three feet in diameter. The trunk was deeply fluted, and at each joint there was a flat plate or diaphragm crossing the stem.

Numerous varieties of tree-ferns, such as still abound in the Southern hemisphere; very tall, coniferous trees, like the great Araucaria of Norfolk Island; several palm-trees, bearing fruit not very different from some forms of dates; these, and a multitude of other plants, have been found buried with the sand and mud that have, in course of time, made up the rocks we now call coal-measures. These, then, with the nondescripts we have endeavored to picture, formed the vegetation of north temperate land during the coal period.

With these plants the remains of a few insects have been found, including among them a scorpion. There were also a number of small lizards, and perhaps some larger reptiles. Little else is known of the inhabitants of the land at this distant period. There may have been many whose remains were not preserved. There may also have been many whose remains are safely buried, but which have not yet been turned up. Judging from the number and variety of additions within the last few years, since attention was directed to the subject, the last hypothesis is probable enough.

How have these ancient forests been converted into coal available for fuel? How have they been buried under such thick masses of stone and clay? How have they been broken up into compartments and tilted at high angles, as they are found to be in our English coal-mines? And, lastly, how have they been brought into their present accessible position? These are questions of great interest, not very easily answered without some knowledge of the general history of the earth in respect to other rocks. Let us consider each in its turn.

The essential difference between wood and coal consists in the replacement of the water always found in fresh vegetation by gases never found there in a free state.

It is perhaps quite impossible, by any artificial drying short of charring, to deprive wood so completely of moisture that the part still left behind shall not interfere seriously with the value of the material as fuel; for so long as any water is present the whole of it has to be evaporated into steam before available heat is obtained, and the heat lost in this process must be deducted from the heat-giving power of the fuel. Coal contains no water, but, on the contrary, it holds a certain proportion of hydrogen and some oxygen gas; but these help combustion rather than hinder it, and are useful for other purposes. There is also another difference between wood and coal, indicated by the closer texture of the latter. The cellular condition of the wood is, in fact, altered, and the water-contents of the cells must be removed or decomposed before coal is produced. This chemical change has never been produced artificially, either in the case of green wood, dried wood, the black wood obtained from ferns and bog, or various deposits in the earth, nor with such vegetation as peat. All these still contain water: they do not contain gas, and they are not dense and compact stony substances.

Nature would seem to require a long period of time and certain conditions of heat and pressure to bring about the required result. The woody matter originally accumulated has been buried with clay and sand. The whole together has been sunk down into the earth, and has then been gradually covered up with newer deposits, until it has reached a depth where the temperature is high enough for the chemical change needed. For thousands and tens of thousands of years the ancient forests have been thus exposed, and at length the work is done, and coal has replaced wood, sand has become sandstone, and clay shale. Who can say how long the beds may have remained after this change, or when the movements took place that have brought the whole again to the surface?

But still the question remains, how have so many successive deposits of vegetable matter been produced in so narrow a space? Perhaps, in the absence of facts bearing on the inquiry, it is safer to leave this great difficulty without an attempt at solution. That sometimes the trees grew on the clay where their roots still remain, and on which the coal now lies, would seem unquestionable. That in other cases the whole mass of vegetable matter has been conveyed from a distance, and has been mixed up with marine remains, is equally certain. We may so easily lose ourselves in conjectures as to the best explanation, not only of the repeated depressions of the surface that admitted of a succession of deposits, but of the mere fact of the accumulation of vegetable matter in a state of decomposition, that we are obliged to imagine rather than able to investigate. It is something in these cases to recognize a difficulty.

The deposits of vegetable matter, sand, and mud, once converted into coal, stone, and shale, in horizontal and parallel layers, the mechanical uplifting could only have been caused by some great force acting from below, and upheaving, with resistless power, the whole mass. But in such upheaval, whether slowly or rapidly performed,—whether a succession of violent earthquakes has jerked mountains into the air, or, which seems more likely, a gentle pulsation has by degrees brought up the mass, at the rate of only a few inches, or at most a few feet, in a century,—in any case there must have been fracture of the brittle minerals, partial upheavals, separations of beds and liftings up of one part higher than another, tiltings up of certain strata and droppings down of others, accompanied by a washing away of loose material from the surface, especially when the elevation has brought surface-beds under the influence of the sea-waves. Thus have been produced all those results that at first seem so strange; and the reader may safely accept this as the explanation of the third and fourth queries.

We may now proceed to the consideration of another matter concerning these ancient forests, and learn, if possible, how far they could have grown in the climates in which they are now found. The great beds of coal are very widely spread, and fossil remains of plants very nearly allied to each other, if not identical, range at no very distant intervals throughout the whole of the north temperate zone, and extend even within the Arctic Circle. Similar trees appear to have inhabited the country now occupied by the European continent, the northern part of North America, and even China and Japan. Similar trees occurring over this wide tract presume a similar climate everywhere and some means of communication. There is no other condition of land conceivable than a vast archipelago,—a countless multitude of islands of various sizes, but with no continued continent, studded over the whole area. Such an archipelago exists to some degree in the South Atlantic Ocean now, and is there accompanied by a condition of depression admitting of the growth of coral islands with extreme rapidity. Such an archipelago, we must suppose, then occupied the whole Northern hemisphere in temperate latitudes. If there were masses of land without mountains in the Tropics, and no land whatever in the Arctic Circle, the conditions would be still more favorable.

And the climate that would belong to lands so placed may be guessed at with tolerable certainty. The outlying islands near Great Britain, in spite of the great mass of continental Europe, possess climates so equable as to astonish all those who first make acquaintance with them. With an average temperature not much higher than that of London, we have here, in spite of cold northerly winds and the ice in the Atlantic, spots where snow is rarely seen and water hardly ever freezes. The vegetation of the South of Europe easily adapts itself there; the orange-tree and the arbutus ripen their fruits in the open air, and delicate flowering shrubs, elsewhere confined to the greenhouse, here adorn the garden during the whole winter.

One step further—a change that should remove these islands from the influence of cold land-winds—would assimilate their climate very closely to that of the islands near Australia, where ferns are the prevailing vegetation, where they grow to gigantic size, and are accompanied by trees perhaps the nearest in many respects to those of the coal period. This change would be effected if, in place of the Alps and the land ranging northward towards the pole, there were a sea covered only with islands of moderate elevation.

There is really nothing, so far as the present knowledge of coal-plants indicates, which requires for their production more than that amount of warmth with moisture and that absence from chilling cold that belongs to islands in temperate latitudes with no adjacent large continent. The conditions of the Southern hemisphere are in no way remarkably favorable in these respects, though much more so than in the north; for there the continuous ice extends actually much farther from the pole than it does in the Northern hemisphere, and floating ice reaches to latitudes which correspond with those of the Mediterranean islands. The extreme of equable climate is certainly not obtained on any part of the present surface of the earth, and the conditions are nowhere such as to suggest that a limit of warmth and moisture has been approached.

On the other hand, it is certain that the present land in the Northern hemisphere must have been submerged during the whole time of deposit of the great series of rocks which we now find overlying the coal measures. It is not only a conjecture, but a certainty, that this was the case, since all these are marine deposits and loaded with marine productions. The changes of level that have brought the coal within reach have been alone sufficient to lift all the land of the Northern hemisphere from deep water.

We are, then, at liberty to assume that our ancient forests grew on islands of various dimensions near the present deposits of coal, if not on those actual spots. These islands, if at no very great distance asunder and if connected by marine currents, might easily have had similar vegetation; they might even have possessed identical species. That such islands should have a rapid succession of forest-growth and a quick accumulation of trees and vegetation in their hollows, with but few animal inhabitants, is probable; and that they should have been subjected to occasional depression is only what we find now in the Southern seas. There is no reason to doubt that there would be warmth and moisture enough under such circumstances to account for a rank growth of ferns and palms, mixed with gigantic pines and perhaps a few forest-trees, resembling those which we still possess.

The extent of accumulation of vegetable matter required to produce a single bed of coal of moderate thickness is, however, so great, and the number of coal-seams in a single district is so considerable, that one is lost in astonishment at the magnitude of the result. Even if the whole growth of wood be taken, the time required to produce an acre of coal a foot thick from an acre of forest would, under any circumstances of growth, amount to many centuries; and it cannot be supposed that any thing like the whole growth could be secured. Look at it as we may, the mere heaping together of the raw material for those scores of millions of tons of fuel annually consumed in England is a subject that must ever present great difficulty to understand, and the more so as we are unable to point to any thing in recent times strictly analogous.

And the interval of time that separated the ancient forests from the human period, when their remains were first to be extracted from the earth as modern fuel, is not one of the least remarkable subjects for contemplation.

Each step in the operation demands so much time and has been followed by such long repose—each bed has had to be so hardened and altered, and afterwards lifted and depressed and lifted again, before other beds were placed upon it in their turn—that one is lost in the endeavor to trace the history and connection of the various movements, and read the succession whose broken links are seen in the different intervening strata.

Perhaps there is no geological question that admits of closer discussion—none in which the evidence adduced is larger in amount or more satisfactory in its nature, and at the same time none in which the general conclusion is more overwhelming in the vastness of all it offers for consideration—than this concerning the origin and history of mineral fuel. No one can for a moment doubt that the rocks containing coal abound with indications of plants, and that they were originally deposits formed in the vicinity of land. No one, again, who has looked closely into the matter has ever ventured to suggest that true coal can have had any other than a vegetable origin. The nature of the vegetation is indicated by numberless examples, and the coal appears to have been derived, partly or chiefly, from the trunks of the trees of which we have the fossil leaves. But the change that has taken place to convert wood or other vegetation into coal has never yet been imitated in human laboratories, and its nature can only be guessed at. The accumulated heaps of sand now converted into sandstone and lying over the coal are sometimes penetrated for many yards by the trunk of some ancient tree, also changed into stone; and yet no one can decide absolutely whether such accumulations of sand were rapid or slow. Among the shales that alternate with the sandstones are numerous and valuable deposits of iron-ore, whose origin is not less obscure than the conversion of wood into coal, but which certainly were not what they now are when the beds were deposited; for many of the oval nodules of rich ore are formed on some small fragment of a fern, or exhibit a fruit of some tree in their centre. All these changes seem to tend to the one great result,—an accumulation of mineral treasure into one spot which had been previously distributed irregularly through a large space,—a double concentration of mineral wealth in two forms most useful to man.

Thus, ancient forests, distributed over groups of islands in the Northern hemisphere, have here and there, by some happy accident, escaped from natural decay and have become buried with mud and sand. The cause, whatever it may have been, that first preserved the woody and leafy matter from decay continued to act at the surface, repeating its effect on each successive deposit that came under its influence, while those heaps already completed passed downwards to greater depth, perhaps by the slow collapse of some vast subterranean cavern. The climatal cause that produced the coarse and rapid vegetation did not cease for a long period, and the forests grew and were destroyed time after time, the whole after each destruction being sealed up by overlying heaps of sand and clay till the uppermost deposit lay some thousand feet over that first formed. The buried vegetation was squeezed by the vast pressure of all this overlying mass, and afterwards by the load of hundreds of fathoms of water. Other deposits succeeded, other climates prevailed; there were great changes among the inhabitants of the globe; even the trees and shrubs were altered, and the zamia took the place of the tree-fern, to be in its turn succeeded by the present Northern vegetation. All this time the buried forests were ripening into coal. Century after century the slow change went on: the woody fibre became lost, the cell-structure of the fibre decayed; the water, unable entirely to escape, was resolved into its elements, and these entered into new combinations, carburetted hydrogen being formed under great pressure, and remaining pent up within the minute interstices of the newly-formed mineral.

Of the millions of square miles of land forming the islands of the ancient archipelago, a few thousands are now covered with coal. Buried beneath hundreds of yards of earth, and for the most part out of sight, this mineral is eagerly sought for, and its value everywhere recognized. North America, both the Northern States of the Union and the British possessions, contains large deposits easily accessible. Great Britain has numerous deposits, far smaller, but of excellent quality; and these also are, for the most part, readily obtained, though at some cost. Belgium, Northern France, and Western Germany have each small slices of the same valuable material. In Southern France and Spain, in Russia and Hungary, and in many other parts of Europe, there is also coal. In various parts of Asia, in South Africa, in Australia, and in some of the islands adjacent, patches occur so similar in all essential points that they seem due to similar causes. In the Tropics, as well as in temperate latitudes, and within the Arctic Circle,—in the south as well as in the north,—mineral fuel, associated with fossil vegetation, has therefore been found; and there is everywhere a remarkable uniformity in the conditions under which the two are present. The unused forest-trees of old times have been converted into fuel for our benefit. There are large stores of it; but these stores are not inexhaustible, nor are they capable of renovation. The modern forests once cut down will, if properly managed, become replaced within a century; but the coal once gone is gone forever. On the other hand, the same work may be going on partly at the mouths of our great rivers, and partly where deposits of various geological age are buried beneath the surface of earth and sea and are removed far away out of our sight.

## Chapter the Fourteenth.

### THE PRE-ADAMITE WORLD.

Now comes another very curious question for our consideration; and it is one that involves some difficulties not yet alluded to. Like other difficulties, these must be fairly and honestly met; for we may be quite sure that it is only in this way that they can be conquered and got rid of. They shall first be stated in as few words as possible, and then we will go on to consider how far they affect us in understanding the geological problem.

In the first place, with regard to man. We are bound to suppose that when a work of art—the shaping of a flint into the form of a weapon—is discovered, it indicates the presence of man in the place at some time or other. If such an object is found in a cavern, buried with bones, covered up with a coat of limestone, and that covering again covered with gravel and other bones, all indicating a gradual accumulation, we should be bound to suppose that the place has had an earlier race of inhabitants than that whose remains are found at the top, and that this earlier race has been displaced. It is clear that the more multiplied such specimens are, the greater would be the probability of there having been a large colony of the early inhabitants. If, too, these sculptured flints are generally alike over a wide district, we might fairly presume that they had been made by a race originally widely spread.

If, again, buried with stone weapons, which carry back the date of the introduction of man to a distant day, there are found the skeletons or other remains of animals of various kinds now quite unknown, and if all these, or many of them, have been preserved without much injury to the most delicate angles of bone, and in such numbers and variety as to make it clear that their presence is not the result of local accident, we must admit that these extinct races were contemporaneous with the ancient human inhabitants. It is well known that in Polar seas there have been found, frozen into mud-cliffs, the complete carcasses of elephants adapted to a cold climate by a coat of warm hair, and that these carcasses occupy positions many hundred miles removed from the nearest country which could now be their permanent home. There is thus independent proof that not only the climate, but the larger quadrupeds, of important districts have greatly changed; and, though no carcasses of men have been dug out of these cliffs, there is little doubt that men lived at this period, and peopled the countries of the north temperate zone. Very long, therefore, before civilized races of men inhabited the world, Geology has proved that the earth was tenanted by an ample population, very different from existing races, although, no doubt, well adapted to the climate and conditions of existence of the time. Very long indeed before even the faintest traces of human remains have been suspected, there were other altogether different groups of living things. No records appear of these in any written book; but they are objects not without ample illustration in that great stone record preserved for our investigation in the rocks, mountains, and plains. We find here all that is needed to reproduce the original. The portrait is veiled, no doubt; but the main outlines may be withdrawn from concealment. We are enabled to bring together and compare the bones, the teeth, the horny skin, the shell, or other parts of animals that have been long buried; and afterwards, with such knowledge as we possess, we may compare these with corresponding parts of living and familiar animals, and arrive at definite conclusions concerning them.

It is no easy task, this that we have here pointed out, and it has required the combined knowledge and ingenuity of many great and learned students of Nature to come to a decision on disputed points. For centuries men studied, and examined, and described, and with difficulty became familiar with Nature's doings with existing races. Certain peculiarities of structure were found to correspond with modes of life, with the food, the method of obtaining food, and other matters. Thus, a particular form and structure of tooth is known to be adapted to a particular kind of food. The stomach, also, must correspond to the teeth, in order that the food may be digested; the head and extremities must be adapted so as to obtain it, and the remainder of the skeleton must also be in exact accordance: so that there is a certain mutual fitness of all parts, by means of which any one important bone or part of the skeleton ought to be sufficient to enable us to describe and picture the whole animal.

And it is not only thus in the case of quadrupeds, some of whom are strong and fierce, some weak and gentle. The bird has a peculiar structure of bone, having reference to its power of flight; the fish has another and totally different structure, enabling it to remain always, and without effort, floating in the water. The shell of the oyster or the lobster offers marked peculiarities of structure. Some animals swim with their shell, some float with it; some rest always on the bottom, some burrow in the mud. In every case, the shell, like the bone, is adapted to the use required of it, and has a corresponding structure; and, indeed, each part of every group of animals appears to have some peculiarity, and a special arrangement and contrivance of its own, enabling it to do its work in the fittest way, and allowing it to be identified even if only a very small part of the whole animal is present.

When, therefore, a bone or a shell is found, and is shown to a competent naturalist,—a person whose study it is to find out and describe these mutual relations,—he is often able to tell at once to what animal it belonged, and even a good deal about the individual peculiarities of the animal itself. If a tooth, the form of the tooth will at once tell an important tale: it was meant to cut and tear, and therefore belonged to a flesh-eating, fierce animal; or it was meant to grind, and belonged to an herbivorous animal; or it could both cut and grind, and belonged to an omnivorous brute. And then its structure: under a powerful microscope, the law of its formation, the relation it bears to other teeth of the same or other animals, its mode of growth, and a hundred facts of its history, are revealed. The state of the tooth will indicate the amount of work it has done; its fangs and shape will tell from what part of the jaws it came; and, by a succession of inferences, we shall learn, at last, what particular species, or at least what natural group, it may be referred to. Of course, some teeth are more easily recognized than others. The elephant's tooth is known by its size, as well as by its peculiar arrangement of hard and soft plates of bone and enamel; the shark's, by its shape, and combination of saw and shears; the crocodile's, by its mode of growth; and so on. In the hands of the comparative anatomist, Nature may be interrogated till she replies with complete accuracy; and if there is any living species known to the inquirer to which the tooth that is examined had belonged, to that species the tooth will, in most cases, be referred.

But if there is no such species known, are we to conclude that the naturalist is at fault, and that he must look yet more minutely at existing creation to discover a species before unknown? Doubtless, we are still ignorant of many facts in natural history, and new species are being daily brought in from various quarters, so that the mere fact of want of identity with a known species is not sufficient to remove an undetermined animal from the world of to-day. Should we, however, find that the remains of animals buried in the earth, in any country, indicate species not only quite unknown, but more nearly allied to some not now found in the country in question,—when, for example, we pick up, and hand in for examination, numerous bones of the elephant, the rhinoceros, and the hippopotamus, found in such beds of gravel as are common in many parts of England, or in caverns in the limestone of Wales, Yorkshire, or Somersetshire,—the case is different. We know pretty well the existing species of these large animals, and it is barely possible that important varieties of them can exist anywhere, either in Central Africa or the Asiatic islands; but that any can hereafter be found which now live, in a wild state, in northern temperate climates, and especially in the smaller islands in our latitudes, is a simple impossibility. The same is the case with the larger and fiercer carnivora, or flesh-eating animals; and yet the bones of large bears and hyenas are tolerably abundant in certain places throughout Western and Northern Europe.

The species of these animals known only by their fossil bones differ a good deal from the familiar and recent kinds; and thus we are led to the first great difficulty with regard to fossils, namely, that they represent and illustrate a natural history of the past,—not consisting merely of fragments of creatures recently living on the spot, nor even of bones of such as are still met with at no great distance in wilder parts of the country where man has not the upper hand. They belong to species once living and abundant in the very spots where their remains alone now occur. They are, therefore, *extinct species.*

Now, it does not follow that animals and races are everywhere absent or really extinct merely because they are gone from countries they once inhabited. No doubt the wolf, the wild boar, the black bear, the beaver, the wild cat, and other animals, have departed from England and become locally extinct; and so long as the land remains cultivated and crowded with men they will never reappear. But they are only removed to a short distance, and it will probably be very long before they are driven out of their holds in the wilder and less-peopled parts of the continent of Europe. It is not so with the elephant and hippopotamus, the rhinoceros, the great cavern bear, the great hyena, the gigantic large-horned deer, and many other animals, whose bones are very common in almost every bed of gravel, and in caverns. It is as certain that the fossil species of these are extinct as that the African and Asiatic elephants, the Polar and the black bear, the hyena of the Cape and that of Abyssinia, are essentially different the one from the other.

We thus learn the first lesson concerning organic remains. They form the earliest chapter in the history of the pre-Adamite world,—the world where men were not, and when the lower natures reigned. And just as in each country now there is a group of animals a large number of which may range widely, while others are strictly confined within narrow limits of space, so in the old times each district had its own group of species now lost. And so, also, in all the successive deposits made at different times, there have been at every period natural groups,—some of species ranging widely in time, some spreading over large areas, and others almost confined to one bed, or to one brief period of time. A due consideration of this very important fact will clear up much that appears incomprehensible in Geology, and will enable the reader to understand how, by the study of the natural group of organic remains or fossils of any district, a knowledge may be obtained as to its relative age, and its place in the great series of stratified fossiliferous rocks.

A long expression is this,—*the series of stratified fossiliferous rocks*,—and a great stumbling-block to many a young geologist. But it has a real and important meaning, and, when clearly felt as well as understood, is a wonderful help to the struggling student.

Let us endeavor to illustrate the matter, as we have done more than once before, by a kind of mechanical diagram. Suppose a heap of books, most of them illustrated, and all written in languages concerning which we are either imperfectly instructed or altogether ignorant. These books, thrown confusedly on a table, may represent a number of deposits of various kinds of rock containing fossils. The fossils are represented by the pictures in the books, and the books, piled in some irregular order, now represent the series of stratified fossiliferous rocks. To identify the books under such circumstances, it will clearly be necessary to examine and compare the pictures. They alone will teach us the state of knowledge of the people, and the object of the work illustrated, and we might infer from them the relative dates of the various books. In some cases we may find the illustrations numerous, clear, systematic, and highly characteristic; in others they are few, expressed in mere outline, difficult to make out, and comparatively uninteresting. On the whole, they may, perhaps, give us an idea of the prevailing tone of the collection of books; and what knowledge we thus obtain is valuable and trustworthy. It must be remembered, however, that with regard to the rocks we have only lately begun to look for these illustrations.

Many of them have been turned over by our forefathers without notice or allusion; out of the whole number actually there we have seen but a small proportion, and did we know all we should still only have glimpses of a complete history. An earnest conviction of this "imperfection of the geologic record" is, perhaps, one of the safest feelings that can be cultivated by those who attempt to question Nature on this subject of fossils.

At the same time, it is quite as important that the true and great value and accuracy of the knowledge thus obtained, and the rapidity of its growth, should give confidence and hopefulness. We may not hope to attain to perfect acquaintance with Nature's scheme, or fathom the infinite depth of her ways. Unbounded wealth of knowledge exists, no doubt, in every department, and much of this wealth we may expect to acquire in the course of time; but let no one suppose that he has exhausted the store, or that others who succeed him may not find even more than himself, assisted as they ought to be by his researches, and enlightened by what he and his fellow-laborers have made clear.

In every department of Natural History, the number and variety of extinct animals determined only by fragments found fossil is already large and exceedingly important. Even with regard to man himself, although, as we have said, no bones have yet been detected, there is good evidence of a long history and association with ancient and lost races, in the flint weapons, cut to a uniform pattern, lately found in gravel and caverns. Of the large quadrupeds, the variety is considerable; and such animals, being prominent and familiarly known, naturally attract attention. Their remains are most abundant in the newest deposits; and, indeed, it is not likely that complete remains of large animals will ever be met with in the earlier rocks, deposited when land probably existed in much smaller proportion than at present in our latitudes. The elephants, mastodons, and other great quadrupeds of similar bulk and structure, have left behind them numerous teeth, and bones, and tusks, in most parts of Europe, in the various surface-beds, chiefly of gravel and mud; and for the most part the extinct species differed from existing kinds more in proportions than actual size. Thus, the American elephant (*Mastodon*) had peculiar teeth, very different in appearance from those of the Asiatic or African, but serving similar purpose. The animal was also longer in the body, and not so tall. The Asiatic elephant of former times resembled the Asiatic species at present living, but was larger, and had tusks of the most portentous length. A minute species of elephant has recently been discovered in Malta. Extinct hippopotami are found in India, varying in size from an elephant to a pig; and there are several varieties of extinct rhinoceroses showing extreme difference of dimensions.

While, however, the elephantine animals in the gravel were thus equal or superior in size as well as variety to those of Asia, the corresponding animals in the clay-beds near London, of much more ancient date, are more varied in form, and very much smaller. Few of them exceeded in size the American tapir, and they seem to have been adapted to live in swampy districts or in water. Still, even here there are exceptions; for a few imperfect specimens have shown that there was with these, in similar deposits, one animal at least double the size of the tapir, and therefore approaching in that respect the smaller elephants.

The Mammoth, the elephant of Siberia,—whose carcass was found in its integrity, at the beginning of this century, walled up in the frozen banks of a river, in latitude 70° N.—was by no means the most ancient of its race. Several species are known to have preceded it and had long ceased to live before it flourished.

Some very singular extinct animals are known, which form links between living species now widely separate. Who would anticipate the existence of a creature with the trunk and general proportions of an elephant, but whose head was decorated with four horns,—two like those of the ox and two like those of the antelope? Such was the *Sivathere*, living in India at a time when a great lake extended south of the Himalayas, in the present Valley of the Ganges. At the same time, and in the same place, there existed a curious combination of the horse and rhinoceros, and numerous giraffes, animals now confined to the interior of Africa.

Other remarkable instances there are of gigantic representatives of existing quadrupeds. Some of these are very striking. Thus, in South America—where we have now a peculiar group of animals, illustrated by the sloth and the armadillo, both of small size—the extinct species, of no very ancient date, include the *Megatherium* and *Mylodon*, sloths larger and much more cumbrous than the elephant, and apparently adapted to serve the same purpose in keeping down tree-vegetation. These creatures, not being able to climb trees, pulled them down and then fed on them. So also the *Glyptodon*, of the same part of the world, was an armadillo multiplied into an animal ten feet long, coated with bony armor some inches thick; and the *Macrauchenia* was an almost equally expanded llama. Australia presents a similar condition of existence,—the extinct kangaroos of that country having been as large as the megatherium, and the wombats as large as the tapir. These were accompanied by a carnivorous quadruped, rivalling the lion in size, but marsupial in its habits, like all the quadrupeds of that remarkable country, in former times as well as now.

Very large animals, nearly allied to the lion and tiger, seem to have extended over the Northern hemisphere at a period not geologically remote, since their bones are found in the gravel and other surface-deposits; and at the same time, as all the principal natural groups of animals seem to have been ever limited geographically, we may conclude that the present great divisions of land and water were more than indicated. It is rarely, except in Australia, that we find extinct marsupials,—rarely, except in South America, that we have bones of extinct *Edentates*; while Asia, at the time we refer to, was just as remarkable for its pachyderms and ruminants as it is at present. Only at that time Asia belonged to Europe, in its zoological relations, much more than it does now, and even the African hyenas and hippopotami overspread the northwestern land. Bears of gigantic size were common; a curious gigantic deer, not unlike the reindeer, but larger, with horns spreading to enormous width, ranged over our own islands and the continent adjacent, and was accompanied by other deer, some still remaining in Northern Europe, but most of them lost forever.

When we pass on to consider the quadrupeds of still older rocks, we must be prepared for a great change. The illustrations pictured in the Stone Record are few, and belong to very small kinds; but whether this small size, and the curious marsupial structure indicated by the skeleton, really mean that nothing more existed at that time, or whether the land in our neighborhood consisted only of small and detached islands instead of large continents, it would not be safe to assert. Certain it is that groups of small islands in an open sea are still without quadrupeds larger than a rat; and there would seem no reason why this should not account for the absence of fossils, without having recourse to the assumption that no larger kinds had been created.

Birds tell the same tale as quadrupeds in all essential points. Their bones being for the most part small and delicate, and the greater number of them living quite in the interior of land, it could hardly be that many of their remains would be found among the fossils. Still, as a considerable group inhabit near the shore, and are frequently flying over the sea, there is nothing improbable in their being preserved. There are, in fact, abundant proofs of their existence, even in rocks very low in the great series, although the actual remains found in such localities are few and unsatisfactory. But there is one very curious fact regarding birds. Though usually adapted for flight, there are some species confined to the land, and these are more or less nearly deprived of wings. Just as, in Australia, there are a number of extinct but gigantic marsupial quadrupeds, so in the islands of New Zealand, not far off, there are numerous remains of gigantic wingless birds, represented at present by smaller wingless birds of very similar habits. In both cases the number and variety of the extinct species is considerable, and the giants must have continued very nearly to our own times.

Besides the bones of birds, their footprints are sometimes retained when they have walked over mud in a state favorable for preserving markings made upon it. We thus learn that in very ancient, if not the oldest, periods of our earth's history, birds of gigantic dimensions, and many of smaller size, have lived in Europe and in North America, or rather, perhaps, in islands in a northern archipelago, whose shores, after many alternations,—after being buried deep under water and lifted high into air,—have at last settled for the present into the sandstones of Cheshire and Warwickshire and corresponding beds in Germany and North America.

Reptiles are, in their mode of living, intermediate between quadrupeds and fishes. Cold-blooded, or, in other words, needing only a slow aeration of the blood, they can exist for some time without taking in fresh breath; and some of them are so contrived as to breathe, as fishes do, by exposing the blood to aerated water in gills. There are many varieties of reptiles still living; their habits and ways of living are distinct from those of higher animals, and they include inhabitants of land and water.

Extinct reptiles are exceedingly numerous, and include varieties quite unknown in the living state. Thus, there are flying species found fossil, and there are also some adapted to reside permanently in the sea. Others again there are exceedingly remarkable in structure, and very characteristic of certain volumes of the Stone Library.

Of all the extinct reptiles, perhaps the most different from any animal now living were the lofty giants of the forest and tenants of the air: the latter, indeed, vampire-like, darkened the sky with their wide outspread wings. Some of the former were not only as bulky as the elephant, although with a more elongated body and a crocodilian head, but they stood erect on legs far higher in proportion than those of any existing reptile. We are in the habit of regarding all reptiles as creeping, or moving with the body almost touching the ground; but in these creatures we have some varieties, of portentous bulk, walking over the earth like veritable lords of creation,—some feeding on trees, and others preying on the smaller reptiles and other animals of their time. Associated with them were crocodiles, and probably lizards, like those still living.

But these singular and eccentric, perhaps repulsive, animals, which seem to have been the principal inhabitants of the land of their time, are neither the oldest, nor are they the most curiously strange, examples of creative power in this department of the animal kingdom. During the deposit of the beds of sandstone now quarried at Liverpool, there lived on the land then existing in the neighborhood a varied group of gigantic frog-like reptiles, whose fore limbs were small, but the hinder paws of such dimensions as to leave prints in the sand occupying nearly a square foot of surface each. The head was large, broad, and flat, and almost like that of the crocodile, but intermediate between it and the frog. Probably about the same time, in the opposite hemisphere, there were creatures nearly as large, approaching the turtles more than the frogs in their structure, but real quadrupeds,—walkers, that is, on four equal legs,— and true reptiles, but by no means creeping things.

It must not be supposed that because in this outline mention is made only of the more singular and less familiar forms, there were no others living, and no repetition, under various conditions, of the general types of structure. Very few fossils are found in those sandstones in which have been retained the footprints that are so remarkable; but other footprints, both of smaller lizard-like reptiles and of birds, are there very common. Some of these markings may have belonged to small quadrupeds; for we know there were some such animals in the rocks containing bones of the gigantic land-reptiles. The illustrations that teach us the nature of land-animals are very obscure and very few in number, and we must not judge of Nature by the amount of evidence hitherto collected in this inquiry.

At a comparatively early period in the earth's history, reptiles inhabited the air like birds, some of them only occasionally, perhaps, touching the earth. The bones of such creatures, as we have said, indicate dimensions of the largest size, as compared with winged birds adapted for flight. The greatest width across the expanded wing-membrane, from tip to tip, amounts, in some cases, to more than twenty feet, and the head was exceedingly large and long in proportion to the body. No remains of these creatures have been found in the sandstones with the footmarks just alluded to; but they are common in all newer deposits as far as the chalk. They seem to have been able to swim, and perhaps to dive; and they were certainly reptiles of prey.

In addition to the land and air species, we also find fossil a considerable and interesting group of marine reptiles. These, too, were some of them very gigantic, approaching even the whales in this respect, while there is every probability that they were much more fierce. Unlike the ordinary hard coat of mail that we find covering most known reptiles, and that appears also to have belonged to those in a fossil state, the marine species were soft-skinned, and exhibit strength rather for attack than defence. There are two principal groups, one approaching much more nearly to the true fishes than the other. The one well known as the *Ichthyosaur*, or fish-lizard, has been handed down to us in unusual perfection, many complete skeletons having been worked out of their stony beds, and numerous indications given even of the skin and the contents of the stomach.

The *Plesiosaur*, although more nearly a lizard, as its name implies, would seem to have been even less like any existing animal than its companion. It has been compared to a serpent in a turtle's shell; but in truth, though the neck was exceedingly long and the head that of a lizard, the body was smooth and naked, the tail not very long, and the extremities like the paddles of a whale. Some of the specimens seem to indicate an animal as much as thirty feet long, and the entire and undisturbed skeletons of many individuals, of various sizes and different proportions, are to be found in museums.

At present almost all the common fishes are provided with moderately hard complete skeletons, and are covered with scales usually small and thin. Most of the fish whose remains are found fossil are, however, remarkable for having had cartilaginous instead of bony skeletons. They were enclosed in a bony box, coated with enamel, by means of which the whole animal was defended against powerful enemies. Few fishes of this kind have been found in modern waters; but the "bony pike" of the North American lakes and rivers is a fair illustration of these knights of ancient times. The fishes whose remains are found fossil offer nothing remarkable in regard to size, many existing species being larger than any known extinct kinds. But in strangeness of form, among those enclosed in a coat of mail, the oldest species have hardly since been rivalled. The bony plates are very large, and their shapes such as accurately to adapt them to enclose the small body of the animal between back-plate and breast-plate. One kind, called *Pterichthys* (the wing-fish), had strong spines, like arms, placed near the head, and a very curious tail, tapering and flattened, almost like that of a beaver. The head was defended by a kind of helmet joining on to the back.

Exceedingly abundant in the old rocks, these fishes seem gradually to have become fewer and less important, being replaced latterly by the scale-covered fish of modern times. Sharks and Rays, however, seem always to have existed, and were generally common. They left behind them not only teeth, but bony and enamelled spines, and even scales,—these being more permanent than modern scales, though often quite detached, and never connecting into complete armor.

There are several curious animals now living, large and strong enough to prey even upon fish, but belonging to a group whose nervous structure places them in a lower position in the series of animals. The cuttle-fish, of which there are many kinds round our own shores and in the Mediterranean, often attain a very large size. Some of them possess, when living, a curious oval flattened plate, called (not very improperly) "the bone," which is constantly found washed up on the sea-shore, quite detached from the animal. Many of them have a black fluid, which they are able to throw out and thereby darken the water when they wish either to escape or confuse their prey.

The Nautilus occupies a shell divided into many small compartments, each of which is pierced with a hole of moderate size, and all of which are crossed by a tube. The animal belonging to this shell is a kind of cuttle-fish, and the whole shell serves as a float to the creature, which inhabits only the outermost chamber, the rest being full of air.

It is not a little interesting to find that, of animals covered with shells, these cuttle-fish seem to have been at all times the most characteristic. They have perhaps been more readily preserved than others, owing to various causes; but, at any rate, it is certain that, in the older rocks, shells built upon a principle almost the same as that of the nautilus are so incredibly abundant and so wonderfully varied as to make it certain that their owners played a very important part in their day. Whether they were accompanied by the commoner kind of shells, which have not been preserved, or whether the conditions of deposit were unfavorable for these latter, we cannot now tell. The geological record is imperfect. The illustrations of particular kinds of animals are numerous and minute, while there are few indications of the existence of the others. The *Ammonites* of geologists include a wonderful variety of curious shells, nearly resembling the nautilus in having a multitude of chambers. They have been found of all sizes, from a coach-wheel down to a pin's head; and where the ordinary forms are absent, there are other shells evidently of the same kind, and differing only in matters of detail. So also the *Belemnite*,—the hard part or bone of another extinct species of cuttle-fish,—though very different from the corresponding part of known living specimens, evidently answered a similar purpose. It is therefore clear that these curious and, for the most part, powerful representatives of a class of animals which we now think very little of, and of which we speak slightingly,—identifying them with the snails, oysters, and limpets,—really at one time played a part hardly subordinate to fishes, being quite as active and perhaps almost as intelligent. Certainly no one now can watch them in the sea, and notice their restless activity,—their long arms covered with suckers, their large bright eyes always on the look-out, their powerful jaws, and perfect means of helping themselves and supplying every important want,—without feeling satisfied that they are well able to perform their part in Nature.

Shells, being very easily preserved among the sand and other material at the bottom of the sea or near a shore, are naturally among the most common of all Organic Remains. They also, and for the same reason, speak most distinctly as to the fact that the animals now living on our shores and in the sea are either not the actual descendants of the former inhabitants, or, if they are, are so much altered by time and circumstance as not to show any family resemblance. They resemble each other, in fact, only in the way that the shells of the British shores resemble those of the Indian Archipelago. Both series evidently served the same purpose,—that of sheltering the animal; but they are provided with different contrivances, and are often built up in a different manner, because the circumstances of existence are exceedingly distinct.

Each group of deposits presents its own group of shells, just as each principal district of the earth has its characteristic species. In each case a few of the species range very widely; but the bulk are possessed of some marked peculiarities, and cannot be removed without either losing these or dying.

What we have here said of shells applies equally well to all other animals, and even to all vegetable productions; and in proportion as they range widely now over the earth's surface, so do they seem to have extended far back in time, while the kinds that are limited in space are very local. The variety of forms in these lower animals is now very great, and has been in old time much greater; but still there are certain general principles and laws that seem to have governed them always; and these are so evidently related to the fitness of each created being for the time and place of its existence, that we learn to trust implicitly to such relations, and assume the conditions of life from the animal, or the structure of the living being from known conditions of existence, without fearing the possibility of error.

When, then, we find in almost all deposits, whether of limestone, sandstone, or clay, or any mixture of the three, the remains of species of animals once inhabiting the sea, preserved without injury, and often very plentiful,—and when we discover that each group of deposits is, on the whole, characterized by some special assemblage of animal or vegetable remains peculiar to itself, and nowhere exactly repeated,—though we must suppose similar states of climate and temperature to have been often repeated,—geologists deduce one of those broad generalizations sometimes called Laws of Nature. The law thus discovered being in perfect harmony with all that is now known of the distribution of life, we may with greater reason accept it and employ it in further inquiries.

From the study and application of this law, very large and important natural-history results have been obtained. Learning first by careful observation the various remains most abundant and most characteristic of the different deposits of one country, and working them into a regular series, these have been compared with corresponding series from another country adjacent. From this comparison, bearing in mind the difference of mineral character, the relative age of the two deposits has been determined; and, in some cases, independent evidence has confirmed the decision thus made. With the peculiar fossils of a deposit are always mixed up a number that are common to other deposits, above or below; but on the whole, as we have said, there is a nucleus that, with a little attention and study, may be recognized with much certainty. Stated in other words, this means that *fossils are characteristic of formations.*

It is a fact, settled by observation, that fossils may safely be used to identify such deposits as were made in various places nearly at the same time. In this way also it has been found possible to prepare geological maps for whole continents, that shall communicate a large amount of truth and not much chance of serious error,—the relative position of all principal beds being made out by the comparison of the fossils found in them.

All kinds of fossils are useful for these purposes; but it will necessarily happen that the remains most easily recognized and least easily injured—those most abundant and most complete in themselves, and not the rarest or the most abnormal—will be the most generally useful. Thus, sea-shells, star-fishes, sea-eggs, and sea-urchins, crabs and other crustaceans, corals, and—when the microscope is at hand—those minute specks, too small to be crushed and too delicate to be destroyed, called *Foraminifera*, are all extremely useful, and often far more so than strange and quaint fishes, reptiles, birds, and quadrupeds. All these are valuable when in sufficient abundance; but number and variety are more important than size and unfamiliar structure.

The pre-Adamite world includes, then, a long series of

creations of beings, each series adapted to the exigencies of its own day. If, as we suppose from the study of fossils, there were once warm, swampy islands in these latitudes, instead of a large continent, we might have in our temperate zone a growth of tapirs, antelopes, and other animals fitted for the climate,—together with monkeys, snakes, and vultures. If, on the contrary, the ice reached far down from the Poles towards Southern Europe, and the climate was less genial, there was a corresponding supply of bears and the larger quadrupeds, adapted to exposure by warm coats of fur, and still finding sufficient food in the twigs of trees. If, again, there was deep water as now in the mid-Atlantic, abundant supplies of minute foraminiferous shells like those in the chalk covered the ocean-floor; while if the water were more shallow, perchance the remains of sharks and other strange marine creatures might be accumulated, together with a rich harvest of shells and shoal-animals. Or, lastly, if a river had emptied itself in the neighborhood, there would be marks of fresh water and the remains of land vegetation, insects, and land-animals alone, or mixed with marine remains. All the peculiarities of deposit would be marked, and most of them could be discovered, by the nature of the organic remains.

No one who has not examined for himself can conceive the vast extent—the incredible wealth and profusion—of Nature in this perpetual production of new forms and structures from time to time, as circumstances have changed throughout the world's history. Of all these a multitude of examples, no doubt, remains; but what are they in proportion to the number that is lost? We grope about in the dark, picking up here a little and there a little; but we can never hope to remove and bring to light all that is left, and there must remain to the last, in the great burying-place of Nature, a far larger series than the most searching investigation of man will ever bring to light. Could we even attain to a complete knowledge of organic remains, we should have made but one step, and that an imperfect and incomplete step, towards an acquaintance with the life that has passed away; for there still must remain large gaps to be supplied of such animals as pass out of existence and leave no durable skeleton or hard part capable of conservation.

We have already alluded to this subject in a previous page as illustrating what has been well called "the imperfection of the geologic record." It is right that the young geologist should know the exact nature and value of the weapons and instruments put into his hand, and for this purpose the limits of the evidence yielded by fossils must be learnt, as well as the extent of that evidence. There is amply sufficient positive knowledge to occupy all our thoughts, and quite enough gaps left to teach caution and humility.

# PART V.
## TREASURES in the GREAT STONE BOOK

# THE GREAT STONE BOOK

## Part V.

## Chapter the Fifteenth.

### GLITTERING TREASURES OF THE EARTH.

The surface of the earth, the air, and the shores and depths of the ocean, afford innumerable objects of beauty and interest. But the earth also contains within its bosom marvellous and beautiful things, belonging to that kingdom of nature in which life plays no part, and possessing even a more tangible and direct value than the others. The earth yields its rich treasures of minerals, metals, and precious stones, serving as convenient representatives of money and property; and these, when their beauty of appearance in any way corresponds with the difficulty of obtaining them, are objects of ambition to great potentates, as well as the admiration of all classes, including among their votaries the poet and the artist, the man of science and the man of fashion, the most civilized races and the uncultivated savage.

Of these objects, let us confine our attention here to one group. Let us talk of gems, precious stones, and jewels, leaving the metals, the many valuable minerals, that are less sightly than gems, and the curious fossils, buried records of former states of existence. Let us consider those stones selected as ornaments of the crown, the cabinet, and the toilet, the gems that glitter before our eyes on gala-days, or are seen in museums and in the shops of the jewellers.

There is great variety in the literature of gems. There is the natural history, and what we may call the personal history, the investigation of the optical properties, the story of the mechanical preparation, of the commercial use, and of the money value. There is the chemistry and the geography, the science and the art, the religion and the mysticism, of jewels: each might serve as the heading of a chapter; but we will endeavor to give an idea of the whole subject, without introducing systematic divisions.

Of all gems the DIAMOND is the recognized queen, the most beautiful, the most valuable, the most durable, and the most useful; the hardest, though capable of being split; the symbol of justice, innocence, constancy, faith, and strength. According to a Jewish tradition, the diamond in the breastplate of Aaron became dark and dim when any person justly accused of a crime appeared before him, and blazed more brightly when the accusation was void of foundation. In the possession of any one the diamond was supposed, in former times, to mark the approach of poison by a damp exudation, and to be a sure defence against plagues and sorcery. Taken internally, it was believed to be itself a poison.

No history dates back to the period at which diamonds were first discovered; but we are told on classical authority that a boy, a native of Crete, bearing the name afterwards given to this precious gem, was one of the attendants of the infant Jupiter in his cradle. The other attendants being promoted to be constellations, Diamond was transformed into the hardest and most brilliant substance in nature. In Hindu mythology the diamond plays an important part.

Diamonds are singularly associated with gold in the earth, but all that come into the market as gems have been obtained either from India or Brazil. The account in the "Arabian Nights" of Sinbad the Sailor obtaining diamonds by fishing for them with pieces of raw meat is repeated as a fact of Indian statistics by the old Venetian traveller Marco Polo. "The persons," he says, "who are in quest of diamonds take their stand near the mouth of a certain cavern, and from thence cast down several pieces of flesh, which the eagles and storks pursue into the valleys and carry off with them to the tops of the rocks. Thither the men immediately ascend, and, recovering the pieces of meat, frequently find diamonds adhering to them." The more ordinary mode of obtaining them at present is by washing away the earth and stones from the gravel in which they are found.

The first Brazilian diamonds were discovered by accident just a century and a quarter ago. They also are found in the surface-gravel, from which they are separated by water in nearly the same manner as in India. Upwards of seventy pounds' weight of these valuable jewels were collected and brought over to Europe in one year, shortly after the discovery of the deposit; and it is estimated that some two tons' weight, valued at sixteen millions sterling, had been obtained from the South American mines up to the year 1850. So abundantly are they there distributed that they have been picked up with vegetable-roots in gardens, the stones in the roads have contained them, and the fowls have swallowed them to assist digestion.

Marvellous as it may seem, diamond is but coal in a crystalline form, and is hardly even so pure as some kinds of anthracite, or stone coal, found in Wales. Like coal, the diamond burns, or combines with oxygen, though only at a very high temperature, and the whole substance then disappears in carbonic acid gas. Unlike coal, however, diamonds are usually transparent, possessing a peculiar lustre, hence called *adamantine*, and reflecting light from their inner surface. The light entering a diamond is bent more than in passing into any other substance in nature. Diamond is electric, even when rough, and possesses phosphoric and luminous properties after being exposed to the sun for some time. It is generally of crystalline form, but coated over in the mine by a thick crust, exceedingly hard. Still, even the children, in countries where they abound, can generally detect the valuable gems in their concealment.

Diamonds require very careful cutting, so as to diminish their weight as little as possible consistently with insuring the greatest amount of internal reflecting surface belonging to their form. Their value as gems depends greatly on the cutting, and this, of course, to some extent, on the original shape. What are technically called "brilliants" are those stones that can be cut without serious loss into the form of two pyramids placed base to base. Of these pyramids a slice of the one intended to be presented to the eye is cut off, while the other, serving to reflect light from its internal surface, although also flattened slightly, is much the more nearly pointed of the two. In fine brilliants the upper pyramid has thirty-two facets, or sides, and the lower twenty-four. Nearly half the diamond is often wasted in cutting a brilliant; but without it a fine stone can hardly be considered as presenting the real beauty that belongs to it. When, however, the form of the stone is such as not readily to admit of this treatment, only one pyramid is cut, and the base is imbedded in the setting, making what is called a *rose diamond*. When there is a double pyramid, the setting simply clasps the *girdle*, or junction of the bases of the two pyramids, and the two sets of faces are both exposed to the action of light. Besides these two kinds, some diamonds are cut flat, with irregular facets: these are called table diamonds, and their value, weight for weight, is very inferior to that of roses and brilliants.

Diamond-cutting is a business in the hands of Jews, and is chiefly carried on in Amsterdam, where, it is said, ten thousand persons are more or less dependent on it as an occupation. Owing to the extreme hardness of the stone, the only means of acting on it are by rubbing two faces of different diamonds together, or cutting the stone by a circular steel saw covered with diamond dust.

Diamonds are not always colorless, though many of those most highly valued are so. Some few that are known of fair size and clear distinct tints are even more costly than those of purest white. There is a difference in the estimate of color. Thus, the celebrated blue diamond of Mr. Hope, weighing one hundred and seventy-seven grains, and the green diamond of the crown of Saxony, the finest known colored specimens, are regarded as more valuable than if they were white. The yellow varieties, on the other hand, generally sell at lower prices than stones of equal weight without color.

The largest diamond known is an uncut stone belonging to the Rajah of Mattam, in Borneo. It weighs more than two ounces and a quarter troy, but would probably be very greatly reduced if properly cut. It is egg-shaped, and indented at the smaller end. The largest regularly cut diamond is a rose, and of yellowish tint: it weighs one hundred and thirty-nine and a half carats,* or nearly an ounce. The finest brilliant is the Pitt or Regent diamond, now in the French crown. It originally weighed four hundred and ten carats, but has been reduced to one hundred and thirty-seven by cutting, and was sold to the Regent of France for about one hundred thousand pounds. Our Koh-i-noor, now only one hundred and two carats, is believed to have been part of the largest real diamond recorded, the unbroken stone having weighed nine hundred carats. It is supposed that the great Russian diamond called the Orloff, now weighing one hundred and ninety-three carats, was originally another part of the same stone.

Diamonds are not always transparent, nor are they only valuable for ornamentation. A vast number are used for watches, and others for cutting glass. There is a ready demand for them to almost any extent; and, in spite of the large supply, the price is by no means falling.

---

* The carat is the weight used all over the world to estimate the diamond. It originated in India, and is equal to about three and one-sixth grains troy, six carats being nineteen grains troy.

Next to the diamond in value, in beauty, and in hardness, and in some cases rivalling or even excelling it in the two former properties, are the gems obtained from crystallized clay. Strange that coal and clay, the two least likely substances to possess any intimate relations with beauty and hardness, should, in their crystalline forms, excel all others in both these respects! Not more strange, however, than true.

Under the name of RUBY and SAPPHIRE the red and blue varieties of crystallized clay are well known to the world. They are almost all obtained from Pegu, Ava, and the island of Ceylon,—a singularly limited region for a mineral which one might expect would be widely distributed. Like the diamond, they are obtained by washing gravel, and all the varieties occur in the same district. These varieties include the Oriental sapphire, the Oriental ruby, the opalescent ruby, the star ruby, the green, yellow, and white sapphires, and the Oriental amethyst. Most of them are extremely rare, and all the finest specimens are believed to be still retained in the East. As, however, these stones of Eastern princes are rarely cut, and no doubt many of them would be found affected with flaws, their real money value, if in the market, would be very inferior to their estimated value.

There is a useful mineral of extreme hardness—the corundum of commerce, from which the hardest and finest emery is obtained—which is an imperfect and opaque crystallization, of the same origin as the ruby and sapphire. The gems themselves are clear, though rarely colorless. Small specimens are much less valuable in proportion than larger sizes, for they are far more abundant; but a perfect ruby of five carats is worth twice as much as a diamond of the same weight, and one of ten carats three times as much.

The ruby was called by the Greeks *anthrax*, or live coal, from its brilliant blood-red color and exquisite beauty, which, like the diamond, is rather improved than diminished when seen by artificial light. From the intense blaze of blood-red, the colors of the ruby pale down by admixtures of blue through rose-red to lilac. Exposed to the rays of the sun, or heated, the ruby, like the diamond, becomes phosphoric. In the Middle Ages it was believed to be an antidote to poison, to dispel bad dreams, and to warn its owner of misfortune by a darkening of its color until the danger was past.

There is a very celebrated ruby set under the back cross in the crown of England. It remains in its natural shape—that of a heart—and has received no polish. Its color is that of a Morella cherry, and it is semi-transparent. It was brought from Spain by Edward the Black Prince, and was afterwards worn by Henry the Fifth at Agincourt. Other rubies of very large size are recorded, but few of them are polished, and fewer still are cut.

The sapphire is an exquisite blue variety of ruby, soft, rich, velvety, and delicate in the extreme by day, but losing much beauty by artificial light, even sometimes changing its tint. Occasionally it sparkles with great vividness in the sun, as a star with distinct rays, but such stones are only semi-transparent. There is a violet variety, called by jewellers the Oriental amethyst. It is a gem of great rarity and beauty, and takes a very brilliant polish, owing to its extreme hardness.

Like the ruby, the sapphire was held by the ancients and during the Middle Ages in high honor. It was considered emblematic of purity. To look at one preserved the eyesight; placed on the brow, it stopped hæmorrhage. The powder of sapphire was a sovereign remedy against plague and poison, and if merely placed over the mouth of a phial containing a venomous insect, the insect died on the instant. It is a Jewish superstition that the first tables of the law given by God to Moses were of this stone. It is certain, at any rate, that both rubies and sapphires have long been employed in the East to engrave upon, notwithstanding their great hardness.

Who has not looked with admiration at the rich, soft, lively meadow-green of the EMERALD? It is a gem which, when pure, comes next in value to those hard, brilliant stones just described; but large specimens without flaw are really almost unknown. It loses nothing by exposure to artificial light.

The emerald is the lightest of all the clear valuable gems. It is soft, and is found in regular crystals, often with the rock in which it has been formed. These crystals are long, six-sided prisms, and, though formerly found in the East, are now met with only in Peru; and, indeed, it is only of late years that even this resource has been available. The largest stone on record was in the Great Exhibition of 1851, and weighed nearly nine ounces. It measured two inches in length, and two and a quarter inches across.

A singular superstition has at all times attached to

emerald-mines. From the age of Pliny, when the Scythians obtained these stones, to our own times, there is a belief that the mines are guarded by demons, griffins, and wicked spirits. The mine "Las Esmeraldas," in Peru, could not be visited by Mr. Stevenson, "owing to the superstitious dread of the natives, who assured me that it was enchanted, and guarded by a dragon, who poured forth thunder and lightning on those who dared to ascend the river" that led to the mine.

In the East, emeralds are admired for extent of surface rather than for beauty of any other kind, and vast multitudes were sent over at the time of the Great Exhibition in 1851, most of which were mere slices of crystals marked with many a flaw. Many of them were set as the ornaments of saddles and other horse and elephant trappings, and others were in jade boxes and cups of agate.

The emerald, like the gems already mentioned, has been regarded as possessing remarkable properties, restoring sight and memory, guarding from epilepsy, putting evil spirits to flight, and, if unable to do good, shivering into atoms; for, in the words of a great authority on these subjects, "Elle doit ou lever le mal ou céder comme s'avouant vaincue par le plus fort dans le combat qu'elle rend."* That is, it ought either to remove the evil or acknowledge itself vanquished. The emerald taught the knowledge of secrets, it bestowed eloquence,

---

* Boetius de Boot. Traité des Pierreries, l. ii. ch. 53, p. 253.

and it increased wealth. Even more than this, we have the poet's warrant that

> It is a gem which hath the power to show
> If plighted lovers keep their faith or no:
> If faithful, it is like the leaves of spring;
> If faithless, like those leaves when withering.
>
> L. E. L.

Such are the recorded qualities of this beautiful gem: we may worship the excellence of the diamond, and wonder at the deep mystery of the ruby or the cold brilliancy of the sapphire, but no one can fail to love the soft beauty of the emerald.

BERYL is a mineral much more commonly found impure and cloudy than capable of use as a gem. When in the latter state, it is of a transparent bluish-green or sea-green color, passing into blue by many shades. It is hence called *aqua-marine*. It resembles in many respects the emerald, but is less valued. It is also more widely distributed. Formerly it was regarded as especially efficacious in liver-complaints, idleness, and stupidity.

The TOPAZ is a beautiful gem of bright citron, clear gold, or deep orange-yellow color, sometimes soft and satin-like, sometimes hard and clear. What is sometimes called the Oriental topaz is really a yellow sapphire; but the gems properly recognized under the name are mostly from Brazil, though also found in Saxony and elsewhere in Europe. They were much valued by the ancients, as well for medicinal purposes as for dispelling enchantments and calming frenzy; but they must have been especially useful if, as supposed, they strengthened the intellect, brightened the wit, and cured the bearer of cowardice.

Topaz is not a very valuable stone; but there are some varieties of color, such as the red, occasionally mistaken for ruby, and the blue, which are of great beauty and interest.

GARNETS are comparatively common stones, and are much used for ornamental purposes. They vary a good deal in composition and color, and the varieties are known by many names. The finest of all is the Sorian or Oriental garnet, called generally *carbuncle*. Its color is a rich blood-red, passing into violet, but acquiring an orange tinge by artificial light. Fine specimens might easily pass for rubies, if they were not readily distinguishable by their greatly inferior hardness. It is often cut in facets, and takes a high polish; and the resemblance to the ruby or sapphire group of gems is increased by an occasional six-rayed star seen in the paler and bluer specimens.

*Hyacinth* is a beautiful orange or scarlet garnet found in Brazil; but it is rare. It is nearly allied to *Zircon*, which has a deep honey tint. All these stones are comparatively soft, and they are less used now than formerly. As a group, they were once valued as a protection against the plague. They are comparatively inexpensive jewels in rings and bracelets.

MOON-STONE, *sun-stone*, *amazon-stone*, and other crystalline varieties of the mineral called felspar, deserve notice as gems which occasionally possess a considerable value. The moon-stone is translucent and opaline, sun-stone contains spangles of mica which look yellow like gold in some lights, and amazon-stone is a fine green crystal with a beautiful play of colors. All have a peculiar silky appearance, and are much harder than the somewhat similar varieties of quartz minerals, which we next allude to.

The group of quartz gems includes many varieties of color, and stones of various degrees of value and interest. Pure QUARTZ, or ROCK CRYSTAL, is rather used to look *through* than to look *at*, although not unknown as an ornament. The lenses of spectacles are made of it, and it is cut into various fanciful forms. Round globes of crystal are the magic spheres in which some gifted seers can learn what is doing at distant spots, and perceive events that have long passed away, as if still in progress. They are curiously bound up with the superstitions of the ancient and modern Egyptians. Tinged with color, but still clear, the same mineral is called by many names. A rose-colored variety resembles the ruby; a purple or violet kind is the *amethyst*. Tinged with brown and yellow, it becomes the *cairngorm* of Scotland. Of a blood or flesh-red color, passing into orange and yellow, it is known as *carnelian;* and a rich brown opaque quartz, glittering with golden spangles within its substance, is called *aventurine*. From its beauty and convenient hardness, carnelian and its varieties are much used by lapidaries, and are brought, either cut or uncut, from many parts of India, and from Arabia, as well as found in Europe.

*Jasper* and *blood-stone*, or *heliotrope*, consist of quartz colored in a more decided manner than the stones just mentioned,—the former being altogether opaque, and of a brilliant blood-red, while the latter is partially transparent, or translucent, spotted only with opaque red.

*Agate* may be best described as a mixture of almost all the different varieties of quartz above mentioned. It is partly transparent, partly opaque, and of various colors; often banded, but the bands broken and interrupted; and containing strange figures, representing moss, landscapes with ruins, and angular marks like fortifications, stars, and even human faces. Agates are found abundantly in Scotland, principally near Perth and Dunbar, but also on many parts of the coast of England, among the pebbles on the sea-shore. They are still more common at Oberstein, in the Palatinate, not far from the town of Bingen, on the Rhine; and multitudes come from Siberia, Ceylon, and India. From the latter locality especially are obtained the large plates of agate used for manufacturing snuff-boxes and other purposes, and also the pieces used for knife-handles.

The *onyx*, *sardonyx*, and *chalcedonyx* are banded agates of peculiar kind, and of considerable interest in the arts as having been selected for some of the masterpieces of engraving executed by the ancients and in the Middle Ages. Using the word *sard* as indicating the red or flesh-color of the carnelian, a sard with one layer or band of white is considered to be an onyx; but if there be two or more bands of different tints, the same name is still applied. The zones of color should be very distinct, separate, and strongly marked, and the colors themselves lively and bright. In the sardonyx there is a red zone, in addition to that which forms the true onyx, and the chalcedonyx is semi-transparent and milky.

In cutting the onyx, the figures are usually sculptured from the white portion, leaving the colored band as a background; and no little ingenuity is required to select the parts of the stone best adapted for the purpose of the artist. With three or four bands, a wonderful amount of variety may be obtained, so that the hair, beard, and drapery of figures are accurately represented. Fine antiques thus sculptured on the onyx are of extreme value, and the art of cutting was also carried on in perfection during the Middle Ages. The works of this kind are true cameos, and of late years they have been imitated by a similar but much easier process of cutting on certain sea-shells, also possessing bands of different color.

Besides cameos or raised figures cut on this class of stones by removing part of the upper belt or zone, other beautiful effects have been produced, such as sculpturing complete figures, taking advantage of the peculiarities of the specimens operated on, and still more frequently bold alto-relievos, and deep cuttings beneath the surface, the latter forming intaglios for seals and other purposes. It is impossible to over-estimate the ingenuity and high art exercised in these works; and the demand for them was at one time so great that onyxes became scarce. Few now carry on the art with success, and thus we must seek for the finest specimens among the antiques or mediæval specimens. One remarkable cameo was cut in the fifteenth century, representing the head of Dejanira, in which the different tints of the stone were made use of to represent, in their natural colors, the flesh and hair of

Dejanira and the lion's skin; while a red streak in the stone, which might otherwise have appeared as a flaw, was so cleverly taken advantage of for the inner side of the lion's skin that it gave it the appearance of having been recently flayed from the animal. It is especially this adaptation of the treatment of the subject to the peculiarities of the stone that characterizes the "glyptic" art as a department of sculpture. It is the department that treats in relief or intaglio these banded stones so capriciously moulded by Nature, taking advantage of their accidents of structure.

It is curious that while almost all other stones called "precious" were worn in former times as amulets, to ward off danger and mischief, and were valued greatly for such purposes, and while almost all the varieties of agate had special uses, the onyx was considered to excite spleen, melancholy, and mental disturbance in the wearer, especially when used as a neck-ornament. As, however, the ordinary agate was worn to calm pain and soothe the mind, and the mere *scent* of some varieties—a peculiarity difficult to ascertain the existence of—would turn away tempests, even arresting the impetuosity of torrents, the line of distinction must have been very nicely drawn. So influential were stones of this kind supposed to be, that the celebrated Milo of Crotona is said to have been indebted to a certain chalcedonyx that he wore for the execution of his feats of wonderful strength. Of the other stones, the beautiful heliotrope, or bloodstone, was thought to render the wearer invisible, while jasper would stop any excess of bleeding arising from natural causes.

All the minerals lately mentioned consist of quartz or

silica, combined, when colored, with a small quantity of metallic oxides and earthy minerals. Thus, the amethyst and other violet and blue colors are produced by manganese, and the rose tint is owing to the same metal. Almost all the reds are due to iron, and the yellow and green to very minute quantities of chrome, copper, or other metals. The brown tint of the cairngorm is the result of a little bitumen.

It is astonishing to consider how very small a quantity of foreign material will sometimes alter the character and appearance of crystals. Thus, the cat's-eye is a gem of greenish tint, milky and opal-like. When cut in a certain way, it presents a floating white band of light, and certain specimens emit one or more brilliant rays, colored or colorless, issuing apparently from one point, and extending to the extremity of the stone. Compared with one of those balls of crystals sometimes cut into the same form, or with the lens of a pair of pebble spectacles, it is hardly possible to imagine that there is so little difference as really exists between the two minerals in their chemical composition. In point of fact, the presence within the crystal of a few delicate threads of white asbestos seems to produce all the modifications, except that of color; and the cause of the color itself is owing to some substance the quantity of which is too small to enable chemists to determine its nature. Certainly the method of small doses, as advocated by homœopathists, is not without a certain analogy in Nature; and doses too small to be appreciated by mortal chemistry are sufficient, sometimes, to produce results on minerals rather startling in their magnitude.

There is one fact with regard to specimens of quartz —or crystals, as they are often called—which is very curious and interesting. Small cavities not unfrequently occur within them, sometimes empty, but often filled with fluid. By exposure to cold, this fluid may be frozen, and very often a slight increase of temperature converts it into a transparent vapor; while by optical methods of examination employed under the microscope, the properties of the fluid can occasionally be detected. Indeed, the cavities have been so large that the fluid could be extracted in sufficient quantity for examination. It might be expected that some new element or compound would be thus obtained,—some secret of Nature's laboratory,—some substance from the interior of the earth, only thus brought within our knowledge, locked up in one of the hard crystalline minerals elaborated far beneath, out of our sight. No such result is obtained, and no such mystery laid bare; for we find almost all the cavities in question to be occupied by water, mixed only with some common salt or acid, held in solution. Vapor of water, then, must be contained in rocks during the whole period of their formation in the earth, much in the same state of admixture in which we know that it is present in the atmosphere to form clouds. Thus these wonders of Nature and treasures of art are the result of some process only the more wonderful because it is so extremely simple, being one by whose agency ordinary familiar substances are worked up, together with water, under certain conditions of heat, bringing about in this way the magic of our most varied and beautiful gems.

Mixed with water in a different way,—the water distributed in every part, and not collected in cavities,—the same mineral, quartz or silica, becomes that very curious and fantastic stone, the opal. The proper color of this gem is a peculiar pearl-gray, showing a fluctuating pale red or wine-yellow tint when seen between the eye and the light. With reflected light, it presents all the colors of the rainbow, showing a flame-red, violet, purple, blue, emerald-green, and golden yellow. The rays of light and color shoot forth from a fine opal (noble opal, in technical language) with the most vivid effulgence; and the more flaws it contains the more does it reflect, and the greater value is attached to it. In some rare cases opals have been found nearly black, but glowing like a fine ruby. Other opals are spangled, and sometimes not more than one color is seen. In all cases, however, the foundation of the stone, independent of the color, which is believed to be a mere optical effect, consists of a peculiar milky translucent mass, characteristic of the gem.

Opals are very rarely found of large size, the dimensions of a hazel-nut or walnut being seldom exceeded. They are never cut in facets, and are generally set surrounded by brilliants, whose bright, dazzling reflections contrast well with the calm, moon-like beauty and rich, soft tints of the central stone. Fine opals are of great value, being considered only next to the diamond. They are softer than crystal, and require extreme care in cutting. They generally consist of about ninety per cent. silica and ten per cent. water, and are very irregular in texture and hardness. There are many varieties, all inferior in value to the noble opal, known by various names. *Fire opal, hydrophane, cachalong,* may be mentioned as among these.

TURQUOISE is a mineral of great beauty, taking rank as a gem, though not crystalline, and always nearly opaque. It is of a fine azure blue or bluish-green color, slightly transparent at the edges, and hard enough to admit of a good polish. It is found in the East, and (of late years at least) chiefly in Arabia and Persia, whence considerable numbers have been obtained. It owes its color to the presence of copper, and was formerly more commonly used and more valued than at present. A superstition was connected with it, as with so many gems, and the possession of this stone, if given to the wearer,—not purchased,—was believed to ward off any threatening danger. Thus, we read in Donne,—

> " As a compassionate turkois that doth tell,
> By looking pale, the wearer is not well."

And again, in the play of "Sejanus," by Ben Jonson,—

> " Observe him as his watch observes his clock,
> And, true as turkois in the dear lord's ring,
> Look well or ill with him."

This stone was also believed to prevent and relieve headaches and appease hatred.

There are some other substances regarded as gems, which though originating with the animal strictly belong to the mineral kingdom; and others, again, which have the same relation to the vegetable world. Pearls are among the former, and amber is an example of the latter. Coral is a more decided animal product.

PEARLS, as all know, are obtained from the insides of certain sea-shells, and they appear to be the result of an effort of the animal inhabitant and constructor of the shell either to repair an injury or to cover up a foreign body which has been introduced. They are, however, mineral secretions, and, once deposited, the constructor would seem to have nothing more to do with them, as they play no part in the organization of the healthy animal. They are obtained both from the Eastern and Western hemispheres, and from shells varying a good deal in their form and structure,—generally, however, in those having two valves. The number of small pearls obtained and sent into the market is exceedingly great, but specimens of any considerable dimensions are as rare as they are valuable. Those of good round form and pure clear color are the best: the pear-shaped are the largest. Pearls do not bear exposure to damp nor to animal exhalations. They should thus be kept dry, and only worn on special occasions.

AMBER is a fossil resin, originally the secreted juice of some extinct species of pine, and it often contains, embalmed within it, remains of insects and even the most delicate parts of flowers. Its exquisite yellow color and beautiful transparency, together with its delicate perfume and some other properties, have caused it to be regarded as a gem. It is found in nodules or lumps on the sea-shore, chiefly in Northern Europe, or in clay-pits at various depths, with lignite and gravel. The specimens containing insects, &c. are highly valued as curiosities, but not as precious stones. Amber was formerly much more in use as a gem than it is now, and in the form of beads, bracelets, and necklaces, it was a common ornament of the person in England in the time of Shakspeare. It is not now altogether out of fashion, and its lightness and elegant simplicity are worthy of some attention. Medicinal properties were at one time attributed to it, and it is still used for perfumes and some medical compounds; but there is no difficulty in manufacturing it artificially.

CORAL, if not a gem, ranks with the class of ornamental minerals we are now considering. It is not, however, like the pearl, an extraneous secretion, unnecessary and useless to the animal that constructs it, but the skeleton or stony framework of the animal itself. The only kind of coral of important value is that beautiful red variety fished up in the Mediterranean. This has been regarded as a talisman against enchantments, witchcraft, venom, the assaults of the devil, thunder, and marine tempests. Ten grains of it, we are told, if given to an infant in its mother's milk, provided it be a first child and this its first food, will preserve it from epileptic and other fits for the whole of its life. Another great authority in matters of this kind believes that coral worn by a healthy man will be of a handsomer and more lively red than if worn by a woman, and that it becomes pale and livid if worn by one who is ill and in danger of death. We can only say with regard to this that we have not ourselves tried the experiment, and that perhaps, like many other experiments, it would succeed only in the hands of the faithful.

There are many curious superstitions and fancies concerning precious stones, besides those we have referred to; and one of them, which, as it is elegant and fanciful in its absurdity, is perhaps worthy of mention in this place, includes almost the whole group of gems used for ornament. It is a Polish idea that every human being is born under the influence of some destiny, that the month of his nativity has a mysterious connection with this, and that when it is desired to make a present to one greatly valued and loved, a ring should be offered containing a gem expressing some such quality as the destiny would indicate. Each precious stone thus has reference to some particular month; and the following list is copied from a memorandum drawn up by a Pole many years ago :—

*January.*—Hyacinth or garnet. Constancy and fidelity in every engagement.

*February.*—Amethyst. Preserves the wearer from strong passions, and insures peace of mind.

*March.*—Bloodstone. Courage and success in dangers and hazardous enterprises.

*April.*—Sapphire or diamond. Repentance and innocence.

*May.*—Emerald. Success in love.

*June.*—Agate. Long life and health.

*July.*—Carnelian and Ruby. Forgetfulness, or cure of evils springing from friendship or love.

*August.*—Sardonyx. Conjugal fidelity.

*September.*—Chrysolite. Preserves from or cures folly.

*October.*—Aqua-marine or Opal. Misfortune and hope.

*November.*—Topaz. Fidelity and friendship.

*December.*—Turquoise or Malachite. Brilliant success and happiness in every circumstance of life.

Another curious superstition concerning gems is that the twelve apostles were symbolized, each under some one. The list is curious; but one can hardly see the meaning of the allusions. It is as follows:—

St. Peter ............................Jasper.
St. Andrew ........................Sapphire.
St. James ..........................Chalcedony.
St. John ............................Emerald.
St. Philip ..........................Sardonyx.
St. Bartholomew ................Carnelian.
St. Matthew......................Chrysolite.
St. Thomas........................Beryl.
St. Thaddeus .....................Chrysoprase.
St. James the Less ...............Topaz.
St. Simeon ........................Hyacinth.
St. Matthias .....................Amethyst.

The stones in this list are sometimes called the Apostle Gems.

*Jet* can hardly be called a gem or precious stone, but, with *malachite, lapis lazuli, jade,* and some other stony minerals, it hovers on the confines of this costly series of natural treasures. Many highly ornamental and beautiful varieties of stones, common enough in other forms, might readily be quoted as coming under the same category, but we must not detain the reader longer by a mere enumeration.

We have now gone through the list of gems or precious stones, elaborated and lying buried in various parts of the earth, and from time to time extracted for the use of man. With few exceptions, all these numerous and varied substances are objects of beauty and luxury, and cannot be regarded in any sense as objects of necessity, or even of great use. We could certainly do without any one of them, and if we had them not we should hardly feel the want. What lesson ought we to draw from this lavish and elaborate ornamentation even of those stones that are mixed up with the dust under our feet? Whence and why this marvellous beauty in things that under ordinary circumstances are not seen by mortal eye or come within mortal ken? It is only when by accident or design some one having wealth, the result of spare and accumulated labor, is enabled to bestow a part of it in rewarding those who discover or render available these hidden treasures, that their beauty is seen and their value recognized, and this notwithstanding that they possess properties of importance distinguishing them from other minerals.

It is no more a right thing puritanically to despise and neglect these gems than it is to refuse to admire flowers, to profess to despise beauty, or to shut our eyes to other clear purposes of nature and nature's God everywhere expressed. We live in a world of beauty; the green carpet of verdure is beautiful, the flower brightening the verdure is beautiful, the butterfly sipping the nectar of the flower is beautiful, the bird pursuing the insect is beautiful, and the blue sky and gorgeous clouds in the heavens are also beautiful. All these are for our use and enjoyment, and it is our duty to study them in order that we may enjoy them. And can it be that those other more durable treasures buried in the earth, distributed only sparingly and found only when looked for properly,—can it be that these were meant to be neglected and despised? Surely such an assumption is contrary to the whole course of nature and the spirit and sentiment of creation.

## Chapter the Sixteenth.

### SOURCES OF METALLIC WEALTH.

The metals, a familiar group of natural substances, having peculiar properties, are obtainable either directly from the earth in what is called a *native* state, or by the aid of chemistry from certain stony minerals, some resembling metals in appearance, others stones in the ordinary sense of the term, with no metallic appearance whatever. Minerals thus yielding metals are called *ores*. Several of the metals are among the most valuable of all natural substances, even in the state in which they are found: others are not less valuable, but in an economic sense only, not being so costly, their value consisting in the largeness of the quantity used, or the amount of labor bestowed in their manipulation. The former are sometimes called noble metals, and they have certain peculiar properties by which they may be recognized. The latter are more homely and plebeian, but they form the main strength of the group.

Of the noble metals, some, such as gold, platinum, and a few others, exist generally in the earth in the metallic state, and these do not tarnish by exposure to ordinary atmospheric influences. They are, for the most part, comparatively rare, and some of them are only known in minute quantities in one or two localities.

Silver and mercury, two other noble metals, are not commonly found pure and alone, being generally mixed with sulphur, or existing in an earthy state as *oxide*. They more readily alter on exposure to the air, and are more common and less valuable, than the others. There are thus two groups.

GOLD is the first of metals, as the diamond is the first of gems; but, whereas the diamond is the rare and exceptional form of coal, a substance infinitely common, gold is very widely spread in the earth, the quantity being small, but the metal always in its true metallic form. Practically, it is not known in nature in any other form. Mixed mechanically with iron, and slate, and quartz rock, or mixed sometimes very intimately, but still not otherwise than mechanically, with other metals, gold is always gold; it is never a mere ore in the ordinary sense of the term.

Australia and California now, South America and Mexico in former times, India and the East at all times, have yielded supplies of this most durable and most valuable metal. Gold, when found, is dug out of the earth much in the way that the diamond and the ruby are. It lies generally mixed up with a quantity of loose stones and rubbish, often at some depth below the surface. It is easily recognized by its color and weight, qualities which together may always decide the question as to its value.

Gold is, indeed, the king of metals. It represents in its own person all the important properties of metals, and can be conveniently made the standard of value for all. When not pure in its native state, it is only mixed with other metals and buried in and obscured by earthy and stony rubbish, from which it is extracted by washing. It is often found in particles so minute as scarcely to be visible to the naked eye; but this fine dust, being pure, is collected easily enough by simple processes. Elsewhere rounded grains (*pepitas*, the Spaniards call them) of sensible magnitude are found, few grains being so large as the head of a small pin. Less frequently it is in flat plates or spangles, very thin, but not so small, and sometimes there are small crystals. It would take a thousand of some of these spangles to make the weight of a grain. Some are larger. Then come the larger, rarer, and more highly valued nuggets, lumps of solid gold, rich, of bright yellow color, and known at once by their great weight, compared with their size. They vary in size from that of a pea to masses worth thousands of pounds sterling. These rare prizes in the great lottery of gold-mining are fallen upon by the merest accident. From the nature of the case, knowledge and experience are of little value in gold-finding, as the metal is not obtained from the vein where it was formed, but from some old river-bed or hollow into which it has been drifted after being transported by water.

Although gold has been profitably obtained in large quantities from very few localities at one time, there is reason to know that such an influx as has deluged the civilized world within the last twenty years is not an event unparalleled in history. No doubt, in former times a smaller quantity entering Europe than has lately been sent would have produced a larger result, for the quantity and value of things represented by coin were then much smaller, and communication much less rapid and perfect. But that two or three times in the world's history gold has poured in unexpectedly, doubling the supply previously existing, and disturbing the equilibrium of prices, is unquestionable. Such influx has one effect, not pleasant, perhaps, but not on the whole unwholesome: it reduces the value of realized property as compared with the value of labor. Wages become higher, and payment for labor of all kinds also becomes higher, because, so many more ounces of gold being in the market, one ounce will no longer purchase so much food as before, and labor must have food. On the other hand, the interest of accumulated money does not increase, but rather tends to diminish. Thus, persons whose income is derived from the interest of accumulated capital are directly injured by gold discoveries. Those whose income arises from land suffer less, as the rent of land will always have reference to the price of food.

Gold is spread very widely over the earth, and is now abundant in Australia, Africa, South America, the countries on the Pacific slopes of the Rocky Mountains, and Siberia, whence the main supply of the world is obtained at present. A considerable quantity has always been added from other districts, and of late years the number of these has increased. The British possessions of North America and New Zealand, most of the rivers of Eastern Europe, especially those coming from the Carpathian Mountains, and the rivers of Spain and Portugal, and, indeed, almost all important rivers throughout the world, have yielded indications of this wealth. Most mountain-districts, even those of the British Islands, are also provided. England, Ireland, and Scotland have all in turn been gold-producing countries. Wales is so now.

Gold in a native state, visible and tangible, is, then, one of the most widely spread of all substances upon the earth. That it is one of the most beautiful and most unalterable is, perhaps, the best reason for the high estimation in which it is held. No exposure to weather, no acids or alkaline substance, except the peculiar mixture of mineral acids called *aqua regia*, will touch it. Although by no means hard, it is wonderfully tough, and is beaten into thin sheets or drawn into wire of almost microscopic fineness. It is capable of being made into sheets so fine that they are actually transparent and transmit a beautiful purple light; and there seems hardly a limit to the fineness of the wire made of it by coating it first with silver, drawing it to extreme fineness, and then dissolving off the silver by an acid which does not touch gold. A mile of such wire would not weigh ten grains (less than the twelfth part of the weight of a sovereign).

Although generally obtained from sands and gravels, by picking out with the hand, washing carefully in water, or catching hold of by mercury, which seems to dissolve it and suck it up as water does salt, gold is sometimes found closely combined with other metals, generally, but not always, in the metallic state. Especially is this the case in Hungary, where it is mixed with a curious and rare metal called tellurium, of no known value. In Brazil and in Siberia gold is found with other very rare metals.

Who has not heard of the incessant efforts of the alchemists to convert worthless substances into gold? Vain efforts they certainly were, and were likely to have been, for they were made in the dark, without a foundation of chemical knowledge, and often in opposition to natural laws now well understood. At present the transmutation of one element into another is regarded as a dream, hardly justified even in a recognized Bedlamite; and no doubt with reason, if the assumption is admitted that all substances called elements are really so. When, however, we see what Nature can do with a few gases in the case of organic life, and the wonderful transmutations there performed, we may be permitted to suspect that perhaps all, or at least many, of the assumed elements will some day yield to a mightier decomposing force than is yet known, and show relations that may restore to our alchemic friends the credit due to them as hard-working investigators of Nature's secrets. Then, gold may be shown to have real relations as well as fanciful resemblances to other substances.

And, after all, the quantity of gold obtained is not great. Look at the ugly but interesting pyramid that disfigured the entrance of the Great International Exhibition. It represented all the gold that has come from Australia. A similar pyramid would represent all that has come from California. A cube, measuring a few yards every way, would represent more than all that has ever been obtained for the use of man since the world began. A block of iron of that size would hardly attract attention, and in a single year more copper might be got out of one mine. Why is gold so scarce in comparison with other metals, and why, being so scarce, is it so very universally distributed? These are queries not replied to satisfactorily by those who study such matters. But one thing is certain: gold is not valuable merely because it is rare. Platinum is much less in quantity, and equally rare. Iridium, rhodium, osmium, palladium, these are all more rare, and cannot be said to have much value, except as curiosities. They have many of the properties of gold, but they lack the rich color, the pliability, the facility of handling, of that metal. Long as the world may last, gold will no doubt continue to be the representative metal, and the metal resorted to for personal ornament by all who can afford to purchase it. It is the most noble and royal of metals.

SILVER is even more beautiful than gold, but it is far less able to resist the influence of acids, gases, and other foreign substances. Unlike gold, also, it is easily tarnished; and it is especially subject to a blackening of the surface by exposure to a sulphur atmosphere. Such an atmosphere as arises from the presence of large numbers of human beings, and the decomposition of many kinds of vegetable matter, tarnishes silver. The consumption of coal and the burning of coal gas set free a considerable quantity of sulphur: so that in peopled districts there is abundant impurity in the air to blacken the surface of this beautiful metal.

Combining more readily with foreign substances, silver is found not only quite as widely distributed, but occurs in a much greater variety of admixtures and far larger quantity than gold. It is found native as a metal, though rarely of the beautiful color for which it is so much admired. The form of native silver is, however, often very fanciful. More frequently it is an earthy oxide or a sulphuret; most frequently it is intimately mixed in small proportion with other metals, &c. It especially affects certain metals, but these are different from those with which gold is associated. Antimony, bismuth, cobalt, arsenic, are among the less common, lead and, to some extent, copper, among the more common, metals thus mixed up with silver. With lead, in its usual form of galena (sulphuret), silver is almost always combined, and with metallic copper it is present in a very singular way, distributed through the native metal abundantly found on Lake Superior, but not forming an alloy with it. As at a very moderate temperature copper and silver combine, there is thus proof either that the metallic copper has not been deposited in these veins in a gaseous or liquid state, or that the silver has penetrated the solid copper since its deposit to occupy blebs and cracks in the metal.

A few of the ores of silver are beautiful as specimens, but they are not used for personal ornament. The metal itself, in its extreme delicacy and adaptability to various purposes, and in the perfect polish it takes, is sufficiently remarkable not to require additional interest from its admixture with other substances.

The properties of silver are many. When well polished, it reflects more and radiates less heat than any other metal. Its use for table-furniture is thus quite as remarkable as its beauty. When pure, it is not so hard as copper, but a very small alloy of copper hardens it without altering its color. It is capable of being beaten into leaves ten thousand of which piled together would not be an inch thick; and it may be drawn into wire finer than the most delicate human hair. A very thin coat of pure silver may be deposited, by the process of electroplating, on the surface of other metals, which thus have the properties of solid silver so long as the surface remains. The salts of silver are much used in porcelain-painting, in chemical manufactures, and in the laboratory.

Silver is very widely distributed. It exists, in quantities that can be determined, in sea-water, in sea-weeds, in the ashes of land-plants, and in some animal substances. It is present in almost all ores of lead and in copper; and a large part of the silver of commerce is obtained, by an ingenious process, from melted lead. The mixed lead and silver being in a large pan in a melted state, the fire is withdrawn, and the metal allowed to cool. Soon crystals of pure lead form and sink to the bottom. If these are removed, the liquid that remains contains all the silver; and by continually removing the crystals the remaining liquid is at last left extremely rich in silver. When the process has been carried on long enough, the silver is obtained by allowing the lead to mix with oxygen gas and pass off as litharge, which is either used in that state or again converted into lead. A slab of silver, weighing nearly half a ton, obtained in this way, was among the minerals at the Great Exhibition of 1851.

MERCURY, or QUICKSILVER, is one of the noble metals. At ordinary temperatures it exists at the earth's surface in the form of a fluid. Near the poles, where the cold is intense, it is solid, and may be hammered like lead; but this is only when the temperature is 40° below zero of Fahrenheit. It dissolves several other metals in the most rapid manner, and forms with them pastes, called *amalgams*. Gold, silver, and tin are among the metals thus acted upon.

Mercury is found sometimes as a metal, and sometimes mixed with sulphur, as a beautiful red stone, called cinnabar, from which the metal is obtained by distillation at a low temperature. In Europe the chief mercury-mines are at Almaden in Spain, in Idria (in Eastern Austria), in the Palatinate (not far from Bingen on the Rhine), and in Hungary. In America, California has lately produced large supplies.

The fact that it remains fluid at all ordinary temperatures renders quicksilver particularly valuable as a measure of heat; and its extreme weight, combined with fluidity, renders it equally useful as a measure of the pressure of the air. It is thus the material used both in the thermometer and barometer; and its high power of reflecting light renders it valuable for mirrors and for an artificial horizon in astronomical instruments.

Besides all these useful properties, mercury is largely used in medicine, as calomel, blue pill, &c., and much more largely in obtaining the precious metals, gold and silver, when they are present in small proportions mixed with earthy matters. Mercury dissolves these metals with great rapidity; and by afterwards applying heat, the mercury passes off into vapor, and can be re-obtained in bottles, while the gold or silver is left behind in a cake.

Mercury is extremely heavy, being thirteen and a half times as heavy as the same quantity of water.

The next group of metals includes those sometimes called *base;* but this is only in a technical and antiquated sense, and because they cannot be reduced into the metallic state by mere application of heat. Of these the most useful and interesting are *malleable;* in other words, they are flattened when struck by the hammer, instead of being broken like a stone. This very real and important practical condition is one that divides the metals into two well-marked groups. Seven of the best-known metals are malleable, and only five are brittle, while there are nine rare and unfamiliar base brittle metals, and only one unfamiliar metal that can be hammered. The property of flattening under the hammer is thus a good characteristic; and it is found that the brittle metals are chiefly useful either to mix with and harden the others, or for properties which seem to have little to do with their metallic character.

Of the metals that may be hammered, we may begin with COPPER, remarkable for its color, its toughness, its power of mixing advantageously with other metals, its high value, and its durability. In itself it is not very hard, but, mixed with a little iron and tin, it becomes almost as hard as steel. Of a dull red color, it assumes the color of gold when mixed with a little of the clay metal *aluminium;* it makes brass when mixed with zinc, and affords several other valuable yellow compounds with zinc, lead, and tin; mixed with tin only, it produces bronze, a most valuable hard alloy, used for guns, for public monuments, and to a large extent now for small coins. At least three thousand tons' weight of metal are required for the latter purpose in England only. Of this the proportion of tin is four parts, and of zinc one part, in a hundred: the rest is copper.

Copper has been in use from time immemorial. Obtained by the ancients from the island of Cyprus, it was called for a time *æs Cyprium*, or the Cyprian metal. Thence the name *Cuprum* was derived, and from this most of the modern European names—copper, cuivre, kupfer, cobre, &c.—have been derived.

Copper is found sometimes in very large quantities, nearly pure, or mixed only with silver and a little quartz. In this state a block weighing 500 tons was lately discovered in the mines on Lake Superior. It is so very tough a substance, that when these large masses are discovered they are very difficult to take out of the mine. As many as forty men, working continually for twelve months, were required to remove the block just alluded to. But the value is very great, varying from £80 to £120 sterling per ton. At £100 a ton, the block in question would be worth £50,000, and well pay any expense of getting, refining, and carrying to market.

The usual mode in which copper is found is either as a hard metallic stone of a yellowish color, called *copper pyrites*, or as a softer and very beautiful green stone, called *malachite*. There are many other varieties, some common enough in certain places, and quite different from these. Among them we may mention a peculiar black earth (black oxide), and a gray stone, the latter metallic in its appearance, and not unlike black lead. From these the copper is obtained by a long and difficult series of operations, beginning with roasting, and involving a frequent refining.

Malachite is a wonderfully beautiful stone, used sometimes as a marble, or even as a gem, and at other times as an ore from which the metal is obtained. The finest malachites are obtained from Siberia, whence the raw material has been quarried for those magnificent specimens of green marble which grace the palaces of the world. The largest quantities come from Australia, where, however, the quality is not so fine.

LEAD is another metal of great value, and tolerably abundant in most parts of the world. Most of the great lead deposits consist of a combination of sulphur with the metal; but though the sulphurets of lead (*galena*) are very widely spread, they are not the only valuable ores. Carbonates are common, especially in those numerous instances where limestones enclose the lead-vein. Lead is never found in a native state as a pure metal, and when obtained from the ore it is generally mixed with silver. It is, however, reduced without much difficulty, as it melts at a low temperature, and, as already stated in speaking of silver, separates readily from that metal while cooling.

Pure lead is used in sheets or pipes for various purposes; but it is dangerous, as pure water dissolves a part of it and becomes very poisonous: when used for household purposes, great care is required. It mixes with many other metals, and forms some useful and important alloys. Thus, with tin it makes pewter and the solder used by glaziers; with tin and antimony it becomes hard, and slightly enlarges while cooling, thus forming a most useful compound for such purposes as type-metal. Alloyed with arsenic, by which it is much hardened, lead becomes available for shot; and other combinations are known. The oxide of lead is called *massicot* and *litharge*, used in making flint glass, and for many other purposes. Another combination, with oxygen, is called *red lead*, and is useful as a pigment, though dangerous from its poisonous properties. Carbonate of lead, as *white lead*, is a valuable paint, though injurious, as are so many of the combinations of lead to those exposed to their influence. A yellow paint is obtained from the *chromate of lead;* and *sugar of lead* (the acetate obtained by the action of vinegar or acetic acid on sheet lead) is used in dyeing, and for many purposes, but is also poisonous.

Lead, like copper, has been used from the most ancient times. It is easily recognized as an ore, owing to its great weight as compared with other stones.

IRON.—Although it seems certain that hard bronze was long in common use for many purposes now supplied by iron, before iron and steel had been generally introduced, it is quite impossible to state when or how this extremely abundant and useful, but most refractory, metal was first discovered. It rarely exists native except in a few stones that seem to have come to the earth from without. It is found, however, in a vast variety of forms, mixed in larger or smaller quantity with almost all earths, and occasionally in vast quantities in different districts. England is especially rich in the earthy ores; Sweden contains extremely large deposits of the oxide, valuable for making the best kinds of steel; but there are few, if any, countries without a supply in some form or other. The common clay ironstones of Great Britain have long been the sources whence iron has been manufactured to supply the world. No sooner had symptoms of exhaustion shown themselves in one district, than fresh deposits, almost indefinitely large, were discovered in another; and there is now no doubt that, while fuel lasts, the ores of iron will not fail.

Iron is wonderfully tenacious: when pure, it requires the full heat of a smith's forge to fuse; but in the form of pig it melts at a much lower temperature. It is very malleable, especially at a high temperature, and when red-hot two surfaces may be united firmly and permanently by hammering. This is called welding, and is a quality possessed by a very small number of metals.

Some of the ores of iron are used in the arts. Thus, a peculiar red or dark-brown ore (*hæmatite*), when reduced to a fine powder, is valuable for burnishing and polishing glass. Yellow ochre is a common pigment. Iron pyrites is hardly so much an ore of iron as of sulphur: it is abundant and much used.

TIN is a metal of considerable value, but, unlike those hitherto mentioned, is limited to a very few localities, and is hardly ever met with except in the one form of oxide. It is a beautiful white metal, more resembling silver than any other, and takes a high polish. It may be beaten into thin leaves, which crackle and give out a peculiar odor when handled. It melts easily, and burns with a bright flame. It coats iron with great facility, and the plates thus covered are called tin-plate. It also coats copper. The salts are valuable in dyeing and calico-printing. The metal is quite as much used to modify others by mixing with them as by itself. Thus, with copper it makes bronze, bell-metal, &c., and with bismuth and lead several curious compounds. Tin has been long known, and was certainly mined in Britain before the invasion of the Romans. It is still obtained chiefly from Cornwall, though considerable quantities are brought from some of the islands of the Eastern Archipelago, and it has been discovered in Australia.

ZINC, as a metal, is of recent discovery, though one of its ores, calamine, was commonly employed to mix with copper from the earliest period, in order to form brass. The metal passes off so rapidly into the air at a low temperature, in the form of a white cloud, that the metallic character was long concealed. Although malleable, zinc is tough, brittle, and unmanageable, except within narrow limits of temperature. At the boiling-point of water it may easily be worked; but at a slightly greater heat it may be pounded in a mortar, and when cold it can hardly be bent. It is a beautiful bluish-white metal, tarnishing slightly on exposure, but not wearing rapidly. It is very much used for baths, window sashes and frames, chimney-pots, and many other purposes. It is also used as an alloy, not only with copper, to make brass, but with other metals of more or less importance.

NICKEL is often seen as a separate metal, but is largely used in the manufacture of *German silver*, of which, however, it only forms four parts out of a hundred, the rest being chiefly copper with a little zinc. Different proportions produce other white metals, much used in other countries in place of silver. This result is singular, as the red color of the copper is completely lost by this slight admixture of other metals. The ores of nickel are rare: some look metallic, but others are earthy. They are chiefly mixtures with arsenic. Nickel is malleable. It is remarkable that meteoric stones, falling on the earth from the atmosphere, consist chiefly of iron, combined with nickel.

COBALT is never used as a metal, its value, which is very considerable, being entirely derived from the use of the oxides as a pigment. They produce the finest and most durable blue color known, especially for staining glass or coloring porcelain, in both which operations the color has to be burnt in. Like nickel, the ores are usually combinations with arsenic. One of them is a tin-white metallic-looking mineral; another is remarkable for its beautiful color, like the bloom of a peach.

These are all the malleable metals. Bismuth, antimony, and arsenic remain to be considered as useful brittle metals, easily melted; and manganese and chromium, also useful, but fusible with great difficulty.

ARSENIC has already been mentioned, as occurring with cobalt and nickel. It is also found native and with many of the metals. As a metal, it is useless. As a mineral, it is one of the most poisonous. Its presence is readily detected by the garlic-like fumes it gives off when heated. There are two ores, one transparent and of a beautiful clear cochineal-red, called *realgar;* the other less transparent, and of a beautiful orange-yellow. It is called *orpiment*, and is used as the basis of the pigment called king's yellow. Although a violent poison, arsenic is habitually consumed without injury by the people in some parts of the Tyrol. It is used as medicine.

ANTIMONY is also occasionally found native, but very seldom. It is almost always mixed with sulphur, and affords a brilliant and beautiful metallic ore. Though not used alone, antimony, arsenic, and the other brittle metals, are of considerable value in hardening the malleable metals for certain special purposes. Type-metal, hard pewter, and Britannia metal, are examples. The lead on which music is engraved is hardened by a small mixture of antimony. Gold cannot be hammered if alloyed with a little of this curious metal.

BISMUTH is another brittle metal, with curious properties. It is found native, generally with arsenic; but its peculiarity is to render any metal mixed with it much more fusible. What is called *plumber's solder* is a mixture of this kind. Eight parts of bismuth, five lead, and three tin, constitute a metal which will melt at a heat below that of boiling water. A little mercury added makes it still more fusible. Tricks are sometimes played by making spoons of this metal and offering them for use. The salts of bismuth are used in dyeing and as a cosmetic.

MANGANESE is a metal never used, and very rarely seen. Its ores are black. They are valuable for various purposes, being very widely diffused and employed in bleaching, dyeing, calico-printing, and in glazing and coloring pottery. The *umber* of commerce is obtained from the ore called *wad*. Oxygen gas is given off readily by heating the ores of manganese. One ore of manganese is capable of taking a high polish, and is used for inlaid work as a spar. Many of the manganese ores, and stones where traces of the metal occur, are remarkable for their pink color.

CHROMIUM is another of the metals, brittle, not easily melted, altogether without any known use as a metal, but valuable in the arts from the color derived from it. The only ore is a combination of the oxide of the metal with iron and earthy substances. It is found in England in serpentine and other green magnesian rocks; but there are many known localities in various parts of the world. It is very extensively used as a pigment for dyeing, and in all those cases in which the color has to be burnt into the material.

Besides the metals and ores we have described, there are many others less common. These are interesting rather to the chemist who analyzes than to the geologist who observes them. They are some of them curious, and have remarkable properties, but rather as earths than metals.

It is a curious fact, determined of late years by a series of observations on the nature of light and color, that many of the metals forming part of our earth are present also in the sun, and even in some of the fixed stars whose light has been examined. As it has been known almost from time immemorial that foreign substances occasionally fall to the earth from or through the air, and these are generally composed of a rare mixture of familiar metals, there is some reason to suppose that various small bodies, composed of similar elements, are floating about in the universe, not far from us, and that these are from time to time brought within our influence. Since no new element has been introduced in the fallen stones, one is thus led to speculate on the possibility of a common origin of our own earth and the other bodies of our solar system, and that some fragments of similar matter, broken away from an old planet, or strayed from a comet, or perhaps in course of collection by a comet, may yield the aerolites or meteorites that have so often caused wonder and alarm. The indications of this state of things are more numerous and complete than is generally supposed.

## Chapter the Seventeenth.

### THE CIRCULATION OF WATER.

Of the many conditions of Nature that require to combine, in order that our earth may be the abode of living beings having the wants and habits of those now dwelling on it, there is none more remarkable than that which has secured for us a constant circulation of water,—in the air, on the earth, and within the earth. The mere fact that with us there are three conditions of matter—solid, fluid, and gaseous—is itself, as far as we can judge, a state of things by no means always met with in planets. The moon does not seem to possess a similar arrangement: Mars probably does, but Jupiter may be regarded as doubtful. We can hardly guess at some of the other planets. Taking the earth as we find it, however, it is very interesting to see how the three states of matter seem always to have characterized every part of its history.

Water in abundance rests on the surface; the air contains water in large quantity; and almost all the rocks contain a certain quantity of water, either in such a state that it courses freely from one part to another, or closely shut in and buried in the very substance of the most solid minerals.

Water is, indeed, present in two distinct ways in rocks. Except lava and such-like material, once certainly fluid from heat, every kind of stone, including granite and marble, contains a certain percentage of water as one of its component parts. The proportion is not large; but, from the universality of the fact, the quantity of water thus locked up is very considerable. But in addition to this, and quite independent of it, there is a far larger quantity of water occupying innumerable cracks and crevices in rocks, running between beds, oozing through narrow channels in all sorts of unexpected places, occupying caverns and veins, existing in pools (often under great pressure) at various depths, issuing in natural springs at hill-sides in some countries, and even on mountain-tops, or reached by artificial borings in all parts of the world. We are so accustomed to find fresh pure water wherever we require it—we are so familiar with the custom of digging a hole into the substance of the earth in order to reach this fluid—that the nature of the continuous supply, and the circulation that takes place in order to insure it, are hardly thought of. These are, however, subjects as interesting as they are important.

The history of the Great Stone Book is given in the preceding chapters. It points out that the earth is made up of numerous beds or strata of rock of different material,—some absorbing water, some letting it pass freely, some stopping it altogether. The additional facts determined concerning the fractures of these rocks, the way the rocks have been tilted, the way in which deep cracks have been sometimes left open and sometimes filled with hard material, the mutual intercommunication that exists far out of sight, and the open passage thus afforded to water, are also illustrated by the history there given.

There is something exceedingly **grand** and deeply **interesting** in following the course of a few drops of water in its circulation though the great terrestrial system. Covering two-thirds of the surface is the great world of water, and above sea and land floats a veil of gases. We do not see all the water. Part of it, **as** we have described, **is** fast locked up in the solid rock; part of it is always held in an invisible state in the air; and part, again, is sometimes visible, sometimes invisible, ranging over earth and through the air, and ready at the **slightest signal to move and distribute itself.**

**Water** is always present in the **air, sucked up and held** by it something in the way that sugar or salt is sucked up and held by pure water. The air itself is a mixture of gases, and the vapor in it is like a third gas. **Just as** hot water dissolves more sugar or salt than cold water, so hot air holds more water than cold air. Air, heated by **the** vertical **rays of** a tropical sun, and passing over the sea, becomes loaded with vapor; and as it afterwards approaches land and comes in contact with cooler air, especially on the sides of mountains, it can no longer hold so **large a** quantity of water as before. Clouds are formed, **and rain** falls. **The air is** cleared and **passes on, cooled** and deprived **of part of its load, to some place where it** is again heated, and where **once** more it absorbs **water.**

The solid materials of the earth we have already considered. Almost all were originally formed in and with water; they have been rendered hard and compact under **water; they have existed** for unnumbered ages always **under water; and** when deprived of water they have **shrunk and cracked.**

All stones contain water. Even the driest and most solid-looking marble used by the sculptor contains at least one part in two hundred of water: in other words, in a block of two hundred weight there is at least a pint of water. Other hard dry limestones contain as much as four parts in a hundred, or half a gallon of water in a hundred weight of stone.

But stones are not only made with and always contain water, but they are very porous and spongy, and suck in great quantities when exposed to rain or soaked in a stream. Thus, Bath stone, of the kind generally met with in buildings, and some other limestones commonly used, will suck in as much as nine gallons of water on a surface a yard square and only a foot thick. When thicker, it will continue to absorb, though not in the same proportion. A surface of chalk will absorb twice as much, and sands are much more porous even than such stones.

Of all the rocks that make up the earth, there are few of those met with at the surface in our country that will not suck up water with extreme rapidity and in very large quantity; and when we come to an actual calculation, the absorbing power of the surface, when dry, is found to be so extremely great as to suck in almost any amount of rain that can fall. It rarely happens, indeed, except in hot summer weather, that the earth is so dry as to absorb at any thing like the rate we have mentioned; but on the other hand, in addition to the means we have considered, there are cracks and crevices innumerable, the consequence of exposure to the weather previously; and thus the water is not only absorbed slowly at the surface, but pours down these open cracks, and gives the rocks in the interior an opportunity of becoming saturated.

Water is, then, present in the earth's interior in extremely large quantity: it is continually being received, because it is continually being removed. Under every **space a** mile square there is water enough present in a thickness of a thousand yards to **fill a pond** of the same area whose depth of water might be many yards or even scores of yards.

Let us now bring together the general **results of this** inquiry, and endeavor to illustrate in a **few words the use and influence of water** in the interior of the earth.

Although not a simple substance, water is a compound of which the composing elements possess affinities so powerful, that the agency of electricity appears to be involved both in its formation and decomposition. The conversion or production of water involves heat, electricity, and chemical action, and this conversion is always going on, for water is everywhere present: no known or conceivable conditions of matter, consistent with the presence of more than very small quantities, appear to be free from it; **hardly any** combinations **of simple substances are altogether without it, and no large quantities** of simple substances **deprived of it exist on or near the** earth's surface.

Water absorbs every thing and is absorbed by every thing. Itself a liquid, it enters into the composition of almost all solids, almost as an essential to solidity. As a **solid, it** has its own special value and properties. It is equally important in the state of vapor, for steam represents power not only available for man's machinery, but

27*

largely used in the workshop of Nature. In every condition and at every change it is connected with heat and electricity. Besides being present in almost all mineral matter, it enters also into the composition of every solid and every fluid of which each part of every living thing is formed.

Let us trace its course from its great receptacle the ocean, where it occupies and conceals depressions which are little more than wrinkled or furrowed markings on the earth, and which, if they could be seen from our satellite the moon, must appear very small, compared with the variations of level on that body.

Kept in incessant motion in all parts of the ocean by tidal influences and winds, water rising as vapor from its surface is received between the particles of mixed gases that form our atmosphere, and there becomes subject to influences of temperature and electricity; and these are constantly changing by the revolution of the earth on its axis, of the moon round the earth, of the earth and moon round the sun, and of our whole system in space.

Lifted as vapor, it is drifted along, either in an invisible or visible form, until it reaches land. Once there, it is set free, and large quantities fall to the earth. Part of what falls is re-evaporated; part serves to quench the thirst of every leaf and root, as well as every mouth and skin, exposed to its influence; part again runs on the surface,—the mountain-torrent, the brook, and the river carrying back this proportion to the parent ocean. Part of it whitens the lofty mountain-top, or collects in icy masses in the sheltered valleys.

But a large part enters the earth. The earth and the

sands are thirsty, as well as the leaf and the skin: they not only drink in an abundant supply, but they convey downwards some portion; and this reaches the interior through the crevices of hard rocks, or the porous substance of those that are softer.

This supply is so ample that abundant springs gush out from the hill-sides, or are ever ready to rise through openings prepared for them by Nature or man.

The ultimate residuum, after all this lavish supply has been granted, is still an important quantity.

And now is forced upon us a view of Nature, and of the operations of Nature in the interior of the earth, which is almost oppressive, from the extreme difficulty the human mind has in grasping a conception so opposed, it may seem, to the evidence of the senses.

We speak of the grave as silent; we think of the ground and the rock as permanent, and almost as if they were eternal. We cannot feel that all beneath our feet is changing, and that there is a kind of life even in dead matter. We cannot see it, but a circulation really goes on in all material substances, and it is consistent with apparent and external repose; for if we examine and carefully describe an object or a state of matter at one time, and afterwards, after a sufficient interval, repeat our investigation, we may find perhaps the same form but a different substance: there may be the same appearance, but there is a new and changed texture.

Nature, indeed, knows no repose. The minute atoms of which solids are formed, however compactly placed they may seem, are removed from each other by a distance which is large in proportion to their size,—large enough, at any rate, to admit of any amount of motion among themselves,—large enough to let atoms of other matter circulate among and replace them,—large enough to allow the combined atoms of hydrogen and oxygen, as water, to penetrate them.

The mud deposited to-day at the mouths of the Rhine, the Ganges, or the Mississippi is a mechanical mixture of lime and clay and water with grains of sand, fragments of wood and bone, marine and fresh-water shells, and particles of iron oxide. With them is the infinity of miscellaneæ that are brought together by fresh water running over a surface of land which is covered with vegetation and with animal life, and ultimately the river terminates its course and deposits its load where it meets the tidal wave of salt water.

This mud deposited to-day will be buried to-morrow, and in the course of centuries will be covered up thickly, and remain permanently buried for a long time.

What then will happen? Will all remain quiet? Having entered Nature's great laboratory, will these materials be left there inert and idle? Such an idea is little in accordance with what we know of the course of Nature, either now or at any period of the earth's history.

First, decomposition will commence, or will go on if it had already commenced, in the organic matter. Gases will be evolved,—these will affect the other compounds otherwise permanent; elective affinities will be called into play, and a general rearrangement will take place of all the particles, until they attain a first state of temporary equilibrium. During all this time they are saturated with water, a heavy column of water presses upon them, and their temperature is more or less equable in proportion to the depth of the deposit.

By degrees the water gets to a certain extent squeezed out of them, and they become solid instead of pulpy. The attraction of cohesion acts, and at last the wet pulpy mud either becomes changed into tough clay, or a sort of half-formed limestone results, or perhaps the mass remains loose sand.

Then come into play those movements of the earth's surface of which there are examples in most countries. The ground sinks, the deposit continues; and at length the mud of yesterday, kept at a steady even temperature of some 200° or 300° under great pressure of earth and water, is exposed to those magnetic currents which circulate through the earth. Then begins a fresh series of changes, crystallization starting at some atom of foreign matter. Clayey mud passes into tough clay, lime-mud passes into beds of limestone, impurities and foreign substances accumulate together in bands, the shells become crystalline and are cemented together; undecomposed wood tends to become coal, silica takes the place of some of the organic matter; the sulphur and phosphorus set free from animal matter enter into new combinations; the mass, in drying, contracts irregularly, and is full of cracks and fissures; and among these water circulates, forced through at a temperature corresponding to the depth, carrying with it from place to place various minerals,—removing them from one point, leaving them behind at others, according to the nature of the chemical operations going on.

After a time the beds sink lower, the clays become subject to greater pressure, the limestones become compact and pass into marble, and the metals, combined with oxygen or sulphur, group themselves together in cavities with other minerals, earthy and crystalline.

One step more: elevation begins. The clays are now subjected to pressure from below as well as from above; and under this double squeeze they become twisted and bent like pieces of cloth, and they also assume a new lamination. They become slates. Some of the sandstones have by this time been converted into quartzite, and the limestone has completed its crystallization. When elevation comes, these hard beds, being brittle, are broken, leaving large open spaces and great cavities beneath the surface. Here also water collects.

Yet again. Far down, at a depth of tens of thousands of yards, and therefore under great pressure, water, in company with the minerals which form granite, accumulates in a mixed mass; and a slow but incessant crystallization goes on, in which the water is entangled with the other minerals and helps to form a part of the substance of each crystal. We may even imitate the effect by bringing the causes to bear.

But in all this there is no melting, such as we have in volcanic rocks. In these latter water is not present in the same way.

They were formed much nearer the surface; they belong to a different class of phenomena. Their origin is detected by the absence of water in them.

Wherever change has taken place at great depth,—

wherever is seen **a rich** variety of minerals and a valuable supply of metals,—there water has acted.

Water carried down in the rocks that descend is worked **up into** new forms, and is only returned to the surface **when it** has done its work and when other supplies from **above** have replaced it.

**And** in time the rocks thus elaborated rise again. Some, sunk only to a small depth, will have been little altered, and will form gravel, surface-clay, **loose sand, or** soft limestone; some, **from greater depth and more altered,** will **show the effect of chemical action by** unmistakable chemical and atomic change, while the wealth **of their fossil organic** remains sufficiently speaks of their **mechanical origin;** others again, **much** deeper, **will have been so** completely altered as **to have** lost all **trace of this** life-origin. It does not the less follow that **they have once** contained fossils as **distinct and as numerous as those of any** recent deposit.

As each **rock** comes again **within the** influence of surface-disturbance, **it** will be worn away **by the river, or** beaten into fragments by the tidal wave; **water will once more destroy what water** originally formed, what **water afterwards modified, and what** will **once more be converted into a deposit at the bottom of the same ever-present but ever-active element.**

In all the great circle of **changes concerning which Geology** informs us, water is, **then, the chief** agent. Heat and chemical action of themselves could do little, **and certainly could not** produce **what is needed for our world. They act** with and **by water, and thus** produce **their results.**

Abstract this important form of matter, and we may imagine what the result would be. The great ocean would be but a salt desert without an oasis,—the land a dry parched rock; there would be no life, animal or vegetable,—not even the smallest animalcule, or the red lichen on the snow. The sky would be without cloud, and the thermic and magnetic currents would cease to vivify the dry bones that would then form but a skeleton of the earth.

Water is the life of the earth, as blood is the life of man. This is a wonderful and instructive analogy, and one which may lead to many useful suggestions in the contemplation of Nature.

# The Shutting-up of the Great Stone Book.

"And this, the naked countenance of earth,
 On which I gaze, even these primeval mountains,
 Teach the adverting mind. The glaciers creep
 Like snakes that watch their prey, from their far fountains
 Slowly rolling on." . . .

 ". Mont Blanc yet gleams on high. The power is there,
 The still and solemn power of many sights
 And many sounds, and much of life and death."

 . . . "Winds contend
 Silently there, and heap the snow with breath
 Rapid and strong, but silently!" . . .

 "The secret strength of things
 Which governs thought, and to the infinite dome
 Of heaven is as a law, inhabits thee!
 And what wert thou, and earth, and stars, and sea,
 If to the human mind's imaginings
 Silence and solitude were vacancy?"
                   SHELLEY'S "MONT BLANC," Stanzas iv. v.

# Chapter the Eighteenth.

## CONCLUSION.

The reader has been introduced to a few of the many remarkable additions to human knowledge that have been made by the study of that Great Stone Book,—the World. The history of the world, from a very early date, if not from the beginning, is a history recorded at every step, but of which the records are buried and concealed as fast as they are made. It is as if each hour of a human being's existence, and each action performed, were instantaneously photographed, and the photographs immediately thrown into a heap as they were prepared. If from time to time, after the original heaping, we suppose this curious and vast collection disturbed,—if the floor on which they were piled should have lost part of its support, or should have partially fallen in, and should be propped up and broken in the operation,—if some members of the series should, from time to time, have been used up for other purposes, and in so far destroyed, —if, when all is over, the surface should be concealed and its appearance changed by dust and mould,—then should we have a case not very dissimilar to that of our earth's surface and its history, and the difficulties met with by geologists in making out the history. Just as no moderate amount of disturbance would be likely to destroy or obliterate much of the detail, or even modify the main outlines of the order, while the relative position or the style of the picture at any period would be a guide that could be trusted to distinguish the earlier from the later representations, so in the history of Nature we are quite satisfied that the evidence we possess is sound and satisfactory, though the details may long remain doubtful and admit of discussion. Making the best use of available material, it has been attempted to reproduce something of reality in these sketches,—to show both how to learn and what to learn in Geology, and to give some notion as to how far the statements which are made have been derived from observation.

Like all knowledge that is worth any thing, that which has brought Geology to its place among the sciences is *cumulative*, or has been derived from the accumulation of isolated facts and points of evidence worked into a connected history. The discoveries of to-day form the basis of future discoveries, and every thing proved suggests something new to prove. There is no finality in such a science. The more we know and see, the wider is our field of vision extended towards those distant and as yet unapproached facts and those further deductions which, when learnt and understood, will only open a yet wider view. If we could ever thoroughly know the history of our own planet, we should perhaps make use of that knowledge to speculate on its relations to other planets, while at present we help our geological speculations by evidence deduced from observations on them. Could we determine the whole succession of extinct species, we might understand the mysterious laws which govern the development of the race as well as the individual; but even that knowledge, great as it is, would but suggest views concerning the nature of life itself. But, though we never can really and fully know all or any of these subjects thoroughly, we are ever approaching more and more nearly towards a knowledge of them. As, from time to time, we make some fresh important discovery concerning them, every such discovery helps us to understand a whole host of phenomena that before seemed obscure, contradictory, and strange; and thus every step secured lays the foundation for another step,—every light thrown upon part of a dark group helps to throw light on the remaining members of the group.

The summing up of the attempts that have been made, in these pages, to enable the general reader to understand and take an interest in the details of the earth's history, may now be presented in a few words; and in stating this result I will endeavor to point out not only what is already known concerning the earth, but what may probably be known, whether soon or at a more advanced period in the history of science, and also what part we cannot hope ever to make out.

And, first, it appears that to observe, compare, and record all that goes on around us, of every kind, is the only path to geological knowledge. There is in Nature so much that is constant, producing so much that is variable,—such infinite difference of effect brought about by such constantly recurring causes,—that, so far as the present can teach, we find all reduced to a narrow limit of ultimate and proximate causation. We find heat and cold, wet and dry, storm and sunshine, always and everywhere working together. There are certain chemical changes produced by these, and others that are mechanical; but, on the whole, the subtle agencies at work above and around us, in the air and ocean, are so efficacious, that no rest is given to any material substance, and a constant circulation is kept up, involving incessant change of the surface. To measure these changes, as far as possible, to find out their ramifications and their connecting links, is a study that is never-ending, and always productive of fresh discovery. It is the most useful, the most suggestive, the most instructive, of all studies of Nature. It is open to every one; it may be carried on by the rich and the poor, the idle and the busy, the well-instructed and the little-instructed among us. It requires only honesty, intelligence, and earnestness. It can never fail; for material is always at hand.

The study of Nature, with a view to find out the mode and extent of action of present causes, is the first and greatest of all preparations for pursuing Geology. It is the only proper preparation; and the more comprehensive and complete it is, the better is the student adapted for carrying out future investigations. No department is too general, none too special, for this purpose. The discovery of the law that regulates the distribution of an insect, a zoophyte, or even an animalcule, may lead to discoveries of the greatest and widest importance. If we knew the laws that governed the introduction of the lower forms of animal and vegetable life,—if we even knew exactly what is the precise line of demarcation between animal and vegetable life, or could clearly see why certain modifications of form of some of these have been induced by changes of circumstance in their development,—the result could not fail to have the most direct and important bearing on the whole history of extinct races, and their distribution in the older as well as newer rocks. If we could determine—a matter clearly within observation, but as yet unattained—the exact amount and rate of changes of level in the land, on certain coast-lines that we know to be subject to upheaval, and could connect that knowledge with alterations on exposed coasts in the vicinity, or measure accurately the change produced by the action of the tidal wave in a given time, there would be a basis for generalizations far more accurate than can be at present attempted. If, indeed, a very small part only of all the numerous opportunities presented in Nature by the progress of events had been carefully and minutely observed and recorded for only a single century, the state of Natural Science at the present day would be far more satisfactory than it is, and Geology would be far more of an accurate science than it can now claim to be. But patient honest observers are rare, and the work they do is quiet and unobtrusive: their results, also, are rarely immediate. Thus it is that, for one useful worker, there are many who prefer vague speculations, and many more who only amuse themselves with technicalities, and waste their energies on the discovery and naming of new species or new subdivisions of a recognized system of arrangement.

The Great Stone Book lies ever before us: it is not closed by any complicated mystery, of which we cannot find the key; it is not written in a character we cannot decipher:—it is illustrated by forms of animated nature, sufficiently like those now living to suggest comparison, but sufficiently different to give individuality to each separate group. The plan of Nature, as there shown, is not different from that plan the operation of which we can trace from year to year, and from century to century, in the experience of generations of men. The methods now adopted to bring about certain results seem always to have been adopted for similar purposes. The Great Overruling Power, to whom we all look as the Final Cause, has ordained from the beginning certain laws,— some affecting all material combinations, mineral as well as organic; others, developed perhaps from them, and involving certain forms of life; others, again, further developed, and only commencing to operate when more complex forms have been elaborated from those that are more simple. It is the privilege of the naturalist to lift the veil that conceals the working of these methods, so far as it is possible to do so. Should, however, any fragment of a system be recognized, so prone are men to generalize that we are apt to assume that a law is discovered; and at once this law is supposed to be universal, and to extend, or to have extended, through all time and space. It may be that the system, thus doubtfully perceived and imperfectly comprehended, is only a part of some larger system; and, under any circumstances, we certainly have no authority to assume that Nature, or the God of Nature, is in any sense bound by it, or unable to supersede or modify it.

Among systems and methods or laws of this kind we

may even name the law of gravitation,—one of the simplest and grandest ever promulgated, and one that is believed to apply to all matter throughout the universe. Of such methods also is the supposed law, according to which, in organic nature, certain peculiarities of structure are handed down from generation to generation in a plant or animal, producing what is called specific distinction. Certainly, it is strange that two sets of animals or plants, sufficiently like in important respects, do not intermingle, but always seem to continue distinct species, while two others, apparently very unlike, belong to each other and are mere varieties. That it is so we know from experience. We may some day discover the real method of Nature in this matter, and learn how it is that, as time rolls on, one species has been succeeded by another, —some species, like some individuals, being hardy and long-lived, while others are weak and short-lived,—some species growing out of others, apparently if not really, and other species suddenly dying or suddenly appearing, as place for them ceased to exist or was created.

That these dark and obscure matters are to be cleared up and rendered intelligible by the study of the records in the Great Stone Book, and that, on the other hand, the curious and difficult problems there presented will be ultimately solved by minute investigations concerning Nature as she now pursues her course, is at least highly probable. It is thus that Geology, and what is usually called "Natural History," are connected together and assist one another; and thus also the various departments of Physical Science are made to bear one upon another, and all are found to assist in clearing up the ancient history of our earth.

In conclusion, if there is one lesson which, more fully than any other, is taught by the Great Stone Book of the World, and which chiefly needs to be impressed on the mind and memory of the geological student, it is this:— Study to become familiar with familiar things; observe the methods now adopted in Nature to bring about certain results; measure and estimate their value and the extent of their action. Learn how at present all things, organic and inorganic, are mutually dependent, so that if any one is changed all the rest are changed in accordance, and weigh well the full meaning of this great fact. In a word, endeavor to comprehend what is meant by the uniform method and the infinite variety of Nature. Here lies the great secret of Nature and the great charm of natural-history labors. None can ever tire of studying Nature; for there is always an abundant store of yet undiscovered facts in the progress of the present creation as well as in the history of the past. On the other hand, none need fear that he may fail at coming to a safe and satisfactory result; for all is the work of one Almighty Power, and has been elaborated from the beginning as part of one vast, comprehensive, and infinitely wise scheme, in which apparent interruptions and interpolations have been foreseen, and are but parts of the full and complete development of an original plan. Surely it is a higher and more noble conception of the Supreme Being, and one more likely to lead to the discovery of truth, to believe in the existence of a plan as perfect as its Designer, than to presume that this earth has been the result of a series of experiments and failures, or has been the scene of great disturbances and convulsions in Inorganic Nature, and of successive creations of what we ignorantly call higher organisms in the world of organic life! We may never in this life succeed in discovering the whole plan, for it is not likely that finite powers can grasp the Infinite Design. But each endeavor that is made, humbly and honestly, will be productive of good: and the student will rise from the study of any part, either of the works or the method, with wider and clearer views, and be better fitted to perform his other duties and be useful to his fellow-men.

THE END.

www.ingramcontent.com/pod-product-compliance
Lightning Source LLC
Chambersburg PA
CBHW031854220426
43663CB00006B/617